Lecture Notes of the Institute for Computer Sciences, Social Informatics and Telecommunications Engineering 186

More information about this series at http://www.springer.com/series/8197

Ifiok Otung · Prashant Pillai
George Eleftherakis · Giovanni Giambene (Eds.)

Wireless and Satellite Systems

8th International Conference, WiSATS 2016
Cardiff, UK, September 19–20, 2016
Proceedings

Springer

Editors
Ifiok Otung
Faculty of Computing
University of South Wales
Cardiff
UK

Prashant Pillai
University of Bradford
Bradford
UK

George Eleftherakis
The University of Sheffield
Thessaloniki
Greece

Giovanni Giambene
University of Siena
Siena
Italy

ISSN 1867-8211   ISSN 1867-822X (electronic)
Lecture Notes of the Institute for Computer Sciences, Social Informatics
and Telecommunications Engineering
ISBN 978-3-319-53849-5   ISBN 978-3-319-53850-1   (eBook)
DOI 10.1007/978-3-319-53850-1

Library of Congress Control Number: 2017933560

Printed on acid-free paper

This Springer imprint is published by Springer Nature
The registered company is Springer International Publishing AG
The registered company address is: Gewerbestrasse 11, 6330 Cham, Switzerland

Preface

There is an exciting range of activities around the world to develop smart, resilient, and innovative wireless and satellite communication systems with capabilities to finally deliver the dream of "broadband anytime, anywhere on earth" and cope with the upcoming data transmission deluge arising from smart homes and cities, driverless vehicles, connectivity for countless billions of sensors and functional items and assets – the so-called Internet of Things (IoT) – and data-rich multimedia services to billions of small mobile devices and fixed larger units anytime anywhere.

The inherent capacity of satellites for broad area coverage makes them an indispensable component of the suite of communication technologies required to achieve truly ubiquitous broadband connectivity by the next decade and satisfy the on-going exponential growth in data consumption around the world. An approach that is both technically sound and economically feasible will have to build on existing telecommunication infrastructure to create a seamless integration of 5G wireless terrestrial networks and smart satellite systems, augmented by wire-line links (including power-line, digital subscriber loop, DSL, cable modem and optical fiber) that provide timely ample-speed data delivery tailored to each service. Such a fully satellite-integrated global telecommunication network will enable smart mobile devices to remain always connected anytime anywhere on earth by automatically switching between Wi-Fi in hotspots, mobile data in areas with adequate terrestrial communication provision, and satellite data in remote or inaccessible locations such as mid-air or mid-ocean. Imagine that passengers on the ill-fated Malaysia Airline Flight 370 that disappeared on March 8, 2014 were able to send text and video messages during their flight. The mystery of what happened to the aircraft might have been easier to solve.

There are, however, significant challenges, not least of which include overcoming the digital divide that still exists within nations and across geographical regions, and delivering broadband services in extreme-latitude regions that are invisible to geostationary satellites and uneconomic by terrestrial means. Furthermore, innovative solutions are needed to facilitate super-efficient utilization of the radio spectrum, security and reliability, use of radio frequencies above Ka-band and dealing effectively with the attendant increased propagation impairments, design of intelligent link-adaptable transmitters, building high-throughput satellite (HTS) systems with capacities approaching one terabit per second (Tbps), interference mitigation, energy efficiency and resource management, and so on.

The 8th International Conference on Wireless and Satellite Systems (WiSATS 2016) was held during September 19–20, 2016, at Hotel Novotel Cardiff Centre, Cardiff, UK; to explore the aforementioned challenges and discuss some of the emerging technical solutions. WiSATS 2016 brought together new and experienced researchers, developers, and leaders of thought within academia, industry, and regulatory bodies in Europe, India, and Japan to cross-fertilize ideas and discuss new work and innovative techniques and solutions that advance the state of the art in wireless and satellite systems. The technical program of WiSATS 2016 was rich and varied, with one major talk to kick off each day followed by technical paper presentations spread across both general and dedicated sessions. Day one of the conference opened with a keynote speech on 5G wireless systems delivered by Prof. Rahim Tafazolli, Director of the Institute of Communication Systems (ICS) at University of Surrey, UK. This was followed by two general technical sessions featuring presentations of various new developments in wireless and satellite systems, and then two special sessions dedicated to the specific areas of "Communications Application in Smart Grid" (CASG) and "Wireless, Computing and Satellite Systems Security" (WCSSS). The day concluded with a conference dinner. Day two began with a talk on the latest developments in mobile satellite communications given by Kyle Hurst, Director of Maritime Business at Iridium, Stevenage, UK. Punctuated with coffee and lunch breaks, the rest of the day was then devoted to various paper presentations and discussions within two general technical sessions. The conference concluded with an awards ceremony for best paper and outstanding contributions to WiSATS 2016.

This publication is a collection of revised articles from the most significant peer-reviewed full papers presented within the two special and four general technical sessions of WiSATS 2016. The articles cover a broad range of related state-of-the-art topics in antennas and mobile terminals, symbol precoding and network coding schemes, energy-efficient strategies in satellite communication and cloud radio access networks, smart grid communication and optimization, security issues in vehicular ad-hoc networks (VANET) and delay-tolerant networks (DTN), interference mitigation in high-throughput geostationary and non-geostationary satellite systems, etc. We hope that this represents a timely contribution to ongoing research and development efforts toward the realization of a fully ubiquitous heterogeneous broadband communications network.

Any international conference on the scale of WiSATS 2016 owes its success to the dedicated work of a great team. We would like to thank all the many volunteers who contributed in various ways to bring WiSATS 2016 to fruition. In particular, we thank members of the conference Organizing and Technical Program Committees and all session chairs and speakers for their invaluable contributions, which helped to make WiSATS 2016 a fantastic, stimulating, enjoyable, and enriching experience for all participants. We are immensely grateful to the reviewers, who gave freely of their time to evaluate submitted papers and make suggestions for improvement. We are also hugely indebted to the contributing authors who submitted high-quality papers and responded positively to reviewers' comments. A final thank you goes to the University of South Wales for their in-kind support and to the European Alliance for Innovation (EAI) for their excellent administration and management of WiSATS 2016.

February 2016

Ifiok Otung
Prashant Pillai
George Eleftherakis
Giovanni Giambene

Organization

WiSATS 2016 was organized by the University of South Wales in cooperation with the European Alliance for Innovation (EAI), the Institute for Computer Sciences, Social Informatics and Telecommunications Engineering (ICST), and CREATE-NET.

General Chair

Ifiok Otung   University of South Wales, UK

General Co-chairs

Sastri Kota   Sohum Consulting, USA
Naoto Kadowaki   NICT, Tokyo, Japan

Technical Program Committee Chairs

Prashant Pillai   University of Bradford, UK
George Eleftherakis   University of Sheffield International Faculty,
                                        City College, Greece

Steering Committee

Imrich Chlamtac   CREATE-NET, Italy
Kandeepan Sithamparanathan   RMIT, Australia
Agnelli Stefano   ESOA/Eutelsat, France
Mario Marchese   University of Genoa, Italy

Publications Chair

Giovanni Giambene   University of Siena, Italy

Web Chair

Kufre Ekerete   University of South Wales, UK

Publicity and Social Media Chair

Andikan Otung   Ciena, London, UK

Workshops Chair

Bamidele Adebisi   Manchester Metropolitan University, UK

Local Chair

Francis Hunt   University of South Wales, UK

Sponsorship and Exhibits Chair

Martin Coleman   sIRG, UK

Conference Manager

Barbara Fertalova   EAI, European Alliance for Innovation

Special Session Organizers

Special Session on Communication Applications in Smart Grid (CASG)

Organized by

Haile-Selassie Rajamani   University of Bradford, UK

Special Session on Wireless, Computing and Satellite Systems Security (WCSSS)

Organized by

Prashant Pillai   University of Bradford, UK

Sponsoring Institutions

University of South Wales
European Alliance for Innovation (EAI)
Institute for Computer Sciences, Social Informatics and Telecommunications
Engineering (ICST)
CREATE-NET

Contents

Communication Applications in Smart Grid (CASG) Special Session

Wireless, Computing and Satellite Systems Security (WCSSS) Special Session

Technical Session 3

Technical Session 4

Technical Session 1

A Compact CSRR Loaded Monopole Antenna with Defected Ground Structure for Mobile WLAN and WiMAX Applications

N.A. Jan[1(✉)], A.M. Saleh[1], M. Lashab[2], F.M. Abdussalam[1], L. Djouablia[2], and R.A. Abd-Alhameed[1]

[1] Faculty of Engineering and Informatics, University of Bradford, Bradford, UK
kakarnayeem@yahoo.com, {A.M.S.Saleh,R.A.A.Abd}@bradford.ac.uk
[2] Skikda University, Skikda, Algeria

Abstract. A physically compact dual band antenna design is presented for use in mobile WLAN and mid-band WiMAX applications. The antenna design is based on a monopole, with a combination of metamaterial inspired features, based on a defected ground structure (GDS) and a complementary split-ring resonator (CSRR). A single CSRR unit cell is placed over a pentagonal monopole antenna, producing a narrow stop-band frequency in the range from 2.40 GHz to 2.49 GHz. The second operating frequency ranges from 3.44 GHz to 6.25 GHz, the broad-banding being due to the influence of the defected ground structure. The antenna design was optimized using HFSS, paying close attention to size constraints, and ease of integration with the radio front end. Simulation results for return loss, gain and radiation pattern are analyzed and presented.

Keywords: Defected ground structure (DGS) · High frequency structure simulator (HFSS) · Complementary split ring resonator (CSRR) · Metamaterial-inspired antenna · Double negative (DNG) behavior

1 Introduction

The antenna design proposed in this paper is intended to address the need for dual-band antennas for use in overlapping WLAN (2.4 GHz, 5.2 GHz, 5.8 GHz) and mid-band WiMAX (3.5 GHz) applications, which do not intefere with one another [1]. Various techniques have been investigated to achieve a suitable miniaturization of the radiating elements. Of interest are etched L-shaped. U-shaped and G-shaped metalization patches [4, 5, 6]; loading planar surfaces with complementary split ring resonator (CSRR) metamaterial [7]; and placing insertions such as shortening pins or resonators in the neighbourhood of the radiating element [8]. The complementary split ring resonator (CSRR) is the dual of the split ring resonator (SRR) [3].

In [9] CSRR along with EBG is used for miniaturization but the antenna is resonatiing in 2.6 GHZ and 3.23 GHz with limited bandwidth and gain results. The antenna design presented in this paper is said to be metamaterial inspired in the sense that only a unit cell of the CSRR metamaterial is needed to realize the design. As compared to [9], the antenna

© ICST Institute for Computer Sciences, Social Informatics and Telecommunications Engineering 2017
I. Otung et al. (Eds.): WiSATS 2016, LNICST 186, pp. 3–10, 2017.
DOI: 10.1007/978-3-319-53850-1_1

presented here has better and widen bandwidth and both the frequencies are adjusted for WLAN and WiMax applications at the cost of small increase in size. The CSRR unit cell structure was designed in HFSS, with the constutuitive parameter extraction being performed through matlab. This design suggests a double negative result at a resonance frequency of 2.45 GHz, which is then utilised to provide the lower band (WLAN) requirement, and to achieve a miniaturised radiator structure. A defected ground structure is then utlised to provide the mid-band WiMAX (3.5 GHz) and upper WLAN (5.2 GHz and 5.8 GHz) service bands, and also constributes to a stable radiation pattern.

2   Metamaterial Unit Cell Design

The geometrical configuration of the CSRR unit cell is shown in Fig. 2. The unit cell is designed and simulated using HFSS. Matlab is used here to retrieve constitutive parameters i.e. effective permeability and permittivity of the unit cell, which determine the response of the material to electromagnetic radiation. The single unit cell, which has no periodicity, normally generates negative permeability only [2]. Unit cell or metamaterial-inclusion can be used for different applications. In [2] though the application of the unit cell is to increase the isolation between MIMO, but in this paper the unit cell is used to attain miniaturization and to make antenna resonate at lower frequency of ISM 2.45 GHz. The unit cell analysed here produces negative permittivity and permeability values from the introduction of symmetrical periodicity in the armatures, and lengths of the unit cell. This unit cell of size 9 mm × 5.5 mm is then etched on top of the monopole to make antenna electrically small and resonant in the ISM 2.45 GHz service band. The optimized parameters of the unit cell are given in Table 1.

Table 1. The optimized parameter of the proposed CSRR unit cell

Parameter	Value (mm)	Parameter	Value (mm)
H	5.5	W_p	4
F	9.75	W_u	2.5
h_1	1.5	g_u	0.5
h_2	1.5	s	0.5

The transmission coefficient of the metamaterial unit cell is given in Fig. 3, it can be seen that the unit cell has a resonance at 2.45 GHz. Extracted values of the effective constitutive parameters with negative real parts at the resonance frequency were observed for this resonance, as shown in Figs. 4 and 5, respectively.

3   Antenna Design and Results

The geometrical configuration of the metamaterial inspired antenna structure is shown in Fig. 1. A finite element model of the antenna was analysed using HFSS. The substrate was a 1.6 mm thick FR4 material with a relative permittivity of 4.4 and loss tangent of 0.02. The pentagonal monopole is loaded with a CSRR unit cell. This metamaterial unit cell displays double negative (DNG) behaviour at a resonant frequency of 2.45 GHz. The feed line is a 50 Ω microstrip stub, with a width of 3 mm. The overall antenna volume is 26 × 25 × 1.6 mm³. The defected ground structure has dimensions of 22 mm × 12 mm, and a further 3 mm-radius semi-circle was cut from each side of the ground to enhance the wideband performance in the upper WLAN frequency range. The optimised CSRR parameters are given in Table 2. Figure 6 shows the 'three step evolution' of the metamaterial inspired design.

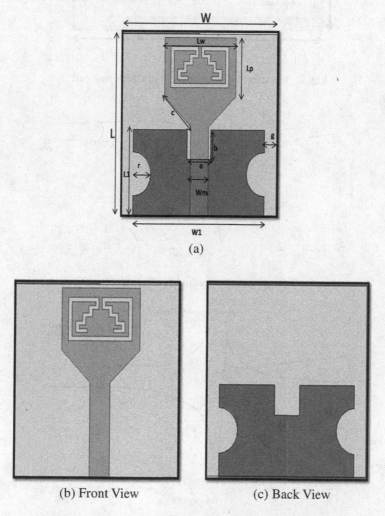

(a)

(b) Front View   (c) Back View

Fig. 1. Monopole antenna loaded with CSRR and DGS.

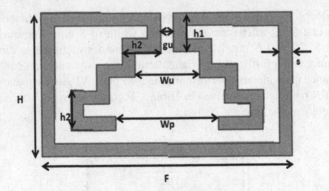

Fig. 2. Geometrical configuration of CSRR unit cell

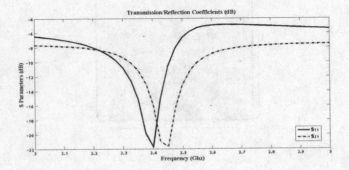

Fig. 3. Transmission/Reflection Coefficient of a unit cell

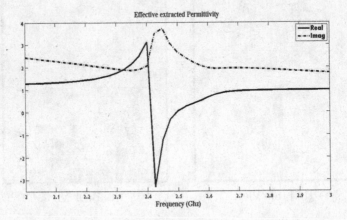

Fig. 4. Effective extracted permittivity of a unit cell

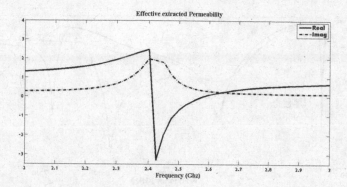

Fig. 5. Effective extracted permeability of a unit cell

Table 2. The optimized parameter of the proposed Metamaterial-inspired antenna

Parameter	Value (mm)	Parameter	Value (mm)
L	25	C	4
W	26	R	3
L_1	12	G	2
W_1	22	W_m	3
a	4	L_w	12
b	4	L_p	8

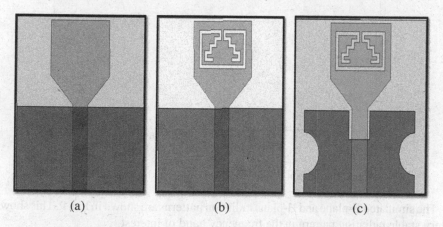

Fig. 6. Metamaterial-inspired antenna design evolution; (a) conventional antenna, (b) Monopole With CSRR, (c) Monopole CSRR with DGS

The results of all the three antennas were simulated in HFSS, these are summarised in Fig. 7. This indicates that the antenna with CSRR loading and DGS has an overall better performance in terms of the realized impedance bandwidth and return loss, as compared to the conventional and CSRR loaded monopole antennas.

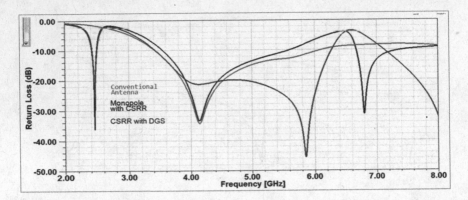

Fig. 7. Reflection coefficient of the conventional, CSRR and CSRR along DGS monopole antenna

Simulated gain values of the Monopole CSRR with DGS antenna is given in the Fig. 8 throughout the whole operational band.

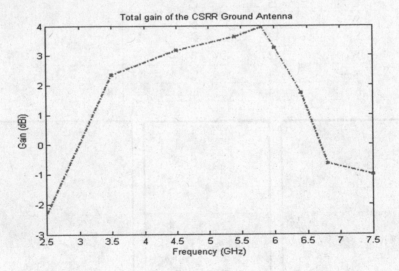

Fig. 8. Total gain of the Monopole CSRR with DGS antenna

The simulated E-plane and H-plane radiation patterns are shown in Fig. 9. This shows a very stable radiation pattern in the frequency band of interest.

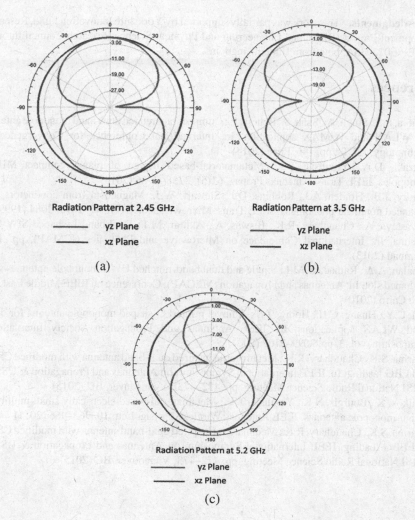

Fig. 9. Simulated E-Plane and H-Plane at (a) 2.45 GHz, (b) 3.5 GHz, (c) 5.2 GHz.

4 Conclusions

A CSRR loaded dual-band monopole antenna with a defected ground structure has been presented for combined WLAN/WiMAX applications. The antenna is fed by a micro-strip feed line. The forecasted antenna volume is 26 mm × 25 mm × 1.6 mm. The simulation model suggests an impedance bandwidth of 3.86% centred on 2.45 GHz for the first band, and a wide upper band from 3.44 GHz to 6.25 GHz. Both bands display a good omni-directional monopole radiation pattern.

Acknowledgments. This work was partially supported by Yorkshire Innovation Fund, Research Development Project (RDP); and Engineering and Physical Science Research Council through Grant EP/E022936A, both from United Kingdom.

References

1. Behera, S.S., Singh, A., Sahu, S., Behera, P.: Compact tapered fed dual-band monopole antenna for WLAN and WiMAX application. In: International Conference for Convergence of Technology (I2CT), pp. 1–6, Pune (2014)
2. Ketzaki, D.A., Yioultsis, T.V.: Metamaterial-based design of planar compact MIMO monopoles. IEEE Trans. Antennas Propag. **61**(5), 2758–2766 (2013)
3. Pendry, J.B., Holden, A.J., Robbins, D.J., Stewart, W.J.: Magnetism from conductors and enhanced nonlinear phenomena. IEEE Trans. Microw. Theor. Tech. **47**, 2075–2084 (1999)
4. Srivastava, A., Chaudhary, R.K., Biswas, A., Akhtar, M.J.: Dual-band L-shaped SIW Slot antenna. In: International Conference on Microwave and Photonics (ICMAP), pp. 1–3, Dhanbad (2013)
5. Shaalan, A.A., Ramadant, M.I.: Single and dual band-notched UWB monopole antennas with U-shaped slot. In: Antennas and Propagation (MECAP), Conference on IEEE Middle East, pp. 1–8, Cairo (2010)
6. Pan, C.Y., Huang, C.H., Horng, T.S.: A novel printed G-shaped monopole antenna for dual-band WLAN applications. In: IEEE Antennas and Propagation Society International Symposium, vol. 3, pp. 3099–3102 (2004)
7. Sharma, S.K., Chaudhary, R.K.: Metamaterial inspired dual-band antenna with modified CSRR and EBG loading. In: IEEE International Symposium on Antennas and Propagation & USNC/URSI National Radio Science Meeting, pp. 472–473D, Vancouver, BC (2015)
8. Ntaikos, K., Bourgis, N.K., Yioultsis, T.V.: Metamaterial-based electrically small multiband planar monopole antennas. IEEE Antennas Wireless Propag. Lett. **10**, 963–966 (2011)
9. Sharma, S.K., Chaudhary, R.K.: Metamaterial inspired dual-band antenna with modified CSRR and EBG loading, IEEE International Symposium on Antennas and Propagation & USNC/URSI National Radio Science Meeting, pp. 472–473, Vancouver, BC (2015)

Development Status of Small-Sized Ka-band Mobile Terminal for Maritime Broadband Communications

Norihiko Katayama[1], Naoko Yoshimura[1], Hideo Takamatsu[2(✉)], Susumu Kitazume[2], Yosuke Takahara[2], Marshall Lewis[3], and Rowan Gilmore[3]

[1] National Institute of Information and Communication Technology (NICT),
4-2-1 Nukui-Kitamachi Koganei, Tokyo 184-8795, Japan
{n.katayama,naoko}@nict.go.jp
[2] JEPICO Corporation,
Shinjuku Front Tower 2-21-1, Kita-Shinjuku Shinjuku-Ku, Tokyo 169-0074, Japan
hideotak@yahoo.co.jp,
{h_takamatsu,kitazume,y_takahara}@jepico.co.jp
[3] EM Solutions, 55 Curzon Street, Tennyson QLD 4105, Australia
{Marshall.Lewis,Rowan.Gilmore}@emsolutions.com.au

Abstract. Most recent development status of small-sized Ka-band mobile communications terminal is presented. The terminal is designed to operate at a minimum target speed of 5 Mbps to/from a Ka-band geostationary satellite, and will eventually be used for the purpose of research activity to explore marine resources within the Exclusive Economic Zone (EEZ) of Japan. The terminal is placed on Autonomous Surface Vehicle (ASV). Because the ASV is "unmanned" and is primarily controlled from a remote ground control station, several mechanisms are embedded into the design for safe and successful operations of the Ka-band terminal. Those key mechanisms are introduced in this paper as they make fault diagnosis easier and increase overall system reliability in case of primary communication channel failure.

Keywords: Mobile communications · Ka-band terminal · Auto-tracking antenna

1 Introduction

Autonomous Surface Vehicle (ASV), as shown in Fig. 1, is an unmanned vessel on the ocean and is currently under development by JAMSTEC (Japan Agency for Marine-Earth Science and Technology) [1]. Target specifications of ASV are tabulated in Table 1.

The primary function of ASV is to relay a communication signal to/from one or multiple Autonomous Underwater Vehicles (AUVs) which can cruise 3,000 m deep seafloors in search for precious marine resources or evidence for earthquake. For this purpose, every ASV has a Ka-band terminal with auto-tracking antenna onboard and is designed to communicate with Ka-band geostationary satellite. The AUV weighs a few tons and can be remotely controlled by ground control station or directly controlled by Research Vessel (RV). On the other hand, Remotely Operated Vehicle (ROV) works at much deeper ocean floors, taking high-definition class pictures and sampling marine

© ICST Institute for Computer Sciences, Social Informatics and Telecommunications Engineering 2017
I. Otung et al. (Eds.): WiSATS 2016, LNICST 186, pp. 11–17, 2017.
DOI: 10.1007/978-3-319-53850-1_2

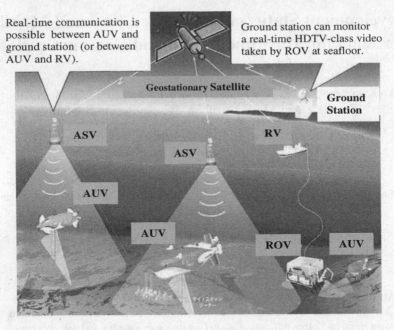

Fig. 1. ASV, AUV, RV, and ROV operations (conceptual view)

Table 1. ASV specifications (target values) [2]

Parameter	Spec
Dimension (L, W, H)	6 m × 2.6 m × 3.2 m
Weight	<3 tons
Operating hours	48 h
Vessel speed	2 knot (cruise), 5 knot (max)
Operating condition	≤Sea State 4, ≤Wind speed 15 m/s

resources. ROV is mechanically cabled to RV and communicates with RV through optical fiber. Figure 2 shows a conceptual view of those operations.

The Ka-band mobile communications terminal will be mounted on ASV, and RF system of the terminal consists of beacon-tracking antenna subsystem and transmit/receive RF subsystem. The antenna subsystem tracks a Ka-band geostationary satellite (WINDS satellite [3] in this case) with tight pointing accuracy and, if the error exceeds the limit, it is designed to immediately cease RF transmission and avoid unnecessary RF interference to neighboring satellites.

The Ka-band terminal is also equipped with a commercially available Machine to Machine (M2M) remote access system, capable of changing a transmission data rate to a lower data rate, for instance, during a heavy rain fade to ensure communication connectivity with a Ka-band satellite. The remote access system also accepts a switch-over command to a redundant Block Up Converter (BUC) in case of a primary BUC failure for some reason.

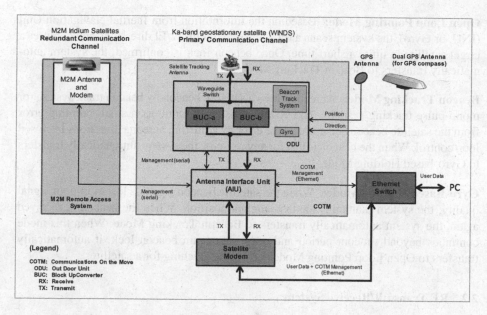

Fig. 2. Overall system diagram of Ka-band terminal

2 Overall System Diagram

Figure 2 shows overall system diagram of Ka-band communications terminal. The system is mainly divided into Communications On The Move (COTM) and Machine to Machine (M2M) Remote Access System. The COTM is further divided into Antenna Auto-Tracking System and RF Transmit/Receive system and they are explained in the following paragraphs. See legend in Fig. 2 for acronyms used in the paragraph.

2.1 Antenna Auto-tracking System

Beacon tracking system (BTS) is employed for Ka-band antenna auto-tracking to realize the tight antenna pointing requirement (i.e. $\pm0.2°$) while operating on the ocean. It is commonly known that BTS uses three axis control (i.e. azimuth, elevation, and polarization) and the reason for having the fourth axis, or ex-elevation axis, is to avoid a "Keyhole Effect". During a primary mode of antenna pointing control, Antenna Control Unit (ACU) drives a motor in each axis based on the sum and difference signals supplied from the BTS system.

The antenna system is also designed to have an "interlock function", which allows RF transmission only when the system locks onto the stable Ka-band beacon and pointing error stays within $\pm0.2°$ limit. Outside the limit, the system is designed to cease RF transmission to avoid unnecessary RF interference to neighboring satellites. Antenna Auto-Tracking System has the following three modes of operations:

Open Loop Pointing Mode: Based on the information from Inertial Navigation Unit (INU, or Gyro), the system scans a tracking antenna in Az/El directions and captures a target satellite in quite a short time. Once beacon lock is confirmed, the system automatically transfers to Beacon Tracking Mode.

Beacon Tracking Mode: Antenna tracks a satellite beacon by beacon track system (or mono-pulse tracking system). The system constantly monitors a small pointing error from the satellite beacon and corrects the error by adjusting antenna directions in closed loop control. When the beacon is lost for any reasons, the system automatically transfers to Gyro-based Holding Mode.

Gyro-Based Holding Mode: When the satellite beacon signal is lost or in poor signal quality, the system maintains the last antenna position. When the beacon is received again, the system automatically transfers to Beacon Tracking Mode. When this mode continues beyond timeout period and does not regain beacon lock, it automatically transfers to Open Loop Pointing Mode and starts searching for a satellite.

2.2   RF Transmit/Receive System

The RF Transmit/Receive System mainly consists of a driver amplifier and BUC. The BUC mainly consists of up-conversion mixer and solid state power amplifier (SSPA) and shows a slightly higher failure rate than other components in the RF Transmit/ Receive system. Since whole Ka-band terminal requires higher level of operational reliability and survivability on severe sea state conditions, we have decided to incorporate a "redundancy scheme" (BUC-a and BUC-b) into the BUC design as shown in Fig. 2. Selecting GaN SSPA, instead of GaAs SSPA, is a part of those efforts because GaN shows a better power added efficiency (typically 25%) and lower heat dissipation, leading to a smaller failure rate. Table 2 shows GaAs and GaN performances in Ka-band frequency. Estimated value of system MTBF (Mean Time Between Failures) is examined in Sect. 3.

Table 2. GaAs and GaN performances (Ka-band)

Parameter	GaAs	GaN
Supplier	Triquint	Triquint
DC input	36 W (6 A at 6 V)	36 W (1.5 A at 24 V)
RF output (saturation)	6 W	9 W
Thermal dissipation	30 W	27 W
Power Added Efficiency (PAE)	15%	25%
Format	Chip or package, 6 W	Chip, 9 W
Linear RF power	1–2 W (backed off)	3 W (backed off)
	3–4 W (with lenealizer)	6 W (with lenealizer)

As a result, the Ka-band terminal has "dual BUCs" as shown in Fig. 2 with a primary BUC (i.e. BUC-a in the figure) producing 20 W of RF power by combining four RF outputs of GaN device and a redundant BUC (BUC-b in the same figure) in standby mode. If a failure occurs in primary BUC, then redundant BUC automatically comes on line. Redundant BUC can also be commanded on line by remote operator's command through Iridium Short Burst Data Service (SBD), which is explained in Sect. 2.3. A waveguide-type RF power combiner is used for combining GaN RF outputs because of its lower RF combining loss and excellent design heritage.

A design method to produce a target EIRP was discussed in detail in a previous paper [4]. Therefore, using the same method described in the reference, EIRP, G/T, and satellite link margin are estimated to establish a 5 Mbps satellite link. Result is shown in Table 3 (below) for a Ka-band terminal having a 54 cm diameter antenna. Note that $EIRP_{ASV}$ = 51 dBW in Table 3 is operational EIRP with output back-off of 1.8 dB included.

Table 3. Estimated EIRP, G/T, and satellite link margin

Parameter	Value (predicted)	Notes
EIRPasv	51 dBW	G_{TX} = 41.9 dBi@28.33 GHz, Psat = 20 W (13 dBW), OBO = 1.8 dB
G/Tasv	13 dB/K	D = 0.54 m
Satellite link margin for 5 Mbps	3.3 dB (ASV to land) 4.9 dB (land to ASV)	FEC 1/2 QPSK; Assumed a 3 dB rain attenuation in satellite uplink link calculation (ASV to land). The same amount of rain effect is assumed in satellite downlink calculation (land to ASV)

2.3 M2M Remote Access System

Machine to Machine (M2M) communication is a technology that allows both wireless and wired machines to speak to, monitor, and control other machines of the same type. There are many M2M services available today, offering superior geographical service coverage with an extremely affordable cost for users.

The reason a redundant communication channel is introduced into our Ka-band terminal design is that M2M communication can provide an alternative communication path in case of a primary communication channel failure. The failure could be a Ka-band transponder failure, hardware failure, and/or software malfunction of Ka-band terminal. Without M2M communication, those situations can be serious for ASV operations: Those failures may leave an unmanned ASV in a helpless situation on the ocean, and it is certainly a problem not knowing where the troubled ASV is located and what kind of operational state the ASV is in. Therefore, to increase overall system availability and reliability, Iridium Short Burst Data Service (SBD) is selected and implemented. Note that Iridium SBD is mainly used to diagnose and recover the overall system performance, and is not suitable for transferring a large amount of data of the primary communication channel.

The following are what redundant M2M communication channel can perform:

Normal Operations: The redundant M2M channel is active and critical system status messages (i.e. current values and alarm status) for each subsystem (i.e. COTM terminal, Ethernet Switch, Satellite Modem, and redundant communication channel) are sent via Iridium SBD once a day. Critical parameters are to be defined. Self-test on Iridium SBD is performed several times a day. System generates alarms/notifications if faults/failures are detected.

Failures: Catastrophic failure prevents the system from being accessed remotely via the primary communication channel, and it can be detected by the system or by human operators. A failure in COTM terminal can be detected and diagnosed by firmware.

Operation After Failure: If a failure occurs, Iridium SBD messages indicating failure will be sent via Iridium satellite network periodically. Remote host may receive a status message or the host can detect a loss of communication over the primary channel. In either case, operator sends diagnostic commands or system recovery commands via Iridium system.

Operation After System Recovery: The system sends SBD message indicating failure is cleared.

3   System MTBF Calculation

Table 4 shows an MTBF (Mean Time Between Failures) value calculated in accordance with MIL-HDBK-217F Notice 2 in a 40°C Naval Sheltered environmental condition. The failure rate is determined by calculating and summing the failure rate of each component in the terminal. Each component has a base failure rate depending on its type (resistor, capacitor, etc.) which is then multiplied by coefficients based on variables such as temperature, component quality, environmental conditions and power rating, as part of the MIL-HDBK-217F Notice 2 standard. Once failures per million hours (fpmh) are thus estimated, MTBF is obtained by calculating 10^6 (h)/fpmh.

Table 4. MTBF of Ka-band Terminal

	Dual BUC, redundant DC converters	
	Commercial	Experimental
Failure rate (fpmh)	352	110
MTBF (hours)	2,838	9,035

During experimental phase of ASV operations, it is assumed that every ASV will go to the ocean and work continuously for two weeks and that the operation repeats six times a year. In the meantime, there is a chance of periodic maintenance for each ASV, which is scheduled four times a year. Based on the operational scenario, 9,035 h is believed to be a good number for the current operational purpose.

The commercial MTBF, on the other hand, assumes continuous operation of ASV in a Naval Sheltered state, showing a smaller value than experimental.

4   Summary

The most recent development status of small-sized, Ka-band mobile communications terminal was discussed for successful operations of Autonomous Surface Vehicle (ASV). The goal is to establish reliable broadband mobile communications between ASV vessel and ground station through a Ka-band geostationary satellite. Having "redundancy scheme" in a BUC design is considered useful to increase overall system survivability of the Ka-band terminal. The authors also believe that incorporating M2M communication into Ka-band terminal design greatly enhances fault diagnosis capability. Finally, MTBF is computed for Ka-band terminal equipped with dual BUC and redundant DC convertor system. Calculated MTBF value is considered adequate for current experimental purpose.

Acknowledgements.   The authors greatly appreciate useful and kind advices, comments, and supports made by JEPICO and EM Solutions. It is emphasized that this development work of Ka-band mobile communications terminal is one of the critical element of Next-generation Technology for Ocean Resources Exploration, which constitutes one of the highly-prioritized Strategic Innovation Promotion Programs (abbreviated as "SIP programs") of Cabinet Office, Government of Japan. Ten SIP programs have been implemented since 2014 and they plan to continue until March 2019.

References

1. JAMSTEC. Research vessels, facilities and equipment. http://www.jamstec.go.jp/e/about/equipment/ships/
2. Workshop on Next Generation Experimental Test Satellite (2015)
3. JAXA. High-speed internet will be available anytime, anywhere. http://global.jaxa.jp/article/interview/vol32/index_e.html
4. Katayama, N., Yoshimura, N., Takamatsu, H., Kitazume, S., Takahara, Y., Logan, J., Ness, J.: Development of Ka-band mobile communications platform for ocean broadband communications. In: AIAA ICSSC (2015)

New and Less Complex Approach to Estimate Angles of Arrival

Mohammed A.G. Al-Sadoon[1], Abdulkareem S. Abdullah[2], Ramzy S. Ali[2],
Ali S. Al-Abdullah[1], Raed A. Abd-Alhameed[1(✉)], Steve M.R. Jones[1],
and James M. Noras[1]

[1] School of Electrical Engineering and Computer Science,
University of Bradford, Bradford BD7 1DP, UK
r.a.a.abd@bradford.ac.uk
[2] Department of Electrical Engineering, University of Basrah, Basra, Iraq

Abstract. Accurate angle/direction of arrival (AOA/DOA) estimation is an important issue which, helps mobile communications, wireless positioning and signal processing systems to improve their performance significantly. This paper proposes a new method to estimate the direction of arrival of signals. The proposed estimator is dependent on applying the eigenvalue decomposition (EVD) approach on the covariance matrix of the received signals and then selecting the eigenvector which corresponds to the largest eigenvalue. This method is called Maximum Signal Subspace (MSS). In a novel step, the sidelobes of the pseudo-spectrum are supressed. The theoretical and mathematical model of the proposed method is proved and then verified by computer simulation. The computer simulation is applied to linear antenna array to demonstrate and justify the validity of the new method. The estimation performance and execution time of this method are compared with three AOA methods.

Keywords: Direction of arrival · Angle of arrival · Eigen decomposition method · Wireless communication · Antenna array · Positioning systems

1 Introduction

Direction finding (DF) relates to estimating the DOA of signal sources that impinging on an antenna array either in the form of acoustic or electromagnetic waves. The need for DOA estimation stems from the requirements of tracking and locating signal emitters in both military and civilian applications, for example, radar systems, public security, seismology, sonar and emergency call locating [1]. Furthermore, wireless technology applications have disseminated into several fields, for instance, sensor networks, environmental monitoring, search and rescue [2]. All these applications motivated and focussed increased attention towards developing direction of arrival techniques for wireless communication systems. The AOA method is the heart of smart antenna systems technology that provides accurate direction information about signal sources for wireless communication network [3]. Smart antenna systems combine multiple antenna elements with a digital signal processing to improve and optimize its reception

© ICST Institute for Computer Sciences, Social Informatics and Telecommunications Engineering 2017
I. Otung et al. (Eds.): WiSATS 2016, LNICST 186, pp. 18–27, 2017.
DOI: 10.1007/978-3-319-53850-1_3

and transmission pattern adaptively according to signal environment response to improve signal to interference ratios [4]. This technology had been found useful in mobile communication systems since it allows increasing the number of mobile users given limited resources [5]. Several angle of arrival techniques have been proposed and developed during last five decades for array signal processing to estimate DOA [6]. The Bartlett or classical beamformer method is one of the earliest techniques proposed to estimate the direction of impinging signals by scanning across an angular space of interest [7]. However, this method suffers from poor resolution and high sidelobe levels. Later, Capon proposed a new approach for the same purpose, which is known as the minimum variance distortedness response (MVDR) method [8]. The principle of this method depends on estimating the signal from one direction and supposing that all other directions are interference. Although this method gives better resolution accuracy than the Bartlett method, its performance significantly drops when arriving signals are correlated or close to each other in angle. This type of techniques was called non-subspace since it does not need to decompose the covariance matrix of received signals. Another class of AOA techniques are called signal subspace methods, which present high accuracy compared with the previous ones. Multiple Signal Classification (MUSIC) was a well-known method, which provides high accuracy for direction estimation [9]. However, this method was a bit complex and required many computational processes since the size of the matrix increases as the number of the incoming signals increases. The complexity of the estimator is another issue that algorithm designers must take care of. Hence, this paper proposes a new and less complex method with good accuracy to estimate the direction of incident signals. This paper is organized as follows: Sect. 2 the mathematical modelling of the direction of arrival signals. The proposed estimator and its mathematical model are given in Sect. 3. Section 4 simulates the proposed estimator and discuss the simulation results. Lastly, in Sect. 5, conclusion and summarized results are presented.

2 Direction of Arrival Mathematical Modelling

When the antenna array receives signals from various directions, the angle of arrival algorithm is implemented to find these directions. Let's assume there are D signals incident on M antenna elements as shown in Fig. 1. These signals will be received by M-elements with M potential weights, w_m. Each kth sample of incident signal $s(k)$ contains on an Additive White Gaussian Noise (AWGN). This can be modelled as in [10].

The received vector signal can be defined as:

$$\bar{x}(k) = \bar{A}.\bar{s}(k) + \bar{n}(k) \tag{1}$$

where

$\bar{A}(\theta_i)$ is total steering matrix of received signals and defined by

$$A = [\bar{a}(\theta_1)\,\bar{a}(\theta_2)\dots\bar{a}(\theta_D)] \tag{2}$$

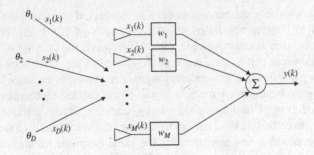

Fig. 1. M-element array with arriving signals.

$\bar{s}(k)$ is a vector of incident complex signals at $k\Delta t$-time is given by:

$$\bar{s}(k) = \left[s_1(k), s_2(k), \dots, s_D(k)\right] \tag{3}$$

$n(k)$ is a zero mean Gaussian noise for each channel and is expressed by:

$$\bar{n}(k) = \left[n_1(k), n_2(k), \dots, n_D(k)\right] \tag{4}$$

$\bar{a}(\theta_i)$ is the array steering vector and is given by [2]:

$$\bar{a}(\theta) = \begin{bmatrix} 1 \\ \exp(j\beta d\sin\theta) \\ \vdots \\ \exp(j\beta d(M-1)\sin\theta) \end{bmatrix} \tag{5}$$

where
d denotes the distance between each two adjacent elements.
β is the spatial frequency and defined by:

$$\beta = \frac{2\pi}{\lambda} \tag{6}$$

The output signal can be expressed as:

$$y(k) = \bar{w}^H \cdot \bar{x}(k) \tag{7}$$

with $\bar{w}$, the array weights, given by [10]:

$$\bar{w} = \left[w_1\, w_2\, \dots\, w_M\right]^T \tag{8}$$

The calculations depend on time samples of the received signals since these signals are time varying. Obviously, when the signal emitters are moving from one place to another, their corresponding arrival angles are changing, and this will cause to change the steering vectors matrix as well. Thus, the covariance matrix $\bar{R}_{xx}$ of uncorrelated receiving signals case is given as follows.

$$\bar{R}_{xx} = E\left[\bar{x}\,\bar{x}^H\right] = E\left[(\bar{A}\,\bar{s} + \bar{n}) \times (\bar{s}^H \bar{A}^H + \bar{n}^H)\right]$$

$$\bar{R}_{xx} = E\left[(\bar{A}\,\bar{s} + \bar{n}) \times (\bar{s}^H \bar{A}^H + \bar{n}^H)\right] \tag{9}$$

$$\bar{R}_{xx} = \bar{A} E\left[\bar{s}.\,\bar{s}^H\right]\bar{A}^H + E\left[\bar{n}.\,\bar{n}^H\right]$$

$$\bar{R}_{xx} = \bar{A}\,\bar{R}_{ss}\,\bar{A}^H + \bar{R}_{nn} \tag{10}$$

And

$$\bar{R}_{ss} = E\left[\bar{s}\,\bar{s}^H\right] \tag{11}$$

$$\bar{R}_{nn} = \sigma_n^2\,I \tag{12}$$

In this situation, $\bar{R}_{ss}$ is a diagonal matrix since the incoming signals are assumed as uncorrelated. When the incoming signals are correlated, the covariance matrix will be different from the previous condition due to $\bar{R}_{ss}$ matrix is non-diagonal. This situation is given by [10].

$$\bar{R}_{xx} = \bar{A}\,\bar{R}_{ss}\,\bar{A}^H + \bar{A}\,\bar{R}_{sn}\,\bar{A}^H + \bar{A}\,\bar{R}_{ns}\,\bar{A}^H + \bar{R}_{nn} \tag{13}$$

And

$$\hat{R}_{ss}(k) \approx \frac{1}{K}\sum_{k=1}^{K}\bar{s}(k)\bar{s}^H(k) \tag{14}$$

$$\hat{R}_{sn}(k) \approx \frac{1}{K}\sum_{k=1}^{K}\bar{s}(k)\bar{n}^H(k) \tag{15}$$

$$\hat{R}_{ns}(k) \approx \frac{1}{K}\sum_{k=1}^{K}\bar{n}(k)\bar{s}^H(k) \tag{16}$$

$$\hat{R}_{nn}(k) \approx \frac{1}{K}\sum_{k=1}^{K}\bar{n}(k)\bar{n}^H(k) \tag{17}$$

3 Proposed Method

After the covariance matrix is computed, a method is required to estimate the DOA of incoming signals. Hence, this paper suggests a new approach to estimate the direction of emitters; this approach (i.e. MSS) can be classified as a subspace method. The method consists of three main steps: first, sample the incoming signals and construct the covariance matrix. Secondly, applying decomposition on this matrix and select the Eigenvector that corresponds to the largest Eigenvalue. Lastly, compute the pseudospectrum and find the location of peaks as shown in Fig. 2.

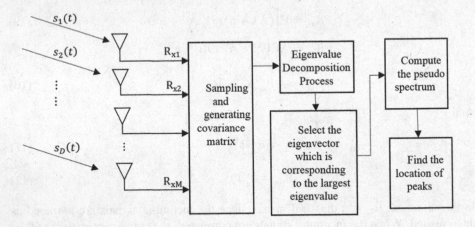

Fig. 2. Proposed method block diagram for direction estimation.

According to the matrix theory, the $\bar{R}_{xx}$ can be diagonalised by a nonsingular orthogonal transformation matrix as follows:

$$\bar{Q}^* \, \bar{R}_{xx} \, \bar{Q}^T = \Lambda \tag{18}$$

where Λ is (M $\times$ M) diagonal matrix consists of real Eigenvalues and is given by:

$$\Lambda = \begin{bmatrix} \lambda_1 & 0 & \dots & 0 \\ 0 & \lambda_2 & \dots & 0 \\ \vdots & 0 & \ddots & \vdots \\ 0 & & \dots & \lambda_M \end{bmatrix} \tag{19}$$

Q is the eigenvectors matrix and can be defined as:

$$\bar{Q} = [\bar{e}_1, \bar{e}_2, \dots \bar{e}_M] \tag{20}$$

where $\bar{e}_i$ is the Eigenvector column with size (M $\times$ 1). For each Eigenvector ($\bar{e}_i$), there is a corresponding Eigenvalue λ_i. These Eigenvalues have to be sorted in descending way (i.e. from largest to smallest) and then selects the Eigenvector, which is associated with largest Eigenvalue. Once this eigenvector is obtained, the DOA can be found from the orthogonality between the Largest Eigenvector (LE) and the antenna array steering vector as follows:

$$P(\theta) = \bar{e}_1 \cdot \bar{a}(\theta) \tag{21}$$

The above equation will search on the maximal points, which represent the angles of arrival. However, these peaks are wide and in addition, there are high sidelobes associated with pseudospectrum of this equation. Therefore, it is better to search for nulls instead of maximal peaks. This can be achieved by subtracting the maximum value of $P(\theta)$ from all other values of $P(\theta)$ to obtain sharp peaks in the direction of received signals as follows:

$$P_{MSS}(\theta) = \frac{1}{P(\theta)_{max} - P(\theta) + \varepsilon} \tag{22}$$

where ε is small scalar value added in order to avoid the singularities.

4   Simulation Results and Discussion

A computer simulation has been performed to verify and demonstrate the theoretical concepts of the proposed method. This method has been applied to a uniform linear array (ULA) consisting of ten isotropic elements (M = 10) with a spacing distance equal to d = 0.5 λ. Two Binary Phase Shift Keying (BPSK) signals are assumed impinging on this antenna array. Four scenarios are considered in the simulation to explain the performance of proposed technique. The first scenario tests the ability of the proposed method to detect incoming signals when they are close to each other. The second scenario evaluates the behaviour of this method at different signal to noise ratio (SNR). The third case presents the estimation accuracy of the suggested method by computing the error between estimated and actual angles. The last one compare the performance and complexity of the proposed algorithm with three common methods. To estimate DOA by using this method, the following steps should be achieved:

- Step 1: Generate D signals with N samples for each signal.
- Step 2: Generate the angle of arrival of D signals randomly.
- Step 3: Compute the steering vectors a (θ) for each signal by applying Eq. 5 and then use Eq. 2 to compute total steering matrix of received signals A(θ).
- Step 4: Generate noise with specific SNR and then add it to the signal.
- Step 5: Compute the covariance matrix of the received signals by applying Eq. (9) for uncorrelated signals condition and Eq. (17) for coherent signals condition.
- Step 6: Use Eigen Value Decomposition (EVD) approach to decompose the covariance matrix and then select the eigenvector that corresponds to the largest eigenvalue.
- Step 7: Apply Eq. 21 and then determine the value of the maximum point. Subtract the value from all the values by applying Eq. 22 to obtain sharp peaks in the direction of arrival angles; ε is set to 0.01.
- Step 8: Compute the locations of the peaks to detect the arrival angles.

4.1 Angular Separation

This section simulates the performance of the suggested method by considering the angular separation between arrival signals. The SNR is assumed 10 dB and the number of samples taken for incident signals is 100; the true location of the direction of signals is represented by "o". Figure 3a shows the performance of the proposed method when the arrival signals are far from each other. While in the second case, it is supposed that there is a small angular separation between received signals as shown in Fig. 3b. It is obvious from these graphs that the proposed method has the ability to estimate the direction of arrival signals accurately even when these directions are close to each other.

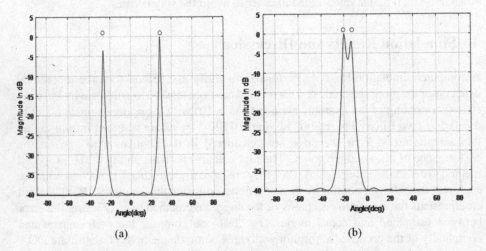

(a)   (b)

Fig. 3. The performance of the MSS method when changing the angular separation between AOAs; (a) Large angular space between AOAs, (b) Small angular space between AOAs.

4.2 Different SNR

This section tests the robustness of proposed method and its ability to work efficiently even if one or more of network parameters have failed. This can be achieved by changing the value of SNR of received signals. Thus, three different SNR values have been considered are SNR = 20 dB, 0 dB, −20 dB; and the number of samples chosen N = 100; the true direction of arrival signals are represented by "o". It is clear from this graph Fig. 4, that this algorithm gives good accuracy even at poor SNR. However, as the SNR increases, the peaks will be sharper and more accurate.

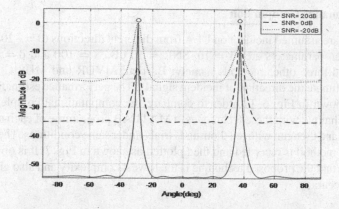

Fig. 4. The performance of MSS method with various SNR.

4.3 Accuracy of Estimation and Error Calculation

The accuracy of estimation is one of the most important factors which should take into our consideration to evaluate the performance of each technique. Accuracy illustrates the deviation degree of the estimated angles from the actual angles. Hence, Ten thousand sets of two angles of arrival have been generated randomly in order to evaluate and examine the resolution of estimation. This simulation section was achieved with the number of samples is 100 and SNR = 10 dB. The average absolute error between the actual and estimated directions is 1.422° and the cumulative distribution function (CDF) is shown in Fig. 5. It is clear from this figure, eighty percent of the average error is less than two degrees and this seems acceptable in most of the application.

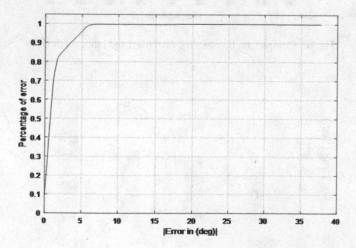

Fig. 5. CDF plot of total average error of the MSS algorithm.

4.4 Performance Comparsion

Two signals are assumed incident on ULA from different directions ($\theta = -20°$ and $10°$); the simulation parameters are M = 10, SNR = 10 dB, N = 100 and d = 0.5 λ. The proposed and three other methods namely: Bartlett, MVDR and MUSIC have been applied to estimate the direction of incident signals. The performance estimation of each method is shown in Fig. 6. In order to compare the computational complexity of the proposed technique with these techniques, a MATLAB programme of each method has been written and then run with ten thousands trials under same conditions. The execution time of each method is recorded and then plotted as shown in Fig. 7. It is obvious from these graphs that the proposed technique is the lowest complexity and also gives a good estimation accuracy.

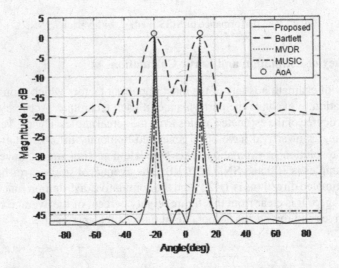

Fig. 6. Comparison between the proposed and other methods.

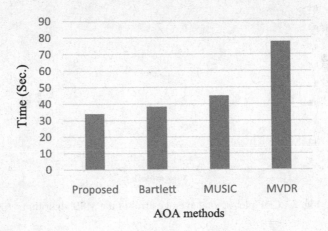

Fig. 7. Execution time comparison.

5   Conclusion

A maximum signal subspace (MSS) algorithm based on the eigenvector associated with the largest eigenvalue is has been proposed. The main benefits of the proposed technique its low computational complexity and does not require to pervious knowledge to the number of arrival signals since it only utilizes one eigenvector, regardless of the number of arrival signals. It has been tested and evaluated with different SNR and different directions of AOAs to demonstrate the theoretical concepts. In order to examine and test the proposed method on a wide range of circumstances, ten thousand values for two different AOA have been generated randomly. The error between actual and estimated angles has been computed and plotted as CDF function. This method has been compared with three common AOA techniques and the results have verified the effectiveness of the proposed method with good resolution, low computational complexity and small estimation error.

Acknowledgments. This work was partially supported by Antenna, Propagations and Radio Frequency Research Group, at Bradford University, United Kingdom and Higher Education Ministry of Iraq.

References

1. Zekavat, R., Buehrer, R.M.: Handbook of Position Location: Theory, Practice and Advances, vol. 27. Wiley, New york (2011)
2. Chen, Z., Gokeda, G., Yu, Y.: Introduction to Direction-of-Arrival Estimation. Artech House, Boston (2010)
3. Balanis, C.A., Ioannides, P.I.: Introduction to smart antennas. Synth. Lect. Antennas $2(1)$, 1–175 (2007)
4. Ghali, M.A., Abdullah, A.S., Mustafa, F.M.: Adaptive beam forming with position and velocity estimation for mobile station in smart antenna system. In: 2011 7th International Conference on Networked Computing and Advanced Information Management (NCM), Gyeongju, pp. 67–72 (2011)
5. Al-Sadoon, M., Abd-Alhameed, R.A., Elfergani, I., Noras, J., Rodriguez, J., Jones, S.: Weight optimization for adaptive antenna arrays using LMS and SMI algorithms. WSEAS Trans. Commun. **15**, 206–214 (2016)
6. Krim, H., Viberg, M.: Two decades of array signal processing research: the parametric approach. IEEE Signal Process. Magaz. **13**(4), 67–94 (1996)
7. Bartlett, M.: An Introduction to Stochastic Processes with Special References to Methods and Applications. Cambridge University Press, New York (1961)
8. Capon, J.: High-resolution frequency-wavenumber spectrum analysis. Proc. IEEE **57**(8), 1408–1418 (1969)
9. Schmidt, R.: Multiple emitter location and signal parameter estimation. IEEE Trans. Antennas Propag. **34**(3), 276–280 (1986)
10. Gross, F.: Smart Antennas with Matlab: Principles and Applications in Wireless Communication. McGraw-Hill Professional, New York (2015)

MIMO Based Multi Band Antenna for Wireless Communication in C-Band, X-Band, K-Band and Ku Band

Kunal Srivastava[1]([✉]), Ashwani Kumar[2], Binod Kanaujia[3], Santanu Dwari[4],
A.K. Verma[5], Mukul Yadav[6], Josyula Lalita[1], and S. Chamarthi[7]

[1] Sri Venkateswara College, New Delhi, India
kunal.1211@gmail.com
[2] Sri Aurobindo College, New Delhi, India
ashwanikumar7@yahoo.com
[3] Ambedkar Institute of Advance Technology, New Delhi, India
[4] ISM Dhanbad, Dhanbad, India
[5] Delhi University, New Delhi, India
[6] Department of Electronics and Information Technology,
Kurukshetra University, Kurukshetra, India
mukul.yadav@deity.gov.in
[7] Department of Instrumentation, Kurukshetra University, Kurukshetra, India

Abstract. This paper presents a design of a multiband MIMO microstrip patch antenna. The isolation between the two ports varies from 12.5 dB to 44 dB for all the available bands. Proposed antenna is useful for C-Band, X-Band, K-Band and Ku-Band applications. The proposed antenna shows the circular polarization behavior at 5.27 GHz (5.26 GHz–5.31 GHz), 6.20 GHz (6.18 GHz–6.22 GHz), 11.89 GHz (11.72 GHz–12.24 GHz), 13.56 GHz (13.46 GHz–13.61 GHz), 16.68 GHz (16.55 GHz–16.85 GHz), 21.17 GHz (21.17 GHz–21.20 GHz) and 22.84 GHz (22.28 GHz–22.93 GHz). The proposed antenna is designed on FR-4 substrate with relative permittivity 4.4 and thickness 1.59 mm.

Keywords: Antenna · Multiple-input–multiple-output (MIMO) · Mutual coupling · Multiband · Micro strip patch

1 Introduction

Emerging technologies in the modern wireless communication systems require products that are capable of providing multiple services within a single device. Multiple-input-multiple-output (MIMO) technology is used to increase the capacity and quality of the channels, which are used in communications. Recently, MIMO antennas have been widely studied and used in wireless local area network (WLAN), mobile communication, wireless broadband network and other mobile communication networks. MIMO antennas aim to produce a high isolation among the multi-antenna elements used in the transmitter and receiver; thus in a limited space the channel capacity of the communication system can be increased without increasing bandwidth [1–5].

© ICST Institute for Computer Sciences, Social Informatics and Telecommunications Engineering 2017
I. Otung et al. (Eds.): WiSATS 2016, LNICST 186, pp. 28–36, 2017.
DOI: 10.1007/978-3-319-53850-1_4

The data rate, operating distance and link reliability can be highly improved without using extra spectrum and transmission power in MIMO technology. It helps to handle large data, video and voice stream. MIMO systems are useful for both Line Of Sight (LOS) and non-LOS (NLOS) indoor wireless communications; they reduce the channel's multipath and increase the data throughput [3, 4]. To date, huge R&D has been done to improve underground MIMO channel performances [3–5].

In recent years, lot of work has been done on integrated and multifunctional wireless communication systems. Multi-band antennas play an important role and are extremely desired, as they can be simultaneously used for different signal frequencies [3, 4]. To the best of our knowledge the work done on the multi-band MIMO antennas is very less in the open literature.

This paper presents new design method to design a multi-band antenna with MIMO for C-Band, X-Band, K-Band and Ku-Band applications.

2   Antenna Design

Proposed antenna has been designed on the FR-4 substrate with relative permittivity $\epsilon_r = 4.4$, thickness 1.59 mm and loss tangent 0.02. A 3-dimensional EM simulator HFSS (v.11) has been used to design the antenna. The dimensions of the antenna are: a = 19.5 mm, b = 11.5 mm, c = 6.5 mm, d = 1.5 mm, e = 13.1 mm, f = 3.0 mm, g = 10.46 mm, h = i = 4.0 mm, j = 5 mm, and w = L = 40 mm as shown in Fig. 1. The proposed antenna has a unique combination of two opposite face C-type rings. The radius of the outer ring is 19.5 mm, ring width is 3 mm and gap between two rings is 2 mm. The width of the 50 Ω line is 10.46 mm, which has been used for feeding the antenna and also for impedance matching. The gap between two rings plays a major role in optimizing the resonant frequency and

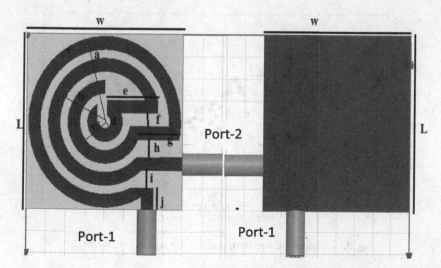

Fig. 1. Layout with dimensions of the proposed antenna (a) Top side (b) Bottom side

isolation between two ports. By changing the gap between the two rings, one can increase the isolation and shift the position of resonant frequency.

Figure 2 shows the |S11| of the antenna while Fig. 3 shows the isolation between two ports. The resonant frequency, bandwidth and % fractional bandwidth are shown in Table 1. From the Fig. 2 it is clear that the antenna is useful for different frequencies between 4.5 GHz to 25 GHz, which cover the C-Band, X-Band, K-Band and Ku-Band. Figure 3 shows the isolation between the Port 1 and Port 2 which is found to vary from 12.5 dB to 44 dB. This shows its effectiveness for the MIMO antenna as well as for multi-band application.

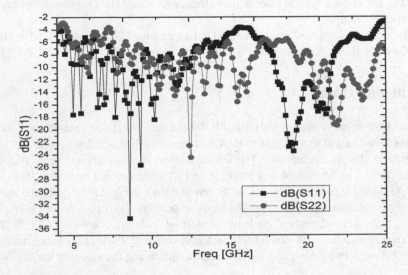

Fig. 2. |S11| and |S22| frequency response of the proposed antenna

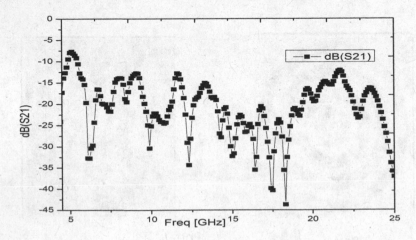

Fig. 3. Isolation between two ports of the antenna |S21| (dB)

Table 1. Performance of the Proposed antenna

Resonant Frequency (Fr) (GHz)	Lower Cutoff of B.W (Fl) (GHz)	Upper Cutoff of B.W (Fh) (GHz)	Bandwidth (GHz)	Percentage Bandwidth ((Fh – Fl)/ Fr)*100
S11				
4.96	4.89	5.08	0.19	3.83
5.47	5.39	5.58	0.19	3.47
6.08	6.04	6.13	0.09	1.48
6.57	6.52	6.77	0.25	3.80
6.96	6.90	7.17	0.27	3.87
7.64	7.58	7.88	0.30	3.92
8.57 & 9.28	8.17	9.45	1.28	14.93 & 13.79
10.14	9.84	10.44	0.60	5.91
11.63	11.37	12.02	0.65	5.58
19.06 & 21.18	17.93	21.56	3.63	20.24 & 17.13
S22				
10.45	10.21	10.80	0.59	5.64
11.46	11.18	11.76	0.58	5.06
12.48	12.19	12.72	0.53	4.24
13.39	13.20	13.59	0.39	2.91
14.29	14.19	14.50	0.31	2.16
15.46 & 16.08	15.27	16.31	1.04	6.72 & 6.46
20.57	20.32	20.96	0.64	3.11
21.77 & 23.50	21.25	24.22	2.97	13.64 & 12.63

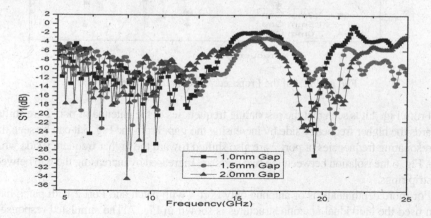

Fig. 4. |S11| of the Proposed Antenna for different gaps.

3 Parametric Study

The effect of the gap between the strips of the rings from 1 mm to 2 mm is shown in Fig. 4. Impedance bandwidth and isolation between the two ports are shown in the Figs. 4, 5 and 6.

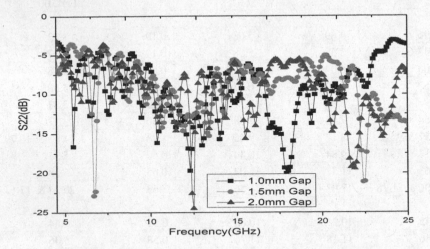

Fig. 5. |S22| of the Proposed Antenna for different gaps.

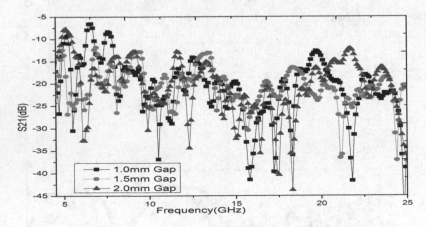

Fig. 6. |S21| of the Proposed Antenna for different gaps.

From Fig. 4 it is seen that the resonating frequencies of the antenna of port 1 are shifted towards the higher frequency side by increasing the gap. From the Fig. 5 it can be seen that the resonating frequencies of port 2 are also shifted toward the higher frequency side while from Fig. 6 the isolation between the two ports are increased by increasing the gap between the strip rings.

For more depth analysis of antenna only Port 1 with patch and Port 2 with patch have been used the individual antenna structures is shown in Fig. 7. The simulated response is shown in Fig. 8.

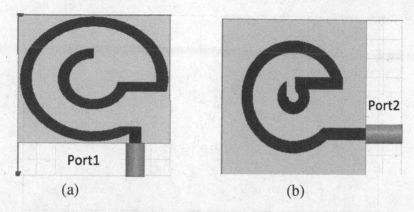

Fig. 7. Proposed Antenna structure (a) with Port 1 (b) with Port 2

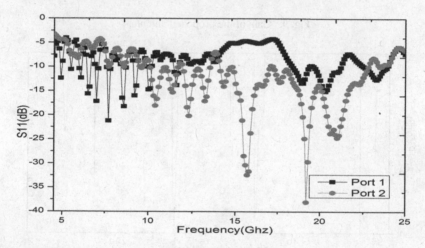

Fig. 8. Antenna structure with Port 1 and Port 2

From Fig. 8 it is clear that the antenna with individual Port 1 resonates in lower frequency range from 4.5 GHz to 12 GHz while antenna with Port 2 resonates from 10 GHz to 22 GHz. As both the ports are connected to the patch, the antenna starts resonating at both the lower frequency as well as higher frequencies, shown in Fig. 2 and Table 1.

This antenna supports ten frequency bands at Port 1, and eight frequency bands at Port 2. Thus, it shows the usefulness for multi-band applications. Most of the multi-band antennas are known to suffer with low gain problems [6, 7] this proposed multi-band antenna, however, is seen to overcome the low gain problems. Gain of the proposed antenna is shown in the Fig. 9. It varies from 1 dB to 24 dB for the entire spectrum of the antenna. This antenna also exhibits the circular polarization for different bands, which is very useful for wireless communication. The axial ratio response of the proposed antenna is shown in the Fig. 10. The axial ratio at resonant frequencies, bandwidth and percentage bandwidth are given in Table 2.

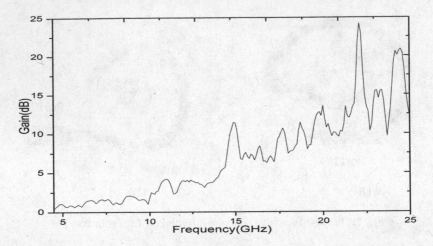

Fig. 9. Gain of the proposed antenna

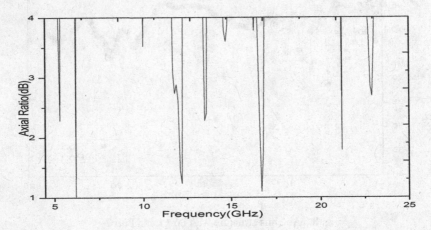

Fig. 10. Axial ratio of the proposed antenna

Proposed antenna shows the circular polarization behavior in C-Band, X-Band, K-Band and Ku-Band. This behavior is suitable for satellite communications, radar, terrestrial broadband, space communications, amateur radio in X-band; satellite communications in K-band; and radar, satellite communications and astronomical observations. The radiation pattern of the proposed antenna for the different frequencies are shown in Fig. 11.

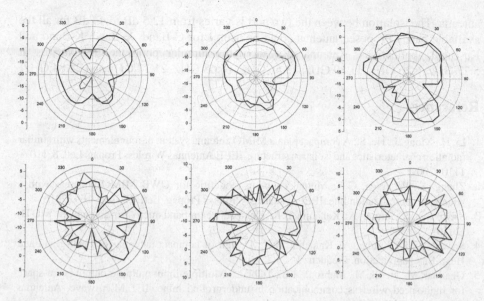

Fig. 11. Radiation pattern of proposed antenna at (a) 5.5 GHz (b) 8.6 GHz (c) 10.5 GHz (d) 14.3 GHz (e) 19.0 GHz & (f) 21.8 GHz

Table 2. Axial Ratio and bandwidth.

Resonant Frequency (Fr) (GHz)	Lower Cutoff of B.W (Fl) (GHz)	Upper Cutoff of B.W (Fh) (GHz)	Bandwidth (GHz)	Percentage Bandwidth ((Fh – Fl)/Fr)*100
5.27	5.26	5.31	0.05	0.94
6.20	6.18	6.22	0.04	0.64
11.89	11.72	12.24	0.52	4.37
13.56	13.46	13.61	0.15	1.106
16.68	16.55	16.85	0.30	1.79
21.17	21.17	21.20	0.03	0.14
22.84	22.28	22.93	0.65	2.84

From the figure it is clear that at lower frequency and higher frequency antenna shows co-polarization. Moreover, at lower frequency E-plane shows unidirectional properties and H-plane show omni-directional properties but at higher frequency it shows some distorted behavior.

4 Conclusion

A multi-band MIMO microstrip patch antenna has been presented. The parametric study has been presented to see the effect of various parameters on the performances of the antenna. The isolation between the two port is varies from 12.5 dB to 44 dB for all the available bands Proposed antenna could be useful for C-Band, X-Band, K-Band and Ku-Band applications. Antenna also show the circular polarization behaviors at 5.27 GHz, 6.20 GHz, 11.89 GHz, 13.56 GHz, 16.68 GHz, 21.17 GHz and 22.84 GHz.

References

1. Li, H., Xiong, J., He, S.: A compact planar MIMO antenna system of four elements with similar radiation characteristics and isolation structure. IEEE Antennas Wireless Propag. Lett. **8**, 1107–1110 (2009)
2. Zhang, S., Pedersen, G.F.: Mutual coupling reduction for UWB MIMO antennas with a wideband neutralization line. IEEE Antennas Wireless Propag. Lett. **15**, 166–169 (2016)
3. Srivastava, K., kumar, A., Kanaujia, B.K.: Compact penta-band microstrip antenna. In: MOTL (2016)
4. Srivastava, K., kumar, A., Kanaujia, B.K.: Design of compact antenna for Penta-Band and Hexa-Band application. Frequenz J.
5. Ghaddar, M., Nedil, M., Mabrouk, I.B., Talbi, L.: Multiple-input multiple-output beam-space for high-speed wireless communication in underground mine. IET Microwave. Antennas Propag. **10**, 8–15 (2016)
6. Yarkan, S., Guzelgoz, S., Arslan, H., et al.: Underground mine communications: a survey. IEEE Commun. Surv. Tutor. **11**(3), 125–142 (2009)
7. Valdesueiro, J.A., Izquierdo, B., Romeu, J.: On 2 × 2 MIMO observable capacity in subway tunnels at C-band: an experimental approach. IEEE Antennas Propag. Lett. **9**, 1099–1102 (2010)

A Staircase-Shaped DGS Structure Monopole Antenna for UWB Operations

Naeem A. Jan[1], Mohammed Lashab[2], Nazar T. Ali[1,3], Fathi M. Abdussalam[1],
Embarak M. Ibrahim[4], Raed A. Abd-Alhameed[1(✉)], and M.B. Child[1]

[1] Faculty of Engineering and Informatics, University of Bradford, Bradford, UK
kakarnayeem@yahoo.com, {r.a.a.abd,m.b.child}@bradford.ac.uk
[2] Electronics Department, Skikda University, Skikda, Algeria
lashabmoh@gmail.com
[3] Electrical and Computer Engineering, Khalifa University, Abu Dhabi, United Arab Emirates
ntali@kustar.ac.uk
[4] College of Electronic Technology Bani Walid, Bani Walid, Libya

Abstract. This paper presents a novel, physically compact, miniaturized, ultra-wideband (UWB) monopole antenna design, which utilizes a defected ground structure (DGS). The defected ground design is realized as a spiral staircase-shaped pattern, and the optimized antenna volume is $26 \times 25 \times 1.6$ mm^3. The resultant antenna operates over the full UWB frequency range from 3.1 GHz to 10.6 GHz, with predicted gains in the range 0.1 dBi to 3.36 dBi across the band.

Keywords: Defected ground structure (DGS) · Ultra-wideband (UWB) · Metamaterial (MTM) antenna · Monopole antenna

1 Introduction

UWB continues to receive widespread attention because of it's immunity to multipath interference, and the ever increasing demand for larger bandwidths and higher data rates. Applications that can benefit from ultra-wideband technology include broadband wireless communication systems, peer-to-peer ultra-fast communications and short range communication systems and sensor networks.

There are several well established techniques for achieving ultra-wideband antenna characteristics. These are now routinely supplemented by the use of techniques based on artificial metamaterials, with specific electromagnetic (constituitive) parameters. Examples include composite righthand/lefthand (CRLH antennas, metamaterial loaded antenna structures, and metasurfaces or electromagnetic bandgap structures (EBG) [1]. EBG approaches date back to the late 1980 s through the work of Yablonovitch and Pendry [2].

EBG structures can be classified into four distinct categories; defected ground structure (DGS), photonic band-gap structure (PBG), high impedance electromagnetic surfaces (HIS) and artificial magnetic conductors (AMC) [3, 4]. The stop-band characteristics of EBG and DGS structures are be used for wide range of antenna applications such as miniaturization, gain enhancement, and promote stable radiation patterns. A

© ICST Institute for Computer Sciences, Social Informatics and Telecommunications Engineering 2017
I. Otung et al. (Eds.): WiSATS 2016, LNICST 186, pp. 37–44, 2017.
DOI: 10.1007/978-3-319-53850-1_5

major feature of EBG/DGS antennas is in establishing large bandwidths, and miniaturisation [5, 6] through the modification and suppression of surface waves. Various compact shapes of monopole antennas with defected ground structure (DGS) have been reported in for UWB applications [7, 8]. However, due to small antenna sizes, the gain in the lower band is always lower than the upper band [8]. In [8] the bandwidth is wide because of the CPW feeding - this feeding enhances bandwidth but not the gain. In this paper a monopole antenna, with a novel defected ground structure, is designed for small size, with positive gain and stable radiation pattern performance across the full UWB service band.

2   Antenna Design and Optimization

The geometrical configuration of the defected ground structure (DGS) is shown in Fig. 1, and the proposed antenna is shown in Fig. 2. The antenna model was simulated using HFSS. The substrate is FR4, with relative permittivity of 4.4, a loss tangent of 0.02, and a thickness 1.6 mm. The front side of the substrate is patterned with monopole and the back side is patterned with the DGS. The cloud shape monopole antenna is chosen for its novelty and a triangular patch is cut on top of the antenna to reduce a footprint without affecting the characteristic of the antenna, which gives rise to wider bandwidth and stable radiation pattern.

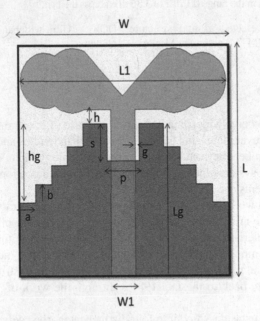

Fig. 1. Geometry of proposed DGS monopole antenna

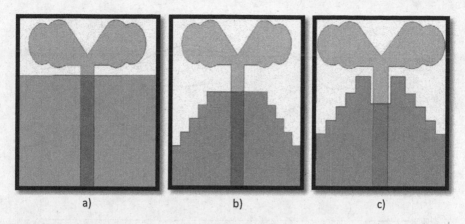

Fig. 2. (a) Simple ground monopole (b) DGS monopole (c) Front (pink) & Back (blue) of modified DGS monopole (Color figure online)

The construction of the defected ground structure was inspired from the arrangement of spiral staircase inside the ancient Mayan "El Caracol" observatory, which will further enhance the bandwidth and radiation pattern. Initially only a three quarter simple and plain ground is etched at the back of the substrate (Fig. 2a), and then the sides of the ground are carved in stairs on both sides, which gives rise to resonances from 3.1 to 6 GHz and 9 GHz and above (Fig. 2b). The middle of the DGS is then modified by cutting a square shape of size (s × p) i.e. (4.1 × 4) mm which produces the UWB frequency response from 3.1 to 10.6 GHz (Fig. 2c). The antenna is fed by a 50 Ω microstrip line of width 3 mm. The antenna volume is $26 \times 25 \times 1.6$ mm^3. The optimized parameters of the DGS and UWB antenna (shown in Fig. 1) are given in Table 1. The simulated reflection coefficients for the three antenna variants are shown in Fig. 3. Initially, there is no radiation with the plane ground plane. For the defected structure, radiation from 3.1 GHz to 6 GHz and then from 9 GHz can be observed. Finally in the modified DGS, a square patch is carved in the middle of the upper part of the DGS, a continuous full band UWB frequency response is obtained.

Table 1. The optimized parameter of the propose UWB antenna

Parameter	Value mm	Parameter	Value mm
L	25	h	1.5
W	26	hg	8.5
L1	25.6	g	0.6
Lg	16.5	s	4.1
a	2	p	4
b	2	w1	3

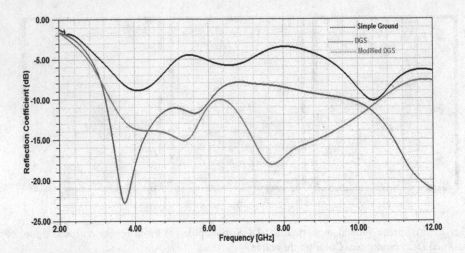

Fig. 3. Reflection coefficient of the monopole antenna with simple plain ground, DGS and Modified DGS.

3 Discussion of Parametric Performance Analysis

Figure 4 shows the comparison of simulated return loss (S_{11}) of the monopole antenna for different spacing sizes, "h", of the defected ground structure (DGS). The structure parameter "h" is the gap between the ground and the upper part of the monopole. Both parts are on opposite sides of the substrate as shown in Fig. 1. The different "h" values used are 1.2 mm, 1.5 mm, 2 mm and 2.5 mm. The graph indicates that the best results are observed for "h" equal to 1.5 mm in the frequency range from 3.1 to 10.6 GHz. For this graph the

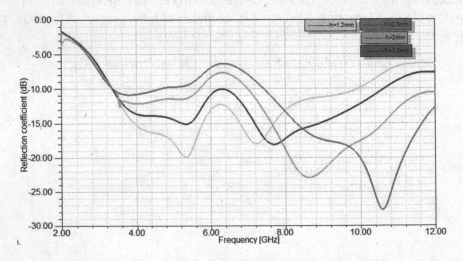

Fig. 4. Reflection coefficient of UWB antenna for different "h"

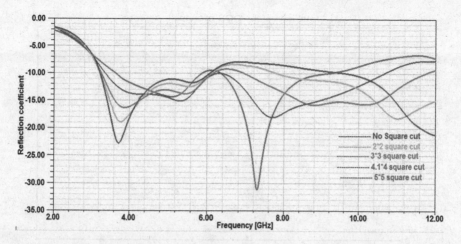

Fig. 5. Reflection coefficient of UWB antenna for different s × p

square shaped cut in the middle of the ground is maintained at 4.1 mm × 4 mm, this removes any discontinuity in the frequency range from 6 to 7 GHz.

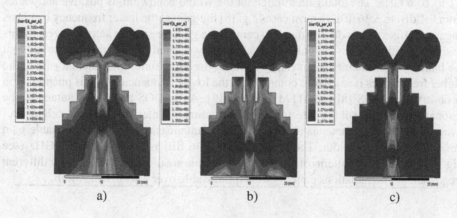

Fig. 6. Current distribution at different frequencies (a) 3.2 GHz (b) 7 GHz (c) 10 GHz

Figure 5, shows the parameter study for the DGS monopole antenna for different "s × p" sizes. Here, "s × p" is the square shaped cut in the middle of the defected ground. Initially a DGS is simulated without any square cut in the middle. Afterwards, four different square cuts of 2 mm × 2 mm, 3 mm × 3 mm, 4.1 mm × 4 mm and 5 mm × 5 mm are sequentially introduced in the middle of the ground. The graph clearly illustrates that the best results are observed for "s × p" at 4.1 mm × 4 mm in the frequency range between 3.1 to 10.6 GHz. From this graph, the gap between the ground and monopole antenna is kept at h = 1.5 mm, which will remove any discontinuity in the frequency range from 6 GHz and above.

Figure 6 shows current distribution at three different frequencies of 3.2 GHz, 7 GHz and 10 GHz. Figure 7 shows the antenna gain across the full UWB frequency band from

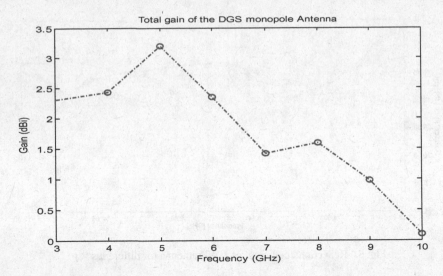

Fig. 7. Total Gain of DGS monopole antenna across the UWB

3.1 to 10.6 GHz. The total gain throughout the whole bandwidth is positive and varies from 0.1 dBi to 3.36 dBi. In most cases e.g. [8] the gain at the lower frequency band has negative values as it is often difficult to control the gain for smaller antenna sizes. In this design a positive gain is not only observable at lower band frequencies, but throughout the band, whilst making the antenna smaller at the same time. The antenna gain at the higher frequencies is smaller as compared to the lower frequencies, as this phenomenon is observed in DGS [8] and MTM antennas [9]. As in DGS and MTM antennas, the resonance is because of the defected ground structure and metamaterial unit cell respectively rather than the antenna alone itself; these antennas can't withhold a stable gain throughout the bandwidth. The peak gain of 3.36 dBi is observed at 5.2 GHz (see Fig. 7). The far fields patterns of the proposed antenna are illustrated in Fig. 8 for different frequencies. The radiations patterns were quite stable over a wide bandwidth.

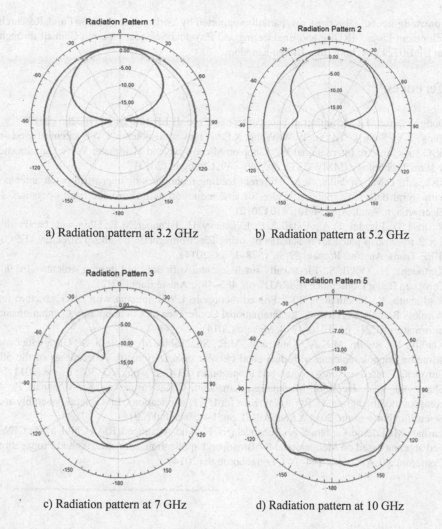

a) Radiation pattern at 3.2 GHz   b) Radiation pattern at 5.2 GHz

c) Radiation pattern at 7 GHz   d) Radiation pattern at 10 GHz

Fig. 8. Simulated E-Plane (Red) and H-Plane (Blue) at (a) 3.2 GHz, (b) 5.2 GHz, (c) 7 GHz. (d) 10 GHz (Color figure online)

4   Conclusion

A miniature monopole antenna, with a novel defected ground structure, has been presented for WLAN 5.2/5.8 GHz and full-band UWB operations. The simulation model was analysed using HFSS, and predicts a working bandwidth operating over the full UWB range from 3.1 GHz to 10.6 GHz. This broad banding is a function of the defected ground structure, which also contributes to the gains observed from 0.1 dBi to 3.36 dBi across the range, and associated pattern stability.

Acknowledgments. This work was partially supported by Yorkshire Innovation Fund, Research Development Project (RDP); and Engineering and Physical Science Research Council through Grant EP/E022936A, both from United Kingdom.

References

1. Dong, Y., Itoh, T.: Metamaterial-based antennas. Proc. IEEE **100**(7), 2271–2285 (2012)
2. Yang, T.Y., Song, C.Y., Lin, W.W., Yang, X.L.: A new band-notched UWB antenna based on EBG structure. In: International Workshop on Microwave and Millimeter Wave Circuits and System Technology (MMWCST), pp. 146–149, Chengdu (2013)
3. Elsheakh, D.M., Abdallah, E.A.: Different feeding techniques of microstrip patch antennas with spiral defected ground structure for size reduction and ultra-wide band operation. J. Electromagn. Anal. Appl. **4**(10), 410 (2012)
4. Nashaat, D., Elsadek, H.A., Abdallah, E., Elhenawy, H., Iskander, M.F.: Ultra-wide bandwidth 2 × 2 microstrip patch array antenna by using Electromagnetic BandGap Structure (EBG). IEEE Trans. Antenns Propag. **59**(5), 1528–1538 (2011)
5. Kimouche, H., Oukil, S.: Electrically small antenna with defected ground structure. In: 9th European Radar Conference (EuRAD), pp. 485–488, Amsterdam (2012)
6. Reghunath, V., Sukumaran, S.K.: Printed monopole UWB antenna with EBG structure for Wireless Body Area Network. In: International Conference on Contemporary Computing and Informatics (IC3I), pp. 1310–1314, Mysore (2014)
7. Khalily, M., Rahim, M.K.A., Kamarudin, M.R., Shaneshin, M., Danesh, S.: Ultra wideband printed monopole antenna with dual-band circular polarization. In: Proceedings of the 5th European Conference on Antennas and Propagation (EUCAP), pp. 365–368, Rome (2011)
8. Shameena, V.A., Jacob, S., Mridula, S., Aanandan, C.K., Vasudevan, K., Mohanan, P., A compact modified ground CPW fed antenna for UWB applications. In: General Assembly and Scientific Symposium, 2011 XXXth URSI, pp. 1–4, Istanbul (2011)
9. Lashab, M., Eddine, C., Jan, N.A., Benabdelaziz, F., Abd-Alhameed, R.A., Child, M.B.: CPW-Fed antenna based on Metamaterial for Broadband application. In: Antennas and Propagation Conference (LAPC), pp. 144–147, Loughborough (2014)

Technical Session 2

Implementation of a Low-Rate Linear Step FM Transceiver on a Software Defined Radio Platform

Yih-Min Chen[✉], Shin-Chi Liao, and Ying-Chang Chen

Department of Communication Engineering, National Central University,
Taiwan Chung-Da Road 300, Chung-Li, Taoyuan, Taiwan
ymchen@ce.ncu.edu.tw

Abstract. Linear FM (Chirp) signals have the merits of constant envelope and insusceptibility to significant carrier frequency offset which particularly suit for low-power low-rate communications. However, the fully digital implementation of the matched filter for the chirp signals is not economically feasible. A low data-rate communication technique using linear step frequency modulated (LSFM) signal was thus proposed which exhibits a complexity reduction in the matched filter implementation with an acceptable performance loss compared to the chirp signals. This paper presents an implementation of such an LSFM transceiver on a realistic commercially available software-defined radio (SDR) platform. Specific system parameters in the LSFM are designed for a furthermore complexity reduction. Implementation cost and experimental results are presented.

Keywords: Chirp communications · Low-rate · Matched-filter · Linear step FM · Transceiver · Software-defined radio

1 Introduction

Wireless communication techniques have been evolving at an exceptional rate recently and will be continually in the near future. Although the mainstream techniques are broadband wireless communications which satisfy the demand of mobile internet services, there are low data-rate techniques due to the growing needs of wireless sensor networks deployment [1]. In a low-rate wireless personal area network (LR-WPAN) standard (IEEE 802.15.4a), the chirp spread-spectrum (CSS) signals are used to support long-range links between sensor nodes.

Chirp signals, also known as linear frequency modulated (LFM) signals, are traditionally used in radar/sonar applications due to its special characteristics in ambiguity function, i.e., pulse compression and Doppler-shift/carrier-frequency-offset (CFO) immunity. Recently the chirp signal has been exploited in communications mainly for immunity against multipath/interference or multiple access purposes [2–8]. The generation of the transmitted chirp signals and the matched filtering in the receiver are mainly relied on the analog surface acoustic wave (SAW) chirped delay lines [9, 10]. In [10], a full-digital implementation of radar chirp pulse compression (matched filtering) using FFT processors is proposed. For a communication system requiring high receiver sensitivity, lower data-rate is mandated and the carrier frequency offset (CFO) between the transmitter and the receiver

© ICST Institute for Computer Sciences, Social Informatics and Telecommunications Engineering 2017
I. Otung et al. (Eds.): WiSATS 2016, LNICST 186, pp. 47–54, 2017.
DOI: 10.1007/978-3-319-53850-1_6

then becomes significant relative to the symbol rate. In this scenario, digital signaling with long symbol period wideband chirps is feasible, which incurs a greater complexity in the digital implementation of the corresponding matched filters. In [11, 12] we have proposed an economic transceiver architecture based on linear step frequency modulated (LSFM) signals, which approximates the chirp signals, and a specific preamble signal designed for symbol/frame/CFO synchronization. The proposed transceiver technique is adequate for physical layer implementation for Low–Power, Wide-Area Networks [13].

This paper presents an implementation of the proposed transceiver on a realistic software-defined radio (SDR) platform which comprises of an RF TX/RX module for RF/Baseband signal conversion and an FPGA for real-time digital signal processing. Implementation cost and experiment results regarding to the receiver performance are given for a specific LSFM system parameters.

2   Chirp Binary Orthogonal Keying with Linear Step FM Signals

In a digital communication system with chirp binary orthogonal keying (BOK), up-chirp and down-chirp signals are typically used to transmit binary data correspondingly. The system model of a chirp BOK communication system with RF frontend and digital modulator/demodulator is shown in Fig. 1. The transmitted baseband signal formulated by

$$s_B(t) = \sum_k s_{a_k}\left(t - k \cdot T_{sym}\right) \tag{1}$$

where $s_{a_k}(t) = \begin{cases} s_{up-chirp}(t), & a_k = 1 \\ s_{down-chirp}(t) = s^*_{up-chirp}(t), & a_k = 0 \end{cases}$, a_k denotes the kth binary data and T_{sym}

is the symbol period. A chirp BOK communication system based on a linear step FM (LSFM) signal is proposed in [11, 12] for simplified the digital matched filter implementation, where the traditional up-chirp (LFM) signal

$$s_{LFM}(t) = \begin{cases} e^{j \cdot \frac{2\pi}{T_{sym}} \cdot \Delta f \left(t^2 - \frac{T_{sym}}{2} \cdot t\right)}, & 0 \le t < T_{sym} \\ 0, & otherwise \end{cases}$$, with Δf denoting the frequency swift range

$(-0.5\Delta f \sim 0.5\Delta f)$ (chirp span) during the chirp/symbol period T_{sym}, is replaced with

$$s_{LSFM}(t) = \sum_{m=0}^{M-1} s^m_{LSFM}\left(t - m \cdot \frac{T_{sym}}{M}\right),$$

$$s^m_{LSFM}(t) = \begin{cases} e^{j \cdot \left(2\pi \cdot f_m \cdot t + \theta_m\right)}, & 0 \le t < \frac{T_{sym}}{M} \\ 0, & otherwise \end{cases} \tag{2}$$

where M $(m = 0 \sim M - 1)$, $f_\Delta = \Delta f / (M - 1)$ and $f_m = -\Delta f / 2 + m \cdot f_\Delta$ denote the number of steps, the frequency step and the instantaneous frequency at the mth step, respectively, while $\theta_m = \theta_0 + \sum_{l=0}^{m-1} f_l \cdot T_{sym} / M$ is the phase adjustment for making the signal continual in phase.

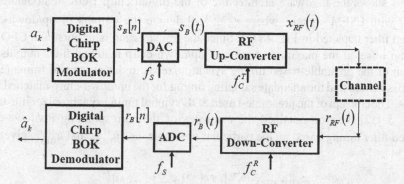

Fig. 1. The system model of a chirp BOK communication system

3 LSFM Transceiver Architecture

3.1 LSFM Transmitter

Figure 2 shows the hardware architecture of the digital chirp BOK modulator (in Fig. 1) with LSFM signals, where $\Delta\omega = 2\pi \cdot \Delta f / f_S$ and $\omega_\Delta = \Delta\omega / (M - 1)$ denote the chirp span and frequency step in digital domain with a sampling frequency $f_S = N / T_{sym}$ and $N = M \cdot N_M$. The frame structure is designed with a specific preamble, i.e., 10101010, which facilitates frame/symbol timing synchronization in a scenario with signification CFO, followed by a payload data stream of P bits length. The main cost of the hardware

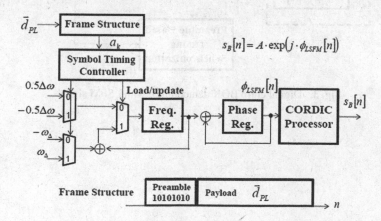

Fig. 2. Digital chirp BOK modulator with LSFM signals

implementation of the digital baseband modulator is thus the phase rotation which can be typically implemented by a CORDIC processor.

3.2 LSFM Receiver

Figure 3 shows the hardware architecture of the digital chirp BOK demodulator (in Fig. 1) with LSFM signals, where $r_M^{down/up}[n]$ denote the outputs of up/down-chirp matched filter depicted in Fig. 4 [12]. Since the transmission is in burst and CFO will cause an offset at the maximum timing of up/down-chirp matched filter outputs, the function of the preamble-based timing synchronizer is to detect start of frame (SOF) transmission and find the adequate sampling timing for the up/down-chirp matched filter outputs. The concept of the preamble-based SOF/symbol timing synchronizer illustrated in Fig. 5 [12]. Having obtained the estimates of the corresponding up/down-chirp matched filter timing based on the particular preamble, i.e., $\hat{n}_{\max}^{up}$ and $\hat{n}_{\max}^{down}$, given by

$$\hat{n}_{\max}^{up/down} = \arg \max_n \sum_{p=0}^{N_p-1} \left| r_M^{up/down}[n - 2 \cdot p \cdot N] \right|^2 \tag{3}$$

the payload data is then detected by the following formula

$$\hat{a}_k = \left| r_M^{up}[\hat{n}_{\max}^{up} + k \cdot N] \right|^2 > \left| r_M^{down}[\hat{n}_{\max}^{down} + k \cdot N] \right|^2 \tag{4}$$

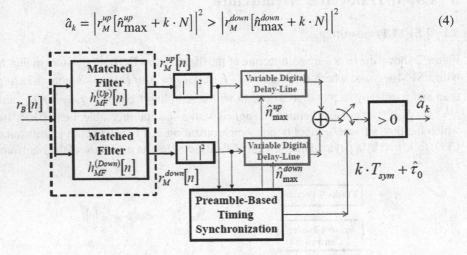

Fig. 3. Digital chirp BOK demodulator with LSFM signals

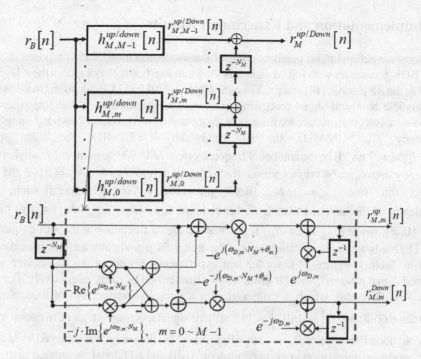

Fig. 4. Low-complexity digital matched filter for up/down-chirp LSFM signals

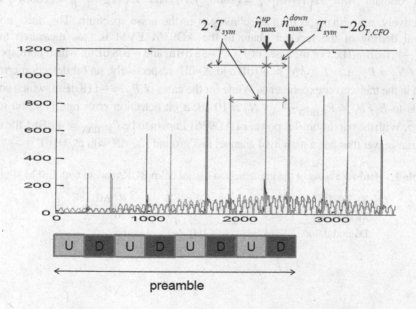

Fig. 5. Illustration of the preamble-based SOF/symbol timing synchronizer

4   Implementation and Experiment Results

The software-defined radio platform used for the implementation of the proposed digital chirp BOK transceiver with LSFM signals is shown in Fig. 6, which comprises the AD9361 EVM as the RF module [14] and the Xilinx/SMIMS AC701 FPGA Evaluation Board as the configurable baseband signal processing module. The specification of the implemented LSFM signals is given as follows: the carrier frequency $f_C = 3$ GHz, the baseband sampling frequency $f_S = 30.72$ MHz, the RF bandwidth $B = 20$ MHz, the chirp span $\Delta f = f_S/4 = 7.68$ MHz, the number of frequency steps $M = 33$, the number of samples per frequency step $N_M = 64$ symbol period which corresponds to $N = M \cdot N_M = 2112$ and the symbol (bit) rate $f_{sym} = f_S/N = 14.5$ Ksymbols/sec. With this specification, the complexity of the matched filter is further reduced since $\exp\left(j\omega_{D,m} \cdot N_M\right) \in \{\pm 1\}$ and $\theta_m \in \{0, \pi\}$, where $\omega_{D,m} = 2\pi \cdot f_m/f_S$ denotes the digital frequency at the mth frequency step. The hardware implementation costs of the digital chirp modulator and demodulator are listed in Table 1. Figure 7 shows the real experimental results of the transceiver with received signal power P_R of -88 dBm, -108 dBm and -118 dBm, respectively. For the $P_R = -88$ dBm case, which is calibrated with a transmission scenario of transmission attenuation 60 dB and $E\left\{\left|s_B[n]\right|^2\right\} = (1800)^2$, the signal spectrum is noticed to rise up from the noise floor. For cases of $P_R = -108$ dBm and -118 dBm, which is achieved by setting the transmission attenuation to the maximum of 70 dB and additional attenuation in digital signal domain with $E\left\{\left|s_B[n]\right|^2\right\} = (1800)^2/10$ and $E\left\{\left|s_B[n]\right|^2\right\} = (1800)^2/100$, respectively, the signal spectrum is submerged in the noise spectrum. The noise power spectral density of the receiver chain in the AD9361 EVM is thus measured to be $N_0 \approx -170$ dBm/Hz. For the cases of $P_R = -88$ dBm and -108 dBm, which corresponds to $E_b/N_0 = P_{R,\min} \cdot T_{sym}/N_0 \approx 40$ dB and 20 dB, respectively, no bit detection error is found in the transceiver experiments. While for the cases of $P_R = -118$ dBm, which corresponds to $E_b/N_0 = P_{R,\min} \cdot T_{sym}/N_0 \approx 10$ dB, a bit detection error rate is found to be $\approx 10^{-2}$. With the maximum TX power of AD9361 known to be $P_{T,\max} = 4$ dBm, the realistic transceiver thus has a margin of channel loss around 122 dB with $P_b = 10^{-2}$.

Table 1. Hardware costs of the implemented digital chirp BOK modem with LSFM signal.

XC7A200T	Slices	DSP48E	RAMB18E
Modulator	943	0	0
Demodulator	1274	160	65

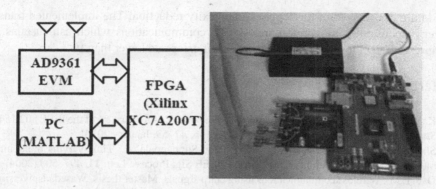

Fig. 6. Software defined radio platform with AD9361 EVM and Xilinx/SMIMS AC701 evaluation board

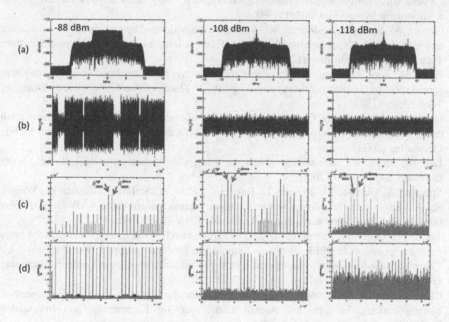

Fig. 7. Experimental results with received signal power of −88/−108/−118 dBm (a) signal power spectrum; (b) real part of received baseband signal; (c) start-of-frame synchronizer output; (d) BOK matched filter output

5   Conclusions

A low data-rate chirp BOK communication technique based on linear step frequency modulated (LSFM) signals exhibits a merit in the matched filter implementation with an acceptable performance loss compared to the traditional chirp signals. In this paper, we present an implementation of such an LSFM transceiver on a realistic commercially available software-defined radio (SDR) platform. Specific system parameters in the

LSFM are designed for a furthermore complexity reduction. The implemented transceiver demonstrates a low-rate wireless data communications which can sustains a margin of channel loss around 120 dB with a bit-error rate lower than 10^{-2}.

References

1. Karapistoli, E., Pavlidou, F., Gragopoulos, I., Tsetsinas, I.: An overview of the IEEE 802.154a Standard. In: IEEE Communications Magazine, pp. 47–53, January 2010
2. Shen, H., Machineni, S., Gupta, C., Papandreou-Suppappola, A.: Time-varying multichirp rate modulation for multiple access systems. IEEE Sig. Process. Lett. **11**, 497–500 (2004)
3. Dao, L.M.: Wireless communications using chirp signals. Master thesis. Waseda University, Japan (2008)
4. Takeuchi, Y., Yamanouchi, K.: A chirp spread spectrum DPSK modulator and demodulator for time shift multiple access communication system by using SAW devices. In: IEEE MTT-S Microwave Symposium Digest (1998)
5. Gugler, W., Springer, A., Weigel, R.: A chirp-based wideband spread spectrum modulation technique for WLAN applications. In: IEEE 6th International Symposium on Spread Spectrum Techniques and Applications (2000)
6. Khan, M., Rao, R., Wang, X.: Non-linear trigonometric and hyperbolic chirps in multiuser spread spectrum communication systems. In: IEEE 9th International Conference on Emerging Technologies (2013)
7. He, C., Huang, J., Zhang, Q., Lei, K.: Reliable mobile underwater wireless communication using wideband chirp signal. In: International Conference on Communications and Mobile Computing (2009)
8. Liu, H.: Multicode ultra-wideband scheme using chirp waveform. IEEE J. Sel. Areas Commun. **24**, 885–891 (2006)
9. Springer, A., Huemer, M., Reindle, L., Ruppel, C., Pohl, A., Seifert, F., Gugler, W., Weigel, R.: A rubuster ultra broadband wireless communication system using SAW chirped delay lines. IEEE Trans. Mircowave Theory Techn. **46**, 2213–2219 (1998)
10. Torroli, P., Guidi, F., Atzeni, C.: Digital vs. SAW matched filter implementation for radar pulse compression. In: IEEE Ultrasonic Symposium Proceedings, pp. 199–202 (1994)
11. Chen, Y.-M.: A low-rate wireless spread-spectrum communication technique using linear step FM signal. J. Adv. Inf. Technol., 44–47 (2014)
12. Chen, Y.-M.: A low-complex digital demodulator for low-rate chirp spread-spectrum communications. In: The 3rd Annual Conference on Engineering and Information Technology, Osaka, Japan, March 2015
13. https://www.lora-alliance.org/portals/0/documents/whitepapers/LoRaWAN101.pdf
14. http://www.analog.com/en/design-center/evaluation-hardware-and-software/evaluation-boards-kits/EVAL-AD-FMCOMMS3-EBZ.html#eb-overview

High Reliability Light Weight Multi-mission Amplifier System

Susumu Kitazume[1(✉)], Yosuke Takahara[1], Chihiro Hayashi[1], and Rowan Gilmore[2]

[1] JEPICO Corporation, Shinjuku Front Tower,
2-21-1, Kita-Shinjuku Shinjuku-ku, Tokyo 169-0074, Japan
{Kitazume,y_takahara,c_hayashi}@jepico.co.jp
[2] EMSolutions, 55 Curzon Street, Tennyson QLD 4105, Australia
Rowan.gilmore@emsolutions.com.au

Abstract. In support of a future ocean broadband projects, a Ka-band mobile satellite communications platform is proposed. To establish a high speed communications link, a high reliability and high power light weight RF amplifier is a key component of the subsystem. The Ka-band High Reliability Light Weight Multi Mission Amplifier system now under development is presented with the technical design and results of ongoing hardware testing. The purpose of this study is to demonstrate that the high reliability of a combined solid state multi-mission power amplifier consisting of many MMIC amplifiers.

Keywords: Ocean broadband · Multi-mission light weight amplifier system · Ka-band · MMIC · High reliability

1 Introduction

As part of continual research in the oceans and seas surrounding Japan, Autonomous Surface Vehicles (ASVs) are proposed to operate at points beyond the horizon and far from land based communication links. To provide high speed communication between these ASV, related research vessels and the land-based research facility, a Ka-band satellite uplink is proposed. Due to the remote nature of ASVs, the RF power amplifier within the communication subsystem will require high reliability and performance that is similar to that commonly needed for satellites.

Currently, Monolithic Microwave Integrated Circuit (MMIC) power amplifiers using GaAs or GaN FET technologies are used in a typical Solid State Power Amplifier (SSPA) for microwave and submillimeter wave applications. In order to realize high power outputs, amplifiers using these solid state elements are required to combine the output power of numerous devices. For the Wideband Internetworking engineering test and Demonstration Satellite (WINDS), the National Institute of Information and Communications Technology (NICT) in Japan developed a SSPA for the Ka-band Broadband Mobile Earth Station. This SSPA combined eight GaAs MMIC devices in parallel to generate 25 W of output power. However, current requirements demand more efficiency light weight and higher output power from amplifiers than the recent technology allows in order to provide a high data rate communication satellite system.

© ICST Institute for Computer Sciences, Social Informatics and Telecommunications Engineering 2017
I. Otung et al. (Eds.): WiSATS 2016, LNICST 186, pp. 55–62, 2017.
DOI: 10.1007/978-3-319-53850-1_7

Additionally, high reliability with a long Mean Time Between Failure (MTBF) is required in order to meet the requirement for continual satellite communications from remote ASVs, even when operated far away from land-based communication links. It is required high reliability and light weight because using remote access operation.

2 Redundant Configurations

Generally, for a reliable microwave amplification system, a fully redundant backup unit is employed. A fully redundant configuration with a redundant backup unit similar to that currently commonly used is shown in Fig. 1. Power Amplifier 1 (AMP-1) is used under normal operation, but upon failure of AMP-1, Power Amplifier 2 (AMP-2) enters normal operation mode by toggling of both the switches RF(IN) and RF(OUT).

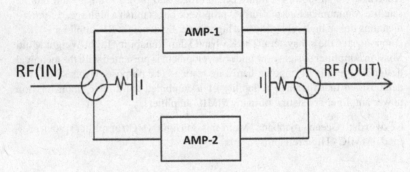

Fig. 1. 100% redundant systems (Normal redundant configuration)

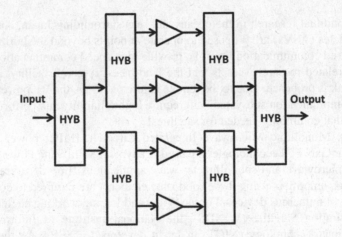

Fig. 2. An example of a power combiner without redundant

A common method to generate higher power output from a SSPA is to use a power combiner to merge several individual MMIC devices. As the output power of each MMIC device is much smaller than the desired output, around 2 or 3 W each as compared to the final output power of 20 to 30 W. For example, four parallel 2 W MMIC amplifiers are required to generate 10 W of output power as shown in Fig. 2. An example of a power combiner with 50% redundant system is shown in Fig. 3. In this case, 33% of amplifiers are not operated during normal operation. Thus the usable output power of this system, in normal operation, is just 2/3 of total system capability.

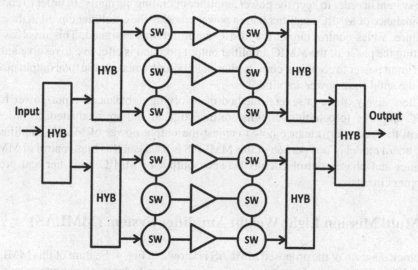

Fig. 3. An example of a power combiner with 50% redundancy.

3 Features of this Multi-mission Light Weight Amplifier System

In order to achieve a highly reliable configuration for microwave amplification operating at a higher output power, both power combining and redundant technology are required. A redundant configuration of 100% or 50% is commonly used. In the case of a 50% redundant configuration, for every two operational channels a redundant channel is not in use during normal operations (no failures). Thus, fully one third of the total system capacity is not used, and implies that this one third can be considered to be superfluous during normal operations. In order to reduce this occurrence within the Multi Mission Light weight Amplifier System (MMLAS) design, all equipment – including redundant parts – are used during all modes of operation. In the other words, all equipment for primary and redundant channels should be active in both cases of normal and failure operation. We are proposing this MMLAS for Ka-band Satellite Communications between ASVs or ocean-going research vessels and a satellite relay system.

This MMLAS is configured to operate all channels – both primary and redundant – during operation, resulting in 150% output power as compared to a 50% redundant system with the same available source capacity. In the event of the failure of an MMIC amplifier, it will be disconnected individually from the amplifier system and the system will still operate normally.

It means that total weight of this amplifier required to get 100% amplification is just 2/3 of weight in case of 50% redundant system. And we can say that the required weight is just half, in case of 100% redundant system.

When a failure occurs within the MMIC amplifier system there is an imbalance of power entering the combiner. This requires that power balancing technology be applied to the system in order to keep the power amplifier operating normally. In order to correct the imbalance of MMIC amplifier output power entering the combiner circuit in the case of failure, a bias control circuit for MMIC amplifier was designed. This involves the adjusting the phase of the MMIC amplifier output port and is effective to resolve unbalanced input power to combiner circuits, thus maintaining a reasonable total output power from the solid state power amplifier.

Alternatively, there is several method of resolving unbalanced input power from MMIC amplifier to combiner circuits are investigated and are evaluated. In order to confirm the basic performance how to adjust the output power of MMIC amplifier, a bread board model of one portion of this MMLAS is used, such as bias control of MMIC amplifier and phase control circuits between output of MMIC amplifier and power combiner circuits.

4   Multi Mission Light Weight Amplifier System (MMLAS)

The block diagram of the proposed MMLAS is shown in Fig. 4. Feature of this MMLAS is as follows. In the case of normal operation without any failures, all output power from the amplifiers is combined to generate the maximum possible output power of this amplifier system.

However, when a failure occurs on any one channel within the combiner, the active circuit is changed to the operation as same as redundant system operation.

In other words, the proposed MMLAS, in the case of no MMIC failures, operates with all amplifier system equipment operating at 100%. In the case of a failure occurring, the amplifier system is operates the same as are 50% redundant system circuit without any weight increase.

5   Block Diagram of Tested Design

Symbolic block diagram of MMLAS is shown in Fig. 4, Case-B. A more detailed block diagram of the MMLAS with switch operation is shown in Fig. 5, which was used for our trial purpose.

6   Case Study of Circuit Operation in the Case of Key Operation

One of key technical issues for the MMLAS is how to combine output powers where the value of individual MMIC amplifiers has changed or where the ratio between two routes of individual MMIC amplifiers has changed. The output power at key points within the power combiner of the Multi-mission Amplifier was studied (see Fig. 5) and

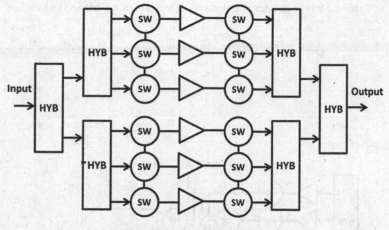

Case A : Modified from Fig. 3

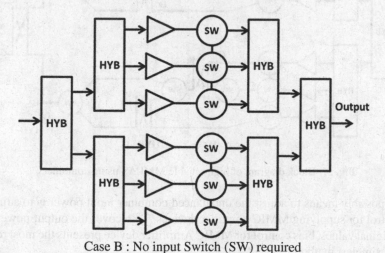

Case B : No input Switch (SW) required

Fig. 4. Symbolic block diagram of a MMLAS with combiner

the results are shown in Table 1. This test uses a unit test case in which the output power from each MMIC amplifier is 1 W.

From this case study, we can see that only one combiner hybrid (Hyb-1) requires adjustment of the input power value to compensate for a single route failure occurring within each channel A and B. We believe that it is enough to consider the case of one route failure for the analysis of this system, although this failure can occur in either or both of the channels. This is the key point which should be reviewed for further study to practically implement this design: how to reasonably operate Hyb-1 in order to combine the two unbalanced input power channels into one output without loss. This will need to be shown experimentally.

Table 1. Power unbalance estimation in the case of normal and failure

Location	Hyb-1		Hyb-2				Hyb-3		Hyb-4		Hyb-5	
	A	B	C	D	C`	E`	E	F	G	H	G`	H`
Normal	3	3	2	1	–	–	2	1	1	1	1	1
Failure (A)	2	3	–	–	2	–	2	1	1	1	1	1
Failure (B)	3	2	2	1	–	2	–	–	1	1	1	1
Failure (A&B)	2	2	–	–	2	2	–	–	1	1	1	1

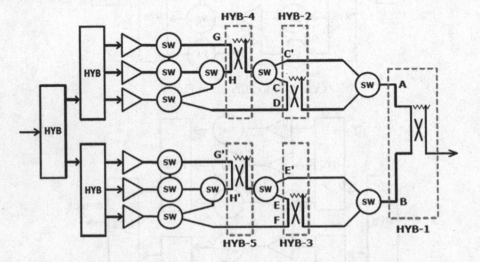

Fig. 5. Block diagram of high reliable MMLAS using combiner

One possibly means to adjust the unbalanced combiner input power is to adjust the bias control for supplying MMIC amplifier devices. To recover the output power back to the original values, bias control for MMIC Amplifier device presents the most reasonable and simplest method.

7   Howe to Operate Output Switch Circuit

Output switch circuit is shown in Fig. 6 as below. In case of normal operation, all three output terminals have equal output power. In the case of failure, where any one of the three amplifiers has failed, the circuit is adjusted such that the output of the two remaining MMIC amplifiers is maximized, with the failed MMIC device having no output.

In case of failure

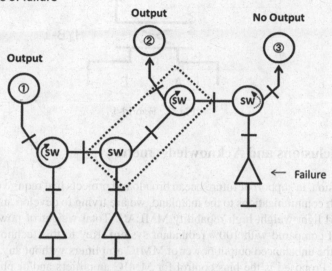

Fig. 6. Output switch circuit operation

8 Test Result

According to the results of the study defined above we have defined how to operate the final combiner hybrid (Hyb-1) within in the proposed amplifier system. This operation should work to combine the two unbalanced input powers at the output of the hybrid only a negligible loss. This is a key point which should be studied to take this idea into practice. The results of the experimental study which compared several circuit conditions is shown in Fig. 7 and Table 2. This test compares the combined input unbalanced power vs measured final output power and calculated values.

Table 2. Input vs output power of typical combiner, measured vs calculated value

Case	Pa [W]	Pb [W]	Tp [W]	MDV [dB]	CV [dB]	Delta [dB]
1	3.0	3.0	6.0	0	0	0
2	2.8	3.0	5.8	−0.15	−0.15	0.00
3	2.3	3.0	5.8	−0.54	−0.15	−0.39
4	2.0	3.0	5.0	−0.88	−0.79	−0.09
5	1.5	3.0	4.5	−1.41	−1.25	−0.16
6	1.0	3.0	4.0	−2.10	−1.76	−0.34

MDV – Measured Degraded Value.

CV – Calculated Value - CV = 10 log(Tp/Tp0); Tp0 = 6 W.

Delta – Difference between MDV and CV – Delta = MDV-CV.

Most probable case of failure happened in this amplifier should be case-4.

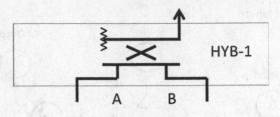

Fig. 7. Hybrid-1

9   Conclusions and Acknowledgement

In conclusion, in support of future ocean broadband projects that require continual, high bandwidth communications to the mainland, we are trying to develop an effective, high power and light weight high reliability MMLAS. Total weight of power amplifier is about half compared with 100% redundant system. Key to this technology is how to combine the unbalanced output power of MMIC amplifiers without any additional loss of power. Proposed is the bias control for MMIC amplifiers and/or phase control for MMIC amplifiers by phase shifter. The bias control of MMIC device is simple way to adjust unbalanced output power in order to adjust the output power to meet required value of combined power. In order to further clarify the test results, investigation into this system will continue. In order to make the test result clear in theoretical, we continue further study.

This is acknowledgement that this study work is developed for NICT (National Institute of Information and Communications Technology) under research and development funding provided by NICT Japan.

References

1. Cross-ministerial Strategic Innovation Promotion Program (SIP), Next-generation technology for ocean resources exploration, 23 January 2015
2. Kuroda, et al.: Ka-b and high power Multi-port Amplifier (MPA). J. Nat. Inst. Inform. Commun. Technol. **54**(4) (2007)
3. Kitazume: Ka-band on-board repeater technologies for communications satellite. ISU Summer Session SLS Houston, 25 July 1997
4. Takagi: GaN HEMTs are still ongoing. In: Asia-Pacific Microwave Conference 2014
5. Szczepaniak, Z.R.: Special power combining techniques for semiconductor power amplifiers. In: Zhurbenko, V. (ed.) Advanced Microwave Circuits and Systems (2010)

Examination of Power Consumption Reduction and Sampling Behavior of Envelope Detection Based Wake-up-Receiver with Duty Cycling Scheme

Josua Arndt[✉], Lukas Krystofiak, Vahid Bonehi,
Ralf Wunderlich, and Stefan Heinen

Integrated Analog Circuits and RF Systems,
RWTH Aachen University, 52074 Aachen, Germany
{jarndt,ias}@ias.rwth-aachen.de
http://www.ias.rwth-aachen.de

Abstract. In most communication scenarios where the transmission time is short compared to the idle listening time for a data transmission, most power is consumed by the receiver. This brings up the need for a wake-up-receiver (WuRx) embedded in the system. This work presents a WuRx designed out of commercial components in order to investigate the needs of an WuRx embedded in a WPAN in a real environment setup including WLAN and LTE communication and considering interferer rejection. A system design is presented that fulfills all requirements and is designed with regard to enabling a duty cycle scheme for the reduction of the power consumption. Investigation of the duty cycling behavior is shown, technical difficulties are named and the resulting sampling rate and the power saving capability are analyzed.

Keywords: Wake-up-Receiver · WPAN · Duty cycling

1 Investigating a Wake-up-Receiver

Personal area networks, as specified in [1], applications like lightning control, monitoring temperature, moisture etc. or IoT (Internet of Things) devices can demand a fast reaction. If the user activates the light it has to react in milliseconds as we are used to the light switching on instantly. For those applications the receiver has always to listen to the channel. In beacon-enabled networks a fast reaction time can be achieved by a big duty-cycle, resulting in a high beacon number to send and the end devices have to wake up frequently. This results in a high energy consumption. A WuRx designed to support a low data rate modulation can be very simple and consume less energy than a high data rate modulation like BPSK or O-QPSK. In this paper, to gain insight in the switching behavior for an integrated design, a WuRx is used which is build out

© ICST Institute for Computer Sciences, Social Informatics and Telecommunications Engineering 2017
I. Otung et al. (Eds.): WiSATS 2016, LNICST 186, pp. 63–72, 2017.
DOI: 10.1007/978-3-319-53850-1_8

of commercial components on PCB to investigate the needs of a system that includes a WuRx and uses the IEEE802.15.4 transmitter to generate the wake-up frame [2]. Some content of this paper is repeated and summarized from the publication [2] in regard to give a better introduction to the topic. The selection of the components was made with regard to the ability to shut-down, to be able to analyze the behavior when a duty cycle scheme is applied. Challenges will be discussed and solutions presented. In Sect. 2 an overview of the requirements will be given and basics of path loss and link margin calculations are presented. In Sect. 3 the system setup, filter design and resulting link margin is presented. In Sect. 4 the measurements of the WuRx are shown. In Sect. 5 the duty cycling of the wake up receiver is explained and results of measurements are presented which substantiate power savings. Section 6 concludes the paper.

2   Design Requirements

A tuned RF is one of the simplest receiver architectures [3]. It accepts incoming RF signals which are filtered, amplified and converted from RF to baseband by an envelope detector (ED). This eliminates the need for a power consuming local oscillator (LO) completely, which is usually the most power hungry component in a receiver. However, this means that this receiver can only process amplitude modulated signals and the architecture calls for a very high selectivity at RF, which will be explained later in detail. This is a result of the behavior of the ED converting all signals at its input directly to Baseband without selectivity.

The designated transmit distance of our WPAN networks with wake-up receivers is between 5 m and 30 m indoors. In our scenario the wake-up receiver works at the same frequency as the main transceiver. To reduce hardware complexity, the main transceiver will be used to generate the OOK signal. As widely known, a higher carrier frequency enables broader bandwidth and therefore a faster data rate as well as reduced diffraction loss, smaller antenna size and overall increased level of integration. But a higher carrier frequency also increases the path loss and therefore the necessary sensitivity of the receiver. Moreover, additional filtering and amplification at high frequencies is more complex and power hungry. The formula for free space path loss in decibel is:

$$\frac{L_s}{\text{dB}} = 20 \, log_{10} \left(\frac{4\pi f d}{c} \right) = 20 \, log_{10}(d) + 20 \, log_{10}(f) - 147.55 \tag{1}$$

with the carrier wavelength $\lambda[\text{m}]$, the carrier frequency $f[\text{Hz}]$, the speed of light $c[\text{ms}^{-1}]$ and the link distance $d[\text{m}]$. To calculate the path loss we consider a direct line of sight and no walls and floors, which is equal to a large room. As shown by [4] the path loss exponent then is smaller than 2, so for simplicity we can use the simple path loss equation formula. Hence with a carrier frequency of 2.48 GHz and a link distance of 10 m the path loss would be 70 dB, at 30 m roughly 80 dB. A better insight of indoor wireless coverage can be found in [5]. For WLAN at 2.467 GHz and a distance of 1 m we get $L_s = -40.29$ dB which is a attenuation of 40 dB. Inserting the system specific transmit power P_{TX}[dB] and the ED sensitivity S_{ED}[dB] we can calculate the resulting link margin L_M[dB]. This can be interpreted as the additional gain necessary to be able to detect a signal at the inserted frequency and distance.

$$\frac{L_M}{\text{dB}} = P_{TX} - S_{ED} - 20 \, log_{10}(d) - 20 \, log_{10}(f) + 147.55 \qquad (2)$$

Setting the link margin to zero and solving the equation for d gives the distance at which the signal can be detected.

$$d = 10^{(P_{TX} - S_{ED} - 20 \, log_{10}(f) + 147.55)/20} \qquad (3)$$

Also considering the overall gain G[dB] and interferer attenuation A_I[dB] of the system and solving the equation for A_I[dB] we can calculate the necessary attenuation for an interferer in a dedicated distance.

$$\frac{A_I}{\text{dB}} = P_{TX} - S_{ED} + G - 20 \, log_{10}(d) - 20 \, log_{10}(f) + 147.55 \qquad (4)$$

For our test system we choose to use the WPAN channel with fewest interferences which is channel 26 at 2.48 GHz. Figure 1 illustrates the down conversion of the RF band to baseband by an ED containing the wake-up signal on WPAN Channel 26 and the two closest interferers, WLAN Channel 13 and LTE Band 7. As shown in the illustration the interferers have potentially higher transmit power than our WPAN node, which has 4 dBm specified as output power of the AT68RF233 transmitter without losses due to the balloon, the antenna or mismatch. As defined in [6] the maximum transmit power for WLAN is 20 dBm and for LTE Band 7 24 dBm as defined in [7]. A narrowband filter in the RF band is necessary to suppress the interferers and only convert down the band of interest. The calculation of the attenuation needed to suppress WLAN signals with transmit power of 20 dBm at a distance of 1 m - for a system using an ED with a sensitivity of −30 dBm - is approximately 10 dB and for LTE with 24 dBm transmit power 13.7 dB, according to Eq. 3.

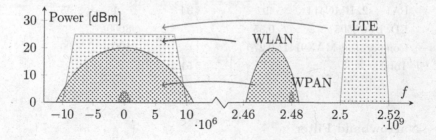

Fig. 1. Down conversion of RF signals to baseband by envelop detection with WLAN and LTE communication as interference

3   System Design

3.1   System Setup

For this work the absolute power consumption of the system is not of interest, since it cannot compete with integrated solutions anyway. The emphasis is on the knowledge gained on how and which parts influence the others. All parts had to be chosen considering manual soldering for fast adaption of changes and debugging.

Figure 2 shows the WuRx with different stages. To achieve a good interferer suppression we designed the WuRx using multiple bulk acoustic wave (BAW) filters with different pass characteristics, which will be explained later. The WuRx sensitivity suffers heavily from the additional attenuation of the bandpass filter configuration. Increased gain is the only way to compensate for the losses, but amplification comes with the cost of power consumption in general.

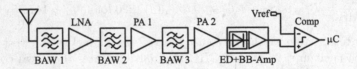

Fig. 2. WuRx system concept with overlapping filters to gain an extremely narrowband filtering

All active components were selected with regard to the switching on/off times and existence of an enable pin. An extraction of some interesting characteristics of the used parts stated in the data sheets are listed in Table 1.

Table 1. Data sheet specifications at 25 °C, 3.3 V, 2.481 GHz

	Current [mA]	Gain [dB]	t_{on} [ns]	t_{off} [ns]
LNA, SKY67159	45.5	17.2	400	150
PA1 + 2, HMC414	494	34	45	45
ED, LTC5508	0.55		8000	
Comparator, MAX9141	0.275		1000	5000
Total	540.3	51.2		

3.2   Narrowband Filter

As mentioned earlier the interferers have higher power than the wake-up signal leading to the necessity of strong suppression. To achieve the necessary inter-ferer rejection we combined multiple BAW filters for different bands which have an overlapping area in the designated frequency range. We chose two BAW filters from Triquint, BAW 885033 (f_c = 2.442 MHz, BAW3) and BAW 885009 (f_c = 2.535 MHz, BAW1/2). The resulting combined attenuation at 2.481 GHz is 16 dB, at 2.467 GHz 63.7 dB and at 2.5 GHz 41.5 dB. Thus, the minimum distance to a WLAN transmitter reduces to 0.7 m and to a LTE transmitter to 14.8 m. Adding more attenuation for LTE would add too much attenuation to our signal. With this configuration the system will still be error prone for LTE, but sufficiently robust against WLAN signals.

3.3   Link Margin

The final performance so far presented here, is achieved with simulated data of the architecture and components described before. With a sensitivity of −25 dBm of the ED, a gain of about 35.2 dB of the amplifier and filter stage, we get a sensitivity of −47.83 dBm at 2.481 GHz. With an assumed wake-up signal power of 4 dBm the equation for path loss gives an ideal maximum link distance of around 15.6 m. With the maximum radiation power of 20 dBm and an attenuation of 12.5 dB WLAN signals are rejected sufficiently above a distance of around 0.7 m. Depending on the distance of the base station the radiation power for mobile phones can reach up to 24 dBm as specified in the 3G standard, to which LTE actually belongs (3.9G). The uplink frequencies for LTE go from 2.5 GHz up to 2.57 GHz in Germany. With a total gain of 10 dB for LTE frequencies, these signals overshadow the desired signal significantly, at equal distance to the receiver. A minimum distance of 14.8 m to the LTE transmitter is necessary to not corrupt the wake-up sequence.

4   Implementation and Measurements

Figure 3 shows the measured gain of the system at the output of the last amplifier. With a gain of 26 dB this results in an ideal range of about 3.41 m with a wake-up signal power of 4 dBm. For 2.467 GHz we have an attenuation of 19 dB and for 2.5 GHz a gain of 3 dB. Table 2 shows the resulting current consumption, Gain and on/off times measured for each stage.

Considering optimum matching and operating points of the power amplifiers the general functionality of the circuit was tested. For the output DC voltage of the ED we get a value of about 275 mV for no incoming RF signal. With regard to the input hysteresis and offset of the comparator the threshold is found to be at 284 mV. With a signal generator directly connected to the board, a sensitivity of −20.0 dBm was measured at 2.481 GHz.

Figure 4 shows the PCB. From the SMA connector at the upper left corner the signal path is routed to the lower right corner and ends in an pin header to be connected to a microcontroller board.

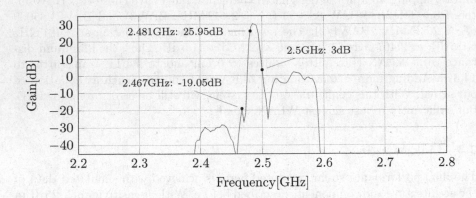

Fig. 3. Measured gain of the complete WuRx

Table 2. Measured electric specifications at 3.3 V supply

	Current mA	Gain dB	t_{on} ns	t_{off} ns
BAW 1+2+3 @2.481 GHz		−16		
LNA	45.5	13.35	397	292
Power Amplifier 1	71.9	12.82	583	371
Power Amplifier 2	73	12.21	772	400
Envelope Detector	0.55		6800	150
Comparator	0.165		3300	5000
Total	191	22.38		

Fig. 4. Wake-up-Receiver PCB

5 Duty Cycling the WuRx

Figure 5 shows the processing of an incoming signal at the input of the first stage. In (a) the incoming wake-up sequence is shown, which is modulated by the transmitter using OOK. The presence of the carrier frequency represents a "1" and the absence a "0". In this example the length of the signal for a bit was chosen to be 200 µs. Therefore, the receiver has a data rate of 5 kb/s. (b) shows the duty cycle for the wake-up-receiver components, that will be switched on and off. One fundamental design aspect of this work is the ability to switch all active components. Thus, the power consumption can be reduced by the factor of the duty cycle, while the receiver is still able to detect a wake-up signal without latency. In this example the on-time was chosen to be 20 µs and the off-time 30 µs, which would decrease power consumption by 60 % The duty cycle has to be adjusted to the used components and the achievable on-off switching times. (c) depicts the filtered and amplified signal and (d) shows the ED output, thus the conversion to DC by the ED. The signal is now nearly reproduced as OOK. The demodulation signal has a low amplitude so it has to be amplified again. Afterwards a comparator converts the signal to an interpretable, digital form. Two different approaches can be taken here. The comparator can be included in the duty-cycle, which decreases power consumption further, leaving the recreation of the wake-up sequence to the following stage, e.g. a logic or microcontroller. This approach is shown in (e). The comparator can also stay on constantly and use its sample-and-hold function to recreate the signal lowering the requirements for the following stage, as shown in (f). At the end of the on-time of the duty-cycle the comparator samples the steady state of the signal and holds it till the next period. As a first value for the sample time 5 µs was chosen, which makes the hold-time of the comparator 45 µs long in this example.

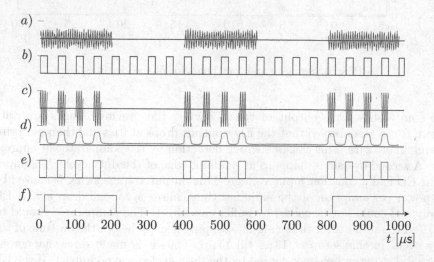

Fig. 5. Sampling wake-up signal with duty cicled WuRx

For the duty cycle all active components were triggered individually, while the rest of the circuit important for the propagation remained constantly on. The signal was measured at the output of the last gain stage, after the ED and after the comparator, to gain insight in influences resulting from the duty cycling. Therefore, a signal generator was connected and adjusted to send a constant signal with a frequency of 2.481 GHz and the output power was set in steps from -47 dBm to -40 dBm to -30 dBm. Additionally, a microcontroller was used to apply the duty cycle to the tested component and served also as trigger source for the oscilloscope. The LNA has an enable time of around 397 ns and a disable time of around 292 ns for all tested output power settings. While the enable time is close to the value given in the data sheet, the disable time is nearly twice as long. For the first power amplifier an enable time of 583 ns and a disable time of 371 ns are measured again for all tested output powers. These values differ heavily from the given 45 ns in the data sheet. Respectively, the second power amplifier has an enable time of 772 ns and a disable time of 400 ns. The ED's measured wake-up time is around 6.8 μs, which is even lower than specified in the data sheet, but still dominates the minimum enable time of the duty cycle. The comparator's enable time is about 3.3 μs, which is again longer than the 1 μs specified in the data sheet and the disable time is around 5 μs.

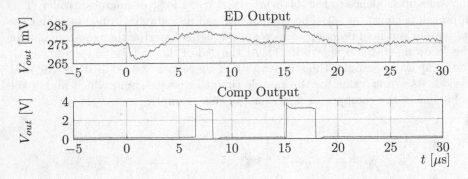

Fig. 6. Swing-in and -out behavior of the circuit

Figure 6 shows the output of the ED when the previous stages are duty cycled. It can be observed that the ED's output drops at 0 μs and than performs a swing in of 12 μs. This causes a wrong detection by the comparator at approx. 7 μs. A second overshoot happens at a falling edge of the duty cycle. The input of the ED had a constant input voltage. This output voltage swing is caused by the power consumption of the amplifier that causes a voltage drop at the ED supply and could not be solved by buffer capacitors. The comparator should be adjusted to sample after the swing-in, stopping shortly before the on-time of the duty cycle, in this setup at 13 μs till 14 μs. Thus it is made sure, that wrong peaks and swing-in behavior caused by the duty cycle have no impact. If the ED is duty-cycled as well, the long wake-up time of about 6.8 μs prevents ringing

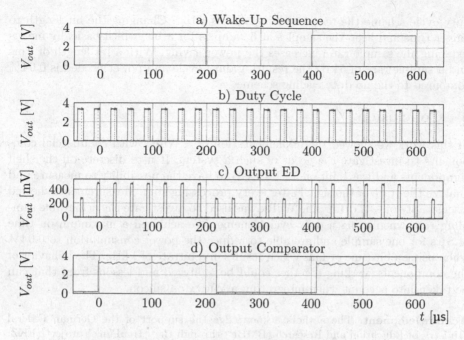

Fig. 7. Sampling wake-up signal with duty cycled WuRx measurement

nearly completely, but for the integrated design which possibly enables a faster activation this should be considered.

Figure 7 shows the measured results of the signal reconstructed by the wake-up receiver. A periodic square wave signal with a length of $200\,\mu s$ was produced with a signal generator, plot (a). The duty cycle, shown in plot (b), was adjusted to 30 % with an on-time of $12\,\mu s$ and an off-time of $20\,\mu s$. The second trace in b), dotted line, shows the period during which the comparator samples the signal, adjusted here to be in the last microsecond during on-time. Plot (c) shows the output of the ED and plot (d) the output of the comparator, the recovered signal. It is noticeable, that the first pulse is longer than $200\,\mu s$ by around $24\,\mu s$ and the second pulse is shorter by about $8\,\mu s$. The reason for this is on the one hand the shift between the signal and the sample time of the comparator and on the other hand the period of the duty cycle. The recovered signal will always be a multiple of the duty cycle plus or minus the sample time of the comparator. If the quotient of the bit length of the signal divided by the period of the duty cycle is not an integer, the recovered pulse will therefore vary in length, which has to be considered during detection. The minimum on-time of the circuit to successfully sample the input signal is $8\,\mu s$, with a sample time of $0.8\,\mu s$. Based on this values different duty cycles can be adjusted and examined, where only the off-time of the circuit is varied and thus the sample rate is changed. To successfully reconstruct the signal pattern with 5 samples at 100 % duty cycle a minimum bit time of $40\,\mu s$ is needed. To get at least 50 % power saving by the duty cycle scheme the resulting bit length is $80\,\mu s$. Changing the bit length to longer time and keep the samples at 5 samples for a bit, which basically means reducing the sample rate, increases the power saving. With a bit length of 1 ms and a sample rate of 5 kHz the resulting duty cycle and power needed is 0.04 % compared to the no duty cycling scheme.

6   Conclusion

In this work we showed the implementation of a WuRx with commercial components to investigate the needs of such a system. It uses discrete off-the-shelf components and was built on a FR4 PCB to have the possibility to measure and analyze the state of the signal after every processing step. Measurements showed a sensitivity of $-47\,$dBm. The WuRx was used to investigate the achievable sampling rate when using a duty cycle scheme. We achieved a maximum on time of $8\,\mu s$ for one sample and are able to reduce the power consumption to 0.04 % when using a bit time of 1 ms which results in a bitrate of 1 kHz. The behavior of the components working together could be analyzed and lessons from that can be taken into account when integrating a WuRx on silicon.

Acknowledgment. The authors acknowledge the support of the German Federal Ministry of Education and Research (BMBF) through the "TreuFunk" project (FKZ: 16KIS0234).

References

1. Gutierrez, J.A., Callaway, E.H., Barrett, R.: IEEE 802.15.4 Low-Rate Wireless Personal Area Networks: Enabling Wireless Sensor Networks. IEEE Standards Oce, New York, NY, USA (2003)
2. Arndt, J., et al.: Implementation of envelope detection based wake-up-receiver for IEEE802.15.4 WPAN with commercial components. Advances in Radio Science (2016)
3. Griggs, J.D.: Ultra-Low Power Wake up Receiver for Medical Implant Communications Service Transceiver. Ph.D. thesis, North Carolina A&T State University (2012)
4. Heereman, F., Joseph, W., Tanghe, E., Plets, D., Martens, L.: Prediction of range, power consumption and throughput for IEEE 802.11n in large conference rooms. In: Proceedings of the 5th European Conference on Antennas and Propagation (EUCAP), pp. 692–696 (2011)
5. Plets, D., Joseph, W., Vanhecke, K., Tanghe, E., Martens, L.: Simple indoor path loss prediction algorithm and validation in living lab setting. Wireless Pers. Commun. **68**(3), 535–552 (2013)
6. 802.11b, IEEE: Ieee standard for information technology - telecommunications and information exchange between systems - local and metropolitan networks - specific requirements - part 11: Wireless lan medium access control (mac) and physical layer (phy) specifications: Higher speed physical layer (phy) extension in the 2.4 ghz band. IEEE Std 802.11b-1999, January 2000
7. ETSI TS 136 101, T.S.: Etsi ts 136 101 v12.5.0 (2014-11). LTE; Evolved Universal Terrestrial Radio Access (E-UTRA); User Equipment (UE) radio transmission and reception (3GPP TS 36.101 ver. 12.5.0 rel. 12) (2014)

Bit Synchronization and Delayed Decision Feedback Equalization for EDGE BTS - Hardware Implementation on TMS320C6424 TI DSP

Laxmaiah Pulikanti[✉], Pradeep Goutam, Bipsa Purushothaman,
K.G. Dileep, and S.V. Hari Prasad

Centre for Development of Telematics,
Electronic City Phase-1, Hosur Road, Bangalore 560100, India
{laxman_p,pradeepg,bipsap,dileepkg,svhari}@cdot.in

Abstract. This paper demonstrates the implementation of bit synchronization and delayed decision feedback equalization for Enhanced Data rates for GSM Evolution (EDGE) system on TMS320C6424 DSP. EDGE makes use of training sequence for channel estimation and inter symbol interference (ISI) cancellation by use of delayed decision feedback equalization. Modulated baseband in-phase (I) and quadrature (Q) signals are generated using Agilent E4438C Vector signal generator and faded using Agilent fading simulator, is used as input to the DSP. Bit Error Rate (BER) performance of uncoded bits for Packet Data Traffic Channel (PDTCH) meets the EDGE standards. Software implementation uses fixed-point C and Integrated Development Environment (IDE) used for development is code composer studio (CCS). Prototyped our design in Texas Instrument TMS320C6424 DSP and verified for all propagation models as per the EDGE standards. The design and hardware implementation of this Demodulator is done for C-DOT indigenous Shared GSM Radio Access Network (SGRAN) Base Transceiver Station (BTS) project.

Keywords: Viterbi equalizer · SGRAN BTS · The design prototyped in DSP · DDFSE · MMSE · DFE · CCS · Centre for Development of Telematics (C-DOT)

1 Introduction

To increase the data transmission rate and to improve network capacity, EDGE was introduced, which uses higher order modulation scheme 8-PSK (phase shift keying) i.e. three bits per RF modulated symbol as opposed to the original one bit per symbol in Global system for mobile communication (GSM). GSM is a digital cellular communications system and one of the most popular personal communication systems which is ubiquitous in the world, especially in Asia. It operates in the 900 MHz and 1800 MHz frequency band, each carrier is spaced 200 kHz and supports eight traffic and data channels per Time division multiple access (TDMA) frame.

The purpose of a detection algorithm is to produce a reliable decision of the input sequence given the received data. With higher modulation scheme used in EDGE, a maximum likelihood sequence equalizer (MLSE), which gives optimum performance,

© ICST Institute for Computer Sciences, Social Informatics and Telecommunications Engineering 2017
I. Otung et al. (Eds.): WiSATS 2016, LNICST 186, pp. 73–82, 2017.
DOI: 10.1007/978-3-319-53850-1_9

become unsuitable for cost effective implementation. Since computational complexity of an MLSE increases with channel spread and signal constellation size. Therefore sub optimal technique such as decision feedback equalization followed by reduced state Viterbi algorithm becomes ideal candidate.

In this paper, we present an economical hardware realization of the Delayed decision feedback equalization in EDGE receiver on Texas Instrument (TI) DSP TMS320C6424 [7]. The multipath propagation of a mobile radio channel may lead to a flat fading or frequency selective fading. In the frequency selective fading case, the width of the multipath delay profile exceeds the bit period which results in a time varying ISI spanning over several bits period. To mitigate this ISI a hardware realization of the MMSE DFE [2] followed by reduced state Viterbi algorithm is discussed.

2 EDGE Transmitter

The modulating symbol rate is $1/T = 1625/6$ ksymb/s (i.e. approximately 270.833 ksymb/s), which corresponds to $3 \times (1625/6)$ kbit/s (i.e. 812.5 kbit/s) [5]. T is the symbol period.

The modulating bits are Gray mapped in groups of three to 8-PSK symbols by the rule

$$s_i = e^{j2\pi l/8} \tag{1}$$

Where l is symbol parameter given by Table 1. The 8-PSK symbols are continuously rotated with 3p/8 radians per symbol before pulse shaping. The rotated symbols are defined as

$$\hat{s}_i = s_i \cdot e^{ji3\pi/8} \tag{2}$$

Table 1. Mapping between modulating bits and 8-PSK symbols parameter l

Modulating bits d_{3i}, d_{3i+1}, d_{3i+2}	Symbol parameter l
(1,1,1)	0
(0,1,1)	1
(0,1,0)	2
(0,0,0)	3
(0,0,1)	4
(1,0,1)	5
(1,0,0)	6
(1,1,0)	7

These symbols are filtered by linearized Gaussian minimum shift keying (GMSK) pulse. Figure 1 shows the mapping of bits into 8-PSK symbols.

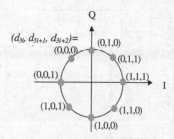

Fig. 1. Symbol mapping of modulating bits into 8-PSK symbol

3 Channel Estimation and Bit Synchronization

The channel estimation and timing synchronization utilize the knowledge of the 78- bit training sequence code (TSC) present in the EDGE burst as in Fig. 2. The channel estimator as in Fig. 3 has the sampled received signal y_k as input. y_k is a sampled sequence which is expected to contain the received EDGE burst. There are eight training sequence codes defined for the normal burst. All the training sequences have good autocorrelation properties.

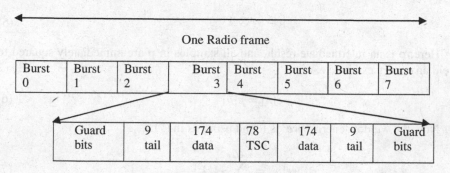

Fig. 2. EDGE Normal burst structure

A sliding window technique is used as in [3, 6] for searching start of the burst. The Eq. (3) represents received signal as $y(t)$, the channel-input data symbols as x_k and the channel-impulse response as $h(t)$; where $n(t)$ is additive white Gaussian noise (AWGN) and T is the symbol duration

$$y(t) = \sum_m x_m h(t - mT) + n(t) \qquad (3)$$

The channel output as given by (3) is sampled at l times of the symbol rate. By grouping $l = OSR$ (oversampling ratio) successive samples into vectors in the channel out, noise and channel impulse response, we can write the sampled output of the channel as

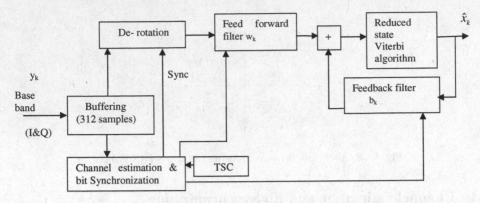

Fig. 3. Functional block diagram of EDGE Receiver

$$y_k = \sum_{m=0}^{\eta} h_m x_{k-m} + n_k \tag{4}$$

Where η is called the channel memory. The first step in the sliding window technique is to convolute received signal y_k with conjugate of known training sequence T_{seq}.

$$p = y_k \otimes T_{seq}^* \tag{5}$$

Here, **p** is an intermediate result, and all samples in **p** are immediately squared to yield an energy estimate **e**.

$$e[n] = p[n]^2 \tag{6}$$

Now the window energy '***we***' is found using as in (7),

$$we[m] = \sum_{k=m}^{m+Len} e[k]^2 \tag{7}$$

Where $Len = \eta \times OSR - 1$. The sample m_{max} in *we* containing the highest energy value is estimated as directly corresponding to the first sample of the channel impulse response in **p**. From m_{max} in *we* and the known OSR, it is now possible to extract an estimate of the channel impulse response and also calculate the beginning of the burst. The number of samples in the estimated h is $(\eta + 1) \times OSR$. In the described procedure the entire y_k sequence is processed. In the actual implementation, however, only a sub-sequence is processed. This is possible since the location of the training sequence within an EDGE burst is known.

4 MMSE-DFE Filter Coefficient Calculation

The name MMSE-DFE [2] implies that the DFE coefficients are derived under MMSE criteria. Here b_k and w_k are the feedback and feed forward filter coefficients derived in minimum-mean square-sense, by making the error orthogonal to the received sequence.

The Eq. (4) can be written as follows:

$$y_k = \begin{bmatrix} y((k+\frac{l-1}{l}T)) \\ \vdots \\ y(kT) \end{bmatrix} \equiv \begin{bmatrix} y_{l-1,k} \\ \vdots \\ y_{0,k} \end{bmatrix}; h_m = \begin{bmatrix} h((m+\frac{l-1}{l}T)) \\ \vdots \\ h(mT) \end{bmatrix} \equiv \begin{bmatrix} h_{l-1,m} \\ \vdots \\ h_{0,m} \end{bmatrix}; n_k = \begin{bmatrix} n((k+\frac{l-1}{l}T)) \\ \vdots \\ n(kT) \end{bmatrix} \equiv \begin{bmatrix} n_{l-1,k} \\ \vdots \\ n_{0,k} \end{bmatrix};$$

By combining N_f (number of feed forward coefficients) output vectors (each containing l samples) together, (4) can be cast in matrix form as follows [2]:

$$\begin{bmatrix} y_{k+N_f-1} \\ y_{k+N_f-2} \\ \vdots \\ \\ y_k \end{bmatrix} = \begin{bmatrix} h_0 h_1 \ldots h_\eta 0 \ldots 0 \\ 0 h_0 h_1 \ldots h_\eta 0 \ldots \\ \vdots \\ \\ 0 \ldots 0 h_0 h_1 \ldots h_\eta \end{bmatrix} \begin{bmatrix} x_{k+N_f-1} \\ x_{k+N_f-2} \\ \vdots \\ \\ x_{k-\eta} \end{bmatrix} + \begin{bmatrix} n_{k+N_f-1} \\ n_{k+N_f-2} \\ \vdots \\ \\ n_k \end{bmatrix}$$

more compactly

$$y_{k+N_f-1:k} = H x_{k+N_f-1:k-\eta} + n_{k+N_f-1:k} \tag{8}$$

the error sequence is given by

$$err_k = x_k - \sum_{i=0}^{N_f-1} w_{-i}^* y_{k+i} + \sum_{j=1}^{\eta} b_j^* x_{k-j} \tag{9}$$

where $(.)^*$ denotes the complex-conjugate transpose. Using the orthogonality principle which states that

$$E\left[err_k y_{k+N_{f-1}:k}^*\right] = 0$$

when the MSE is minimized, we get

$$b^* R_{xy} = w^* R_{yy} \tag{10}$$

where R_{xy} is input-output cross correlation matrix and R_{yy} is autocorrelation matrix.

For minimized error the feed forward filter is given by [2]

$$w_{opt}^* = b_{opt}^* R_{xy} R_{yy}^{-1} \tag{11}$$

$$w^*_{opt} = \begin{bmatrix} 0 & b^*_{opt} \end{bmatrix} H^* \left(HH^* + (1/SNR')I_{lN_f} \right)^{-1} \tag{12}$$

where $SNR' = SNR/l$.

The following is the "Cholesky" (lower-diagonal-upper) factorization:

$$R \equiv (1/SNR')I_{N_f+\eta} + H^*H = LDL^* \tag{13}$$

By performing the cholesky factorization of Eq. (12) and find the N_f th column of L, that is required to compute the feedback filter. Once the feedback filter is computed, the feed forward filter is calculated using (12).

4.1 Computing the Feedback Filter [2]

Initial Condition (T/2 Spaced case):

$$G_0(D) = G(D) = \begin{bmatrix} \dfrac{1}{\sqrt{SNR'}} & h^*_1(D^*) & h^*_0(D^*) \end{bmatrix}$$

where $SNR' = SNR/2$.

Recursion:

$$\text{For } i = 0, 1 \ldots N_f - 1$$

$$d_i = \left| G_i(0) \right|^2$$

$$l_i(D) = D^i G_i(D) G^*_i(0) d_i^{-1}$$

$$\begin{bmatrix} \alpha_i & \beta_i & \gamma_i \end{bmatrix} = d_i^{-1/2} G_i(0)$$

$$DG_{i+1}(D) = G_i(D) \begin{bmatrix} \alpha_i D & -\beta_i & -\gamma_i \\ \beta_i^* D & (\alpha_i + |\gamma_i|^2/(\alpha_i + 1)) & -\beta_i^* \gamma_i/(\alpha_i + 1) \\ \gamma_i^* D & -\beta_i \gamma_i^*/(\alpha_i + 1) & (\alpha_i + |\beta_i|^2/(\alpha_i + 1)) \end{bmatrix}$$

Output:

$$b_{opt}(D) = l_{N_f-1}(D).$$

4.2 Computing the Feed Forward Filter [2]

From (12) the feed forward filter is given by

$$\begin{aligned} w^*_{opt} &= [0 \ldots .010 \ldots 0] L^* \left(H^*H + (1/SNR')I_{N_f+\eta} \right)^{-1} H^* \\ &= d_{N_f-1}^{-1} u^*_{N_f-1} H^* \end{aligned} \tag{14}$$

where $u^*_{N_f-1}$ is the $N_f th$ row of $L^{-1}_{(N_f+\eta)\times(N_f+\eta)}$. Since L is a monic lower triangular matrix, we have

$$w^*_{opt} = d^{-1}_{N_f-1}\left[v^*_{N_f-1}\; 0_{1\times\eta}\right]H^* \qquad (15)$$

where $v^*_{N_f-1}$ is the $N_f th$ row of the inverse of the $N_f \times N_f$ leading sub matrix of L. w^* can be computed efficiently using the following relation [2]:

$$w^*_i = d^{-1}_{N_f-1}\sum_{k=0}^{\min(\eta,N_f-1-i)} v^*(k+i)h^*_k : i = 0, 1, \dots N_f - 1 \qquad (16)$$

5   DDFSE

The delayed decision feedback sequence estimation (DDFSE) [1] can be regarded as a hybrid between MLSE and DFE. It's like a Viterbi algorithm working on a truncated (at a length μ) channel impulse response and using a DFE on each branch of the trellis subtracting the post cursor ISI caused by samples $x_{k-\mu-1}, x_{k-\mu-2}, \dots, x_{k-\eta}$. Where η is the length of the channel and μ can vary between zero and η.

Equation (17) gives the calculation of branch metric, B, where r_k (feed forward filtered and down sampled of y_k) is the observation at time k, x_k is the symbol at time k and b_k is the feedback filter response.

$$B = (r_k - t_k)^2 \qquad (17)$$

Where $t_k = \sum_{i=0}^{\mu} b_i x_{k-i} + \tilde{z}_{k-\mu-1}$ and $\tilde{z}_k = \sum_{i=0}^{\eta-\mu-1} b_{i+\mu+1}x_{k-i}$

Description of the Algorithm [1]:

The DDFSE algorithm recursively finds an approximation to the maximum likelihood sequence estimation problem. It is based on a trellis with a reduced number of states. At time $k + 1$, the algorithm stores for each possible state (for first μ taps)

(1) the best path leading to that state,
(2) the metric of that path,
(3) an estimate of the partial state (using $\eta - \mu$ taps).

The recursion step involves the following.

(a) Computing for each (state, next state) pair the sum of the path metric plus the branch metric given by (17). The estimate, $\tilde{z}_{k-\mu-1}$, is obtained from the estimate of the partial state (using $\eta - \mu$ taps).
(b) For each value of (next state) the best (smallest) metric sum is determined and the (state) which gives rise to the best (smallest sum) edge is selected.
(c) For each value of (next state) an estimate of the partial state is made by applying the partial state estimator the (state) chosen in (b). As in the Viterbi algorithm,

the path leading to each (next state) is found by extending the best path determined in (b).

6   Hardware Realization

The hardware realization of the receiver is done on a 10 layer PCB board with combination of Altera Cyclone 3 FPGA as in [8] and fixed-point TI DSP TMS320c6424 processor [7] that runs at 700 MHz as shown Fig. 4.

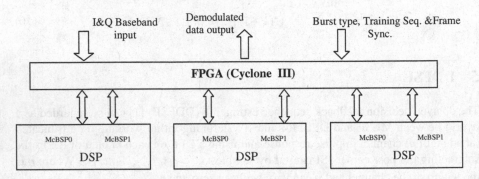

Fig. 4. Hardware realization Architecture

Here FPGA acts as glue logic for interfacing between DSP with other cards of SGRAN BTS. FPGA receives two samples per symbol input data (interleaved I&Q), from down converter (converts RF signal to Baseband). Baseband I and Q samples of 16-bit each is serially buffered to DSP using multi-channel buffered serial port (McBSP) @17.33 MHz.

Received samples are aligned to uplink radio frame (3 times offseted from downlink radio frame) considering all hardware delays in the system using master frame sync of the BTS in DSP. Further DSP performs channel estimation, bit synchronization and DDFSE equalization. Selected parameters for DDFSE are channel memory length (η) of 7 and μ of 1. The total number of 8-PSK modulation symbols is 8 and therefore number of Viterbi states is 8^μ i.e. 8 states. The equalized and demodulated data is streamed back to FPGA using same McBSP interface. Currently the system is able to implement two Transceivers (TRX) in one TI C6424 DSP.

The interface rate calculation is as follows:

{[16-bit (I) + 16-bit (Q)] × 2(over-sampling) × 156.25(no. of samples in burst)}/ 0.577 ms (burst period)) = 17.34 Msps. For two TRX, total Bandwidth required:

17.34 × 2 = 34.68 Msps. Each McBSP port of DSP can handle maximum up to 51 Msps. Hence two McBSPs can efficiently handle the required data rate for two TRX.

DSP Resource requirements:

The synchronization and equalization algorithm requires 145 K cycles per burst. So per TRX, the computation required: 145 K × 1733.33 (no. of bursts per sec) = 251.33 M cycles per sec (Mcps). So for two TRX, the computation required: 251.33 × 2 = 502.66 Mcps. DSP can process up to 700 Mcps hence single DSP can easily process synchronization and equalization for two TRX.

7 Performance Analysis and Results

Performance analysis test setup of the system is shown in Fig. 5. The Digital signal interface module (DSIM) receives the uplink EGPRS signal as per the standard from Agilent ESG through PCI card. DSIM digitizes the faded data for different profiles as per settings in Fader Simulator Application on computer as in Fig. 6. The DUT serially receives the digitized I&Q from DSIM and demodulate data bits as explained above sections and feeds back the bits to Agilent ESG.

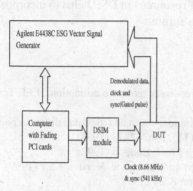

Fig. 5. Measurement Test setup   **Fig. 6.** Agilent fading profiles

The ESG performs the BER measurements on payload PRBS that it has generated for uplink. The BER of the uncoded bits (PDTCH) shall have the limits as in [4] and the measurements for all propagation profiles are given in Table 2.

Table 2. BER performance

Propagation profile	Specification (PDTCH)	Measured
Static	<2%	0.01780%
RA130(1)	<7%	3.55840%
RA130(2)	<7%	3.84180%
HT100(1) 12 tap	<9%	5.56870%
HT100(1) 6 tap	<9%	3.72750%
HT100(2) 6 tap	<9%	4.86170%
TU50(1) 12 tap	<8%	1.45160%
TU50(2) 12 tap	<8%	1.42030%
TU50(1) 6 tap	<8%	1.92890%
TU50(2) 6 tap	<8%	2.44850%
EQ100	≤3%	2.9250%

Agilent ESG setting:
Frequency = 1.8 GHz, Amplitude = 2 dBm, Payload = PN9, Total bits = 1 Mbits.

8   Conclusions

The implemented demodulator is able to successfully demodulate the data bits meeting the GSM recommendation for all propagation profile as in [4]. Uplink Frame alignment in DSP helps to save significant buffer space requirement in down converter, improving the system design. Viterbi is performed in forward and reverse path from the middle of the burst to reduce the trace back time in trellis. Apart from main DSP which supports two TRX, two more DSP's are added in Architecture for more capacity and flexibility of supporting six TRX. External memory access is not required since code size is less than DSP RAM size of 128 KB. Optimum use of resources in DSP helps to incorporate the implementation of GSM receiver diversity in future.

References

1. Duel-Hallen, A., Heegard, C.: Delayed Decision-Feedback sequence estimation. IEEE Trans. Commun. **37**(5), 428–436 (1989)
2. Al-Dhahir, N., Cioffi, J.M.: Fast computation of channel-estimate based equalizers in packet data transmission. IEEE Trans. Signal Process. **43**(11), 2462–2473 (1995)
3. Steele, R.: Mobile Radio Communications. Pentech Press, London (1992)
4. GSM Recommendation 05.05.: Radio Transmission and Reception. Version 8.5.1 (1999)
5. GSM Recommendation 05.04.: Modulation. Version 8.5.1 (1999)
6. Goutam, P., Babu, K.M.N.: Bit synchronization and viterbi equalization for GSM BTS-hardware implementation on TMS320C6424 TI DSP. In: Digital Information and Communication Technology and it's Applications, pp. 319–323. IEEE Press, Thailand (2012)
7. Texas Instruments. http://www.ti.com
8. Altera Corporation. http://www.altera.com

Precoding of Correlated Symbols for STBC Systems Design

Kelvin Anoh[1(✉)], Bamidele Adebisi[1], and Godfrey Okorafor[2]

[1] School of Engineering, Manchester Metropolitan University, Manchester, UK
{k.anoh,b.adebisi}@mmu.ac.uk
[2] Novena University, Kwale, Nigeria
nwajigo@novenauniversity.edu.ng

Abstract. A problem with transmitting correlated symbols over multiple transmit channel paths is that there is no diversity gain achieved at the receiver. Precoding technique provides a smart approach to achieving diversity gains at the receiver even when correlated symbols are transmitted; by phase variation, amplitude variation or both provided by the precoder. The space-time block code (STBC) technique, for example, is well-known when transmitting the same symbols by making them appear as different symbols using conjugation. We observe that correlated symbols can be transmitted over multiple transmit channel paths over STBC scheme while still achieving diversity. The correlated symbols can be made to appear as different symbols by using precoders; this enables diversity and improves data rate. Combining the proposed with the equivalent channel matrix (EVCM) permits the proposed design to outperform the conventional precoding of uncorrelated symbols technique by 2 dB at all bit error ratio (BER) for 2×1 and 2×2 antenna configurations. This is useful in increasing data rates with better BER performance.

Keywords: STBC · Correlated · MIMO · Precoding

1 Introduction

Since the advent of 4G technology, a lot of work has been done towards achieving a 5G design [1–3]. Most of these works have been done on beamforming especially for mmWave and 5G [3, 4]. Beamforming is a precoding technique that involves weighting some input symbols to enable some transmissions in the desired directions or to specific users [5]. The beamforming precoding technique has been investigated widely for STBCs [6–8]. In the use of STBC to design multi-antenna systems, the scheme enables that the same symbol is sent to the receiver more than once by making that same symbol look like another one; by conjugation. To transfer decoding complexity from the receiver to the transmitter, an equivalent channel matrix (EVCM) is usually derived. This technique also enables linear processing and simplifies receiver design. With the EVCM, the implementation of STBC reduces to sending N_T-unique symbols to the receiver over the channel (EVCM) matrix. When combined with precoding, the preocder weights are multiplied by these symbols and equivalently received in the receiver. Conventional transmit precoding, for instance angular beamforming

© ICST Institute for Computer Sciences, Social Informatics and Telecommunications Engineering 2017
I. Otung et al. (Eds.): WiSATS 2016, LNICST 186, pp. 83–91, 2017.
DOI: 10.1007/978-3-319-53850-1_10

differentiates among these symbols by assigning different phases to each transmit symbol block [9]. If these possibilities and differentiations already exist among the symbols (e.g. EVCM and phase difference), we consider that these differences already provided enough diversity for transmitting different symbols than transmitting the same symbols as different symbols over many timeslots as in [10]. Consequently, suppose that the N_T-transmit symbols are correlated. One, the data rate is increased, the amplitude of the symbols are also amplified accordingly but not reduced to $K < L$ symbol lengths like when using the conventional STBC technique; $K = (L/N_T)$. We investigate these in this paper for standard orthogonal-STBC (OSTBC) with two transmit antennas $(N_T = 2)$.

In Sect. 2, we present the system model and discuss the method of multi-antenna precoding that we propose in Sect. 3. The simulation method and results are described in Sect. 4 with the conclusions following.

2 System Model

In our design, we consider an STBC system equipped with two transmit antennas $(N_T = 2)$ and some N_R receivers. Since there are N_T transmitting branches and N_R receivers, we summarize the $N_R \times N_T$ MIMO system in linear form as follows

$$\bar{\mathcal{Y}} = \bar{\mathcal{H}}\bar{\mathcal{C}} + \bar{\mathcal{Z}} \tag{1}$$

where $\bar{\mathcal{Y}}$ is the received signal at the receiver, $\bar{\mathcal{H}} \epsilon \mathbb{C}^{N_R \times N_T}$ is a flat fading multi-path channel and $\bar{\mathcal{Z}} \sim \mathbb{CN}(0, \sigma_z^2 I_{N_R})$ is the additive white Gaussian noise with zero mean and variance σ_z^2. The received signal $\bar{\mathcal{Y}}$ is $\bar{\mathcal{Y}} \epsilon \mathbb{C}^{N_R \times L}$. The multi-spatial data, $\bar{\mathcal{C}} \epsilon \mathbb{C}^{N_T \times L}$ is formed from weighting some un-precoded phase-shift keying (PSK) input symbols. These weights of the multi-spatial data constitute the precoders and can be discussed as

$$\bar{\mathcal{C}} = w \times \bar{c} \tag{2}$$

where $w \epsilon \mathbb{C}^{N_T \times 1}$ is the transmit precoder and $\bar{c} \epsilon \mathbb{C}^{1 \times L}$ is the un-precoded PSK symbols. Since the precoder enables the realization of multi-spatial data streams in (2), then one can easily rewrite (1) as

$$\bar{\mathcal{Y}} = \bar{\mathcal{H}} \sum_{i=1}^{N_T} (w_i \bar{c}_i) + \mathcal{Z} \tag{3}$$

Each of the $\bar{c}_i \ \forall i = 1, \cdots, N_T$, constitutes the ith transmitting branch symbol corresponding to the ith precoder. Let the un-precoded symbols be the standard STBC code described in [10], we rewrite $\bar{c}$ as

$$\check{\mathcal{C}} = \begin{bmatrix} c_1 & c_2 \\ -c_2^* & c_1^* \end{bmatrix} \tag{4}$$

where $(\cdot)^*$ represents complex conjugate. Herein (4), each of the $c_i \, \forall i = 1, \cdots, N_T$ constitutes the ith transmitting timeslot symbol of the OSTBC Alamouti code. It can easily be verified that (4) enables orthogonal processing such as $|\check{\mathcal{C}}|^2 = diag \, (|c_1|^2 + |c_2|^2, |c_1|^2 + |c_2|^2)$. Using (4) an EVCM can be derived so that the linear system in (1) can be rewritten as

$$\mathcal{Y} = \mathcal{H}\mathcal{C} + \mathcal{Z} \tag{5}$$

where $\mathcal{H} = [\mathcal{H}_1 | \mathcal{H}_2]$ represents the channel states at two different timeslots and $\mathcal{C} = w \times c$; $c_i(l) \epsilon \mathbb{C}^{N_T \times L} \forall l = 1, \cdots, L$. We showed in [11] that an equivalent channel matrix can be derived to simplify detection in the receiver as

$$\mathcal{H} = \begin{bmatrix} h_1 & h_2 \\ h_2^* & -h_1^* \end{bmatrix} \tag{6}$$

Both (4) and (6) are used for $N_T = 2$ and $N_R = 1$ designs. We described designs that enable (6) to be used for MIMO system in [11]. Using (6) in (5) for a conventional STBC [10], $\mathcal{C} \epsilon \mathbb{C}^{N_T \times K}$ and $\forall N_T \, \mathcal{C}_i \neq \mathcal{C}_j$ because $c_i \neq c_j \, \forall i = 1, \cdots, N_T$ and $c_{i,j}(k) \epsilon \mathbb{C}^{1 \times K} \, \forall k = 1, \cdots, K; K = (L/N_T)$. Note that $\forall N_T, \, i \neq j$.

Since there are N_T separate beams sequel to the precoder (w) each equipped with a unique phase angle and amplitude, we consider the case where $\forall i = 1, \cdots, N_T \, c_i = c_j$ where $c_{i,j}(l) \epsilon \mathbb{C}^{1 \times L} \forall l = 1, \cdots, L; \forall N_T, \, i \neq j$. We argue that since the precoder has uniquely different phases and amplitudes, then $\forall N_T \, \mathcal{C}_i k \neq \mathcal{C}_j$ still holds thus achieving diversity that does not exist when only $c_i = c_j, \forall i = 1, \cdots, N_T$ is used. We maintain that although $\mathcal{R}_{c_i c_j} = \sum (c_i - \mu_{c_i})(c_j - \mu_{c_j}) = I$ when the precoder is applied, then $\mathcal{R}_{\mathcal{C}_i \mathcal{C}_j} = \sum (\mathcal{C}_i - \mu_{\mathcal{C}_i})(\mathcal{C}_j - \mu_{\mathcal{C}_j}) \neq I; \mu_x = \int xp(x)dx$ is the statistical mean and I is an identity matrix. Moreover, since $K < L$, then the proposed scheme provides higher data rate advantage with the amplitude improved so that the BER becomes better than the traditional STBC combined with the precoding scheme.

3 Method of Multi-antenna Precoding

Singular value decomposition (SVD) provides an elegant method for realizing well-performing precoders [5]. For instance, the precoder weights are unitary matrices that are also positive definitive. When used with the channel matrix, the SVD provides unitary matrices (or the precoders) that simplify channel compensation at the receiver. As an example, consider the EVCM channel matrix, $\mathcal{H}$, its SVD can be expressed as [12–14]

$$\mathcal{H} = \mathcal{U}\Omega\mathcal{V}^{\mathcal{H}} \tag{7}$$

where $\mathcal{U}$ and $\mathcal{V}$ are unitary matrices of the $N_T \times N_T$ dimension of the transmitter and $N_R \times N_R$ dimension of the receiver respectively. It is easy to verify that $\mathcal{U}^{\mathcal{H}}\mathcal{U} = I_{N_R \times N_R}$ and also $\mathcal{V}^{\mathcal{H}}\mathcal{V} = I_{N_T \times N_T}$. Given the EVCM in (6), $\mathcal{H}$ is a square matrix. Then, the diagonal matrix $\Omega \epsilon \mathbb{R}^{N_T \times N_T}$ corresponds to the power allocated to each of the N_T channels. The input signal ($\mathcal{C}$) can also be represented, following (3), as

$$\mathcal{C} = \mathcal{V} \times (I_{N_T} \otimes c) \tag{8}$$

where $\otimes$ is the Kronecker product operator, $\mathcal{C} \epsilon \mathbb{C}^{N_T \times L}$ and $\mathcal{V}^{\mathcal{H}}$ is a vector of the eigen-decomposition of the channel $\mathcal{H} \epsilon \mathbb{C}^{N_R \times N_T}$ for a flat fading channel model. At the receiver, the detection of the transmitted symbols can be explored that by using (7) in (5)

$$\begin{aligned} \hat{c} &= \mathcal{U}^{\mathcal{H}} \mathcal{y} \\ &= \mathcal{U}^{\mathcal{H}} \mathcal{H} \mathcal{C} + \mathcal{U}^{\mathcal{H}} \mathcal{Z} \\ &= \mathcal{U}^{\mathcal{H}} (\mathcal{U} \Omega \mathcal{V}^{\mathcal{H}}) \mathcal{C} + \mathcal{U}^{\mathcal{H}} \mathcal{Z} \\ &= \mathcal{U}^{\mathcal{H}} (\mathcal{U} \Omega \mathcal{V}^{\mathcal{H}}) \mathcal{V} c + \mathcal{U}^{\mathcal{H}} \mathcal{Z} \\ &= \Omega c + \mathcal{U}^{\mathcal{H}} \mathcal{Z} \end{aligned} \tag{9}$$

The result provides N_T parallel independent subchannels. Suppose that $\mathcal{V}^H$ is used at the transmitter for precoding the input symbols, it is clear that $\mathcal{V}^H$ provides different phase and amplitudes for each transmitting branch. Thus, if the input symbols are correlated, then precoding each symbol with $\mathcal{V}^H$ provides uncorrelation among these symbols. Then, if we rewrite $w_t = \mathcal{V}^H$ as the precoder at the transmitter and $w_{\mathcal{H}}^r = \mathcal{U}$ for compensation at the receiver, the received signal can be expressed as

$$\begin{aligned} \hat{c} &= w_r^{\mathcal{H}} \mathcal{y} \\ &= w_r^{\mathcal{H}} \mathcal{H} \mathcal{C} + w_r^{\mathcal{H}} \mathcal{Z} \\ &= w_r^{\mathcal{H}} \mathcal{H} w_t c + w_r^{\mathcal{H}} \mathcal{Z} \end{aligned} \tag{10}$$

On the other hand, since $w_r^{\mathcal{H}}$ is a unitary matrix, the estimated noise term $\hat{\mathcal{Z}} = (w_r^{\mathcal{H}} \mathcal{Z})$ remains Gaussian. For MIMO systems, if the detecting matrix $w_r^{\mathcal{H}}$ maximizes the objective function $|w_r^{\mathcal{H}} \mathcal{H} w_t|$ at the receiver given w_t, then the receiver is said to attain maximum ratio combining (MRC) [15]. Clearly, given the objective function $|w_r^{\mathcal{H}} \mathcal{H} w_t|$, the detecting matrix $w_r^{\mathcal{H}}$ enables the receiver to achieve maximal output for $N_T = 2$. This may not be necessarily true for higher order designs of STBC systems except when the scheme has been enabled to achieve full-diversity such as in [16–19].

The SNR at the receiver can be well-described as

$$\gamma = \frac{\mathbb{E}\left\{|w_r^{\mathcal{H}}\mathcal{H}w_t c|^2\right\}}{\mathbb{E}\left\{|w_r^{\mathcal{H}}\mathcal{Z}\mathcal{Z}^{\mathcal{H}}w_r|\right\}} = \mathbb{E}\left\{|w_r^{\mathcal{H}}\mathcal{H}w_t|^2\right\}\frac{E_c}{\sigma_{\tilde{z}}^2} \tag{11}$$

where $E_c = \mathbb{E}\left\{|c|^2\right\}$ and $\sigma_{\tilde{z}}^2 = \mathbb{E}\left\{|\mathcal{Z}\mathcal{Z}^H|\right\}$; $\mathbb{E}\{\cdot\}$ is the statistical expectation mean of the precoded symbols at the receiver. For MIMO designs, the exact SNR at the receiver can be expressed as $\gamma_{MIMO} = \sum_{j=1}^{N_R} \sum_{i=1}^{N_T} \gamma_{i,j}$. Considering M-ary PSK symbols, the error probability can be described as [6]

$$P_{psk} = \frac{1}{\pi} \int_0^{(M-1)\pi/M} \prod_{i=1}^{N_T} \xi_i(\gamma_i, b_{psk}, \theta)d\theta$$

where $\theta = \pi/2$, $\xi_i(\gamma_i, b_{psk}, \theta) = -b_{psk}\gamma/\sin^2\theta$ and $b_{psk} = \sin^2(\pi/M)$. Define the original un-precoded PSK symbol, $s = \mathbb{C}^{1\times L}$ where L is the length of the input symbols. For multiple antennas dispensing with correlated symbols $\mathcal{C}(l)\epsilon\mathbb{C}^{N_T\times L}$; $\mathcal{C} = \mathcal{V} \times (I_{N_T} \otimes c)$. For conventional STBC symbols, $\mathcal{C}(k)\epsilon\mathbb{C}^{N_T\times K}$ where $K < L$ and $K = L/N_T$; $k = 1, \cdots, K$. For the precoded conventional STBC design equipped with $N_T = 2$ and $N_R = 1$, the SNR is as defined in (11). On the other hand, for correlated symbols similarly equipped, then

$$\gamma_{corr} = \frac{N_T\mathbb{E}\left\{|w_r^{\mathcal{H}}\mathcal{H}w_t c|^2\right\}}{\mathbb{E}\left\{|w_r^{\mathcal{H}}\mathcal{Z}\mathcal{Z}^{\mathcal{H}}w_r|\right\}} = N_T\mathbb{E}\left\{|w_r^{\mathcal{H}}\mathcal{H}w_t|^2\right\}\frac{E_c}{\sigma_{\tilde{z}}^2} \tag{12}$$

Comparing (11) and (12), it can be observed that the received SNR for the correlated symbols is better than the uncorrelated symbols by N_T. If the system operates with $N_R > 1$ then $\mathcal{C}(k)\epsilon\mathbb{C}^{N_R N_T\times\frac{L}{N_T}}$ for the uncorrelated and the SNR is

$$\gamma_{uncorr, MIMO} = \sum_{n-1}^{N_R}\sum_{i=1}^{N_T}\gamma_{i,n}$$

while $\mathcal{C}(l)\epsilon\mathbb{C}^{N_R N_T\times L}$ so that the SNR for the correlated input symbols becomes

$$\gamma_{corr} = N_T\gamma_{uncorr,MIMO} = \sum_{n=1}^{N_R}\sum_{i=1}^{N_T}(N_T\gamma_{i,n}) \tag{13}$$

The above results show that the SNR increases with increasing both the number of transmitting antennas and the number of receivers. If the receiver is constrained in size, for example mobile phones, tablets or laptops in such a way that the integration of many multiple receiving antennas is problematic due to mutual coupling, then the number of transmitting antennas can be increased to improve throughput at the receiver. These results are demonstrated using simulation described in Sect. 4.

4 Simulation Results and Discussions

The simulation environment involves a randomly generated input symbols of length L demultiplexed into N_T branches to realize some uncorrelated symbols; this reduces the symbol length for each branch to $K = (L/N_T)$ such that $K < L$. Thus, the ith-branch input symbol constitutes a symbol vector $c_i \epsilon \mathbb{C}^{1 \times \frac{L}{N_T}} \forall i = 1, \cdots, N_T$ and $c_i \neq c_j$ for all transmitting branches; this enables the standard STBC symbols that are uncorrelated. A multipath flat fading channel with $\mathcal{H} \sim \mathcal{CN}(0, \sigma_h^2 I)$ distribution was generated and used to construct an EVCM. With the EVCM only the $c_i \epsilon \mathbb{C}^{1 \times K} \forall i = 1, \cdots, N_T$ uncorrelated symbols are used and these are precoded before combining them with the EVCM channel. On the other hand, since the precoding involves different weights of different amplitudes and phases, the default input symbols of L length are used when realizing the correlated symbols. This fact enables that the gain in the receiver can be increased by N_T. As a consequence, this technique doubles the data rate against the uncorrelated design for $N_T = 2$ and improves the processing time since the multiple conjugation operations to recover the original symbols are not required. The receiver involves only a linear processing which further makes the design elegant.

Using simulation we show that with the precoding, multiplying the received signal Y with $w_r^{\mathcal{H}}$ is equivalently a diagonal matrix as the conventional channel compensation if the channel matrix can be derived; meanwhile only $w_r^{\mathcal{H}} \mathcal{H} w_t = \left(\mathcal{H}^{\frac{1}{2}} \right)^{\mathcal{H}} \mathcal{H}^{\frac{1}{2}}$. In Fig. 1 the results for transmitting correlated and uncorrelated precoded symbols are compared. Alongside, the result of default OSTBC is presented also. Since $w_r^{\mathcal{H}} \mathcal{H} w_t$ is only equivalent to $\left(\mathcal{H}^{\frac{1}{2}} \right)^{\mathcal{H}} \mathcal{H}^{\frac{1}{2}}$, then the received SNR of the default STBC will be slightly better than that of the uncorrelated precoded design and correspondingly their BER. These are achieved in Figs. 1 and 2.

First, observe that our results in Fig. 1 are consistent with the ones reported in [10] for 2×1 mid 2×2 antenna configurations. Comparing the proposed design with the standard OSTBC for 2 antennas with one receiver, it can be seen that the correlated symbol consistently achieved 2 dB performance gain over the standard OSTBC equipped with one receiver. In (12) and (13), we showed that the received SNR is a function of both N_T and N_R. Consequently, comparing the designs for 2×2 antenna configurations, the correlated symbol precoding technique achieves 2 dB better than the uncorrleated symbols. These investigations are limited to BPSK modulation. Next, we investigate these designs for higher spectral efficiency using QPSK modulation in Fig. 2.

With a similar design environment as in Fig. 1 for a QPSK design in Fig. 2, it can be seen that the proposed consistently outperformed the default-OSTBC by 2 dB for 2×1 and 2×2 antenna configurations. If the EVCM is considered in terms of the standard STBC matrix, there are 2 timeslots and 2 antenna spaces so that the system attains full spatial rate (and also full diversity since $w_r^{\mathcal{H}} \mathcal{H} w_t = \lambda I_{N_T}$ and $\mathcal{H}^{\mathcal{H}} \mathcal{H} = \sigma_h^2 I_{N_T}$, where λ is the eigenvalue from the SVD decomposition of the EVCM). In each of the timeslots, more symbols are transmitted with the correlated symbols than in the uncorrelated symbols per timeslot thus achieving a higher data rate. It follows also that in addition to achieving diversity gain, the SNR is improved in the order of transmitting antennas.

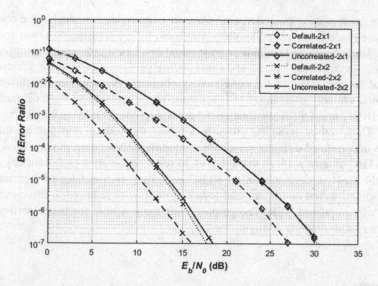

Fig. 1. Comparison of Precoded Correlated and uncorrelated symbols for MIMO STBC with 2 Transmit antennas (BPSK)

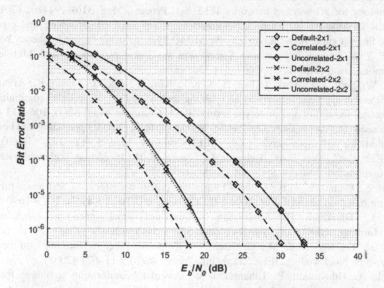

Fig. 2. Comparison of Precoded Correlated and uncorrelated symbols for MIMO STBC with 2 Transmit antennas (QPSK)

5 Conclusion

In this paper we have introduced the concept of precoding correlated symbols over STBC scheme. Although corrected symbols sent over many transmitting channels do not provide any diversity at the receiver, we introduced a novel approach to enabling diversity by transmitting precoded symbols over uncorrelated channels. The correlated symbols are made uncorrelated by precoding them before transmission over multipath channels. These precoding weights provide variations in both phases and amplitudes of the symbols so that diversity gain and some coding performance gain are achieved. We found that the data rates of the correlated symbols are N_T multiples of those of the uncorrelated symbols over an OSTBC scheme. These translated into 2 dB gain when we used BPSK and QPSK modulation schemes for 2×1 and 2×2 antenna configurations. Thus, although STBC provides a smart method of transmitting the same signals as uncorrelated different signals by conjugation, precoding of correlated signals over an STBC scheme realized through EVCM reduced the error probability by N_T and doubles the BER performance of an STBC design. This translates to increased data over the same spectral conditions and lower signal power required to drive more data symbols with improved BER. The proposed has the potential for better performances with higher order antenna configurations.

References

1. Razavizadeh, S.M., Ahn, M., Lee, I.: Three-dimensional beamforming: a new enabling technology for 5G wireless networks. IEEE Sig. Process. Mag. **31**(6), 94–101 (2014)
2. Obara, T., Suyama, S., Shen, J., Okumura,Y.: Joint fixed beamforming and eigenmode precoding for super high bit rate massive MIMO systems using higher frequency bands. In: IEEE 25th Annual International Symposium on Personal, Indoor, and Mobile Radio Communication (PIMRC), pp. 607–611 (2014)
3. Roh, W., Seol, J.-Y., Park, J., Lee, B., Lee, J., Kim, Y., Cho, J., Cheun, K., Aryanfar, F.: Millimeter-wave beamforming as an enabling technology for 5G cellular communications: theoretical feasibility and prototype results. IEEE Commun. Mag. **52**(2), 106–113 (2014)
4. Alkhateeb, A., Mo, J., Gonzalez-Prelcic, N., Heath, R.W.: MIMO precoding and combining solutions for millimeter-wave systems. IEEE Commun. Mag. **52**(12), 122–131 (2014)
5. Jay Kuo, C.-C., Tsai, S.-H., Tadjpour, L., Chang, Y.-H.: Precoding Techniques for Digital Communication Systems. Springer, London (2008)
6. Zhou, S., Giannakis, G.B.: Optimal transmitter eigen- beamforming and space-time block coding based on channel correlations. IEEE Trans. Inf. Theory **49**(7), 1673–1690 (2003)
7. Liu, L., Jafarkhani, H.: Application of quasi-orthogonal space-time block codes in beamforming. IEEE Trans. Signal Process. **53**(1), 54–63 (2005)
8. Jöngren, G., Skoglund, M., Ottersten, B.: Combining beam- forming and orthogonal space-time block coding. IEEE Trans. Inf. Theory **48**(3), 611–627 (2002)
9. Innok, A., Uthansakul, P., Uthansakul, M.: Angular beamforming technique for MIMO beamforming system. Int. J. Antennas Propagation (2012)
10. Alamouti, S.M.: A simple transmit diversity technique for wireless communications. IEEE J. Sel. Areas Commun. **16**(8), 1451–1458 (1998)
11. Anoh, K.O.O., Abd-Alhameed, R.A., Okorafor, G.N., Noras, J.M., Rodriguez, J., Jones, S. M.R.: Performance evaluation of spatial modulation and QOSTBC for MIMO systems. EAI Endorsed Transactions on Mobile Communications and Applications **15**(6), e5 (2015)
12. Du, K.-L., Swamy, M.N.S.: Wireless communication systems: from RF subsystems to 4G enabling technologies. Cambridge University Press, New york (2010)
13. Goldsmith, A.: Wireless communications. Cambridge University Press, New york (2005)

14. Proakis, J.G., Salehi, M.: Digital Communications. 5th edn. (2008)
15. Love, D.J., Heath Jr., R.W., Strohmer, T.: Grassmannian beamforming for multiple-input multiple-output wireless systems. IEEE Trans. Inf. Theory **19**(10), 2735–2747 (2003)
16. Anoh, K.O.O., Jones, S.M.R., Abd-Alhameed, R.A.A., Mapoka, T.T., Okorafor, G.N., Ngala, M.J.: A simple space-time coding technique for wireless communication systems. Internet Technol. Appl. (ITA) **2015**, 405–410 (2015)
17. Park, U., Kim, S., Lim, K., Li, J.: A novel QOSTBC scheme with linear decoding for three and four transmit antennas. IEEE Commun. Lett. **12**(12), 868–870 (2008)
18. Pham, V.-B., Qi, Bo-Yu., Sheng, W.-X., Wang, M.: An improved full rate full diversity qostbc with linear decoding in mimo systems. Wireless Pers. Commun. **69**(1), 121–131 (2013)
19. Pham, V.-B., Sheng, W.-X.: No-zero-entry full diversity space-time block codes with linear receivers. Annals of telecommunications-annales des télécommunications **70**(1–2), 73–81 (2015)

Communication Applications in Smart Grid (CASG) Special Session

Optimization of Community Based Virtual Power Plant with Embedded Storage and Renewable Generation

Oghenovo Okpako[✉], Paul Inuwa Adamu, Haile-Selassie Rajamani, and Prashant Pillai

Faculty of Engineering and Informatics, University of Bradford, Bradford, UK
{ookpako,p.i.adamu,H.S.Rajamani,P.Pillai}@bradford.ac.uk

Abstract. The current global challenge of climate change has made renewable energy usage very important. There is an ongoing drive for the deployment of renewable energy resource at the domestic level through feed-in tariff, etc. However, the intermittent nature of renewable energy has made storage a key priority. In this work, a community having a solar farm with energy storage embedded in the house of the energy consumers is considered. Consumers within the community are aggregated in to a local virtual power plant. Genetic algorithm was used to develop an optimized energy transaction for the virtual power plant with respect to differential pricing and renewable generation. The results show that it is feasible to have a virtual power plant setup in a local community that involve the use of renewable generation and embedded storage. The results show that both pricing and renewable generation window should be considered as a factor when setting up a virtual power plant that involve the use of storage and renewable generation at the community level. Also, when maximization of battery state of charge is considered as part of an optimization problem in a day ahead market, certain trade-off would have to be made on the profit of the virtual power plant, the incentive of the prosumer, as well as the provision of peak service to the grid.

Keywords: Prosumer · Battery · Virtual power plant (VPP) · Genetic algorithm (GA) · Smart grid · State of charge · Solar generation

1 Introduction

Access to clean energy is becoming important. This is due to the current global challenge of climate change caused by the emission of greenhouse gases from fossil fuel. The need for clean energy has ensured that vital consideration is given to energy produced from renewable energy sources. There is a current drive to promote much use of renewable energy, for example, the European Union has renewable energy usage as part of its strategy to cut down greenhouse gas emission by 80% by the year 2050 [1]. Also, most governments are currently encouraging the use of renewable energy through the provision of feed-in tariff, etc. However, renewable energy sources like solar, wind etc. are intermittent in nature, and would require energy storage devices. Energy storage

© ICST Institute for Computer Sciences, Social Informatics and Telecommunications Engineering 2017
I. Otung et al. (Eds.): WiSATS 2016, LNICST 186, pp. 95–107, 2017.
DOI: 10.1007/978-3-319-53850-1_11

becomes key in maximizing the use of renewable energy. It can be used to smoothen peak and trough of renewable generation.

There is a current global restructuring of electric power utilities [2, 3]. This is envisaged to change the consumer role to that of a prosumer, and as well promote the deployment of distributed generation. The prosumer role involves both energy consumption and energy production. Energy storage becomes an asset to the prosumer as it could be to buy cheap energy from the grid during off-peak period, or store excess renewable generation, which could later be sold at peak period for better prices [4–6].

The concept of using small unit of energy storage at the domestic side of the electricity grid to participate in the power market was proposed by Kempton [7]. According to Kempton, the battery electric vehicle is not just a load on the utility grid, but an alternative power source. Work on different energy management strategies for dealing with battery electric vehicles has been done by these authors [8–10]. However, battery electric vehicles are usually mobile and could be limited in their potentials to maximize the use of renewable energy. As a result, it is proposed in this work to have battery energy storage embedded inside the home of the prosumer.

At the domestic side of the grid, prosumers lack the capacity to participate directly at the wholesale power market. Prosumers would need to be aggregated by a virtual power plant (VPP) at the community level. The VPP aggregates small units of distributed energy resource and flexible load for participation in the power market by offering flexibility. Prosumers participation in the power market is done through the VPP. In [11], it is demonstrated that it is possible to have a pricing scheme that provides financial incentive for both the VPP and the prosumer. However, there was no clarity on how VPP operation is affected with both pricing and renewable energy generation. Also the possibility and effect of including battery state of charge as part of an optimization problem for a community VPP was clearly not understood.

In this paper, it is proposed to use genetic algorithm to optimize the energy transaction of a community VPP with respect to differential pricing and renewable generation. The algorithm was tested under various scenarios. These includes an objective function where only the prosumer net cost is considered, and also an objective function where both the prosumer net cost and battery state of charge were considered.

This paper is organized as follows; Sect. 2 is a description of the model, Sect. 3 is the mathematical modelling, Sect. 4 is the VPP optimization, Sect. 5 is the results and discussion, and Sect. 6 is the conclusion.

2   Framework of Virtual Power Plant Model

Figure 1, is a diagram describing the VPP model developed in this work. From Fig. 1, N is the total number of prosumers within the community aggregated as a VPP. Ed_1 to Ed_N is the discharge energy from prosumer 1 to N battery. Ec_1 to Ec_N is the charge energy for prosumer 1 to N battery. Pp_{sell} is the prosumer sell price of energy from battery, or the price at which the VPP buys energy from the prosumer's battery. L_1 to L_N is the load demand of prosumer 1 to N. Pp_{buy} is the price at which the prosumer buy energy from the VPP to meet its load, or the price at which VPP sells energy to the prosumer to meet load demand. E_{imp} and E_{exp} are the amount of energy imported from the grid, and exported to the grid by the VPP. Pv_{imp} and Pv_{exp} are the VPP import and export price of energy to the grid. Epv is the solar energy generation from the community solar farm which is assumed to be free for both parties (prosumer and VPP).

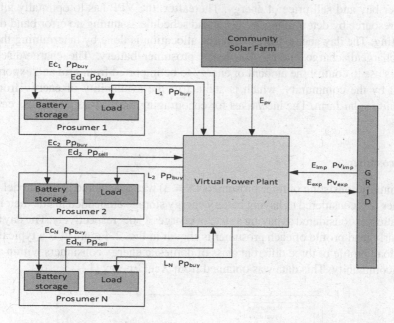

Fig. 1. Architecture of the virtual power plant model.

2.1 Virtual Power Plant

In Fig. 1, the VPP can buy energy in bulk from the grid (E_{imp}) at price Pv_{imp} and from the prosumers (Ed_1 to Ed_N from prosumer 1 to prosumer N) at price Prsell respectively. The energy bought from the grid is use to meet the prosumer's energy demand (L_1 to L_N) as well as to charge their battery. The energy bought from each prosumer's battery (Ed_1 to Ed_N from prosumer 1 to prosumer N) are aggregated by the VPP. The aggregated energy is first used within the community to meet each prosumer's load demand respectively before its excess can be sold to the VPP and then exported (traded in the power market). The solar farm is owned by the community. Energy produced from the solar farm is only use for charging of the prosumers battery and meeting of their load demand. The VPP only imports energy from the external grid when the energy produced from the community solar farm is not enough to meet the prosumers battery charging and load requirement.

In this work, the VPP was considered as having a day ahead forecast of the energy produced from the community solar farm. The VPP has a day ahead forecast of each prosumer half hourly load profile. In addition, the VPP has a day ahead forecast of the price Pvexp at which the external grid would buy its energy (i.e. the day ahead forecast price paid by the grid to the VPP for exporting energy), as well as the day ahead forecast of the price Pvimp at which the grid would sell energy to the prosumer (i.e. the day ahead forecast price paid by VPP to the external grid for importing energy). Both import and export prices for energy are agreed between the VPP and the grid in the wholesale power market. Based on the day ahead import and export price, the VPP agrees a day ahead prosumer buy and sell price of energy. Thereafter, the VPP has to optimally allocate energy resource by determining its day ahead schedule assuming no error band during forecasting. The day ahead energy resource allocation is done by determining the day ahead charge/discharge energy from each prosumer battery. The charge/discharge energy is use to control the amount of energy to be imported from grid and exported to the grid by the community, which is subject to the availability of energy from the community solar farm. The incentives for encouraging the VPP as a business entity is profit.

2.2 Prosumer

A community consisting of three prosumers (N = 3) was considered in this model. Each prosumer was considered as having battery energy storage embedded inside their home. Each battery is considered as having a state of charge of 30% respectively. The day ahead half hourly load profile of each prosumer is shown in Fig. 2. Figure 2, is a typical half-hourly load profile of three different class of domestic energy consumers within a residential community. This data was obtained from Xcel Energy [12].

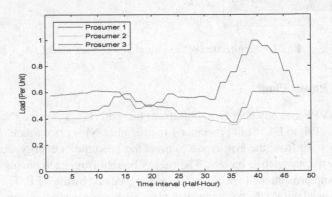

Fig. 2. Forecasted hourly load profile of each prosumer.

Each of the prosumers has a different hourly load profile. The motivation of the prosumer as a participant in the VPP, is to minimize its net cost (energy purchasing cost). In this work, a lower net cost represents an incentive received by the prosumer for participating as part of a VPP in its local community.

3   Mathematical Tool Used in Modelling

3.1   The VPP Energy Balance

The VPP energy balance equation during the time interval t is calculated in (1) as follows.

$$E_{imp_t} + E_{pv_t} + \sum E_{d_{i,t}} = E_{exp_t} + E_{npv_t} + \sum \left(E_{c_{i,t}} + L_{i,t} \right) \tag{1}$$

$$
\begin{cases}
\text{if } (E_{pv_t} + \sum \left(E_{d_{i,t}} - E_{c_{i,t}} - L_{i,t} \right) < 0, E_{imp_t} = +ve \\
\text{if } (E_{pv_t} + \sum \left(E_{d_{i,t}} - E_{c_{i,t}} - L_{i,t} \right) > 0), E_{imp_t} = 0, E_{npv_t} = +ve \\
\text{if } \left(\sum \left(E_{d_{i,t}} - L_{i,t} \right) \right) > 0, E_{exp_{i,t}} = +ve \\
\text{if } \left(\sum \left(E_{d_{i,t}} - L_{i,t} \right) \right) < 0, E_{exp_{i,t}} = 0
\end{cases}
$$

Where i is an integer. t is the time interval. E_{imp_t} and E_{exp_t} are the amount of import energy and the amount of export energy in per unit during t. $E_{c_{i,t}}$ and $E_{d_{i,t}}$ are the amount of charge and discharge energy in per unit respectively allocated to prosumer i battery by the VPP during t. $L_{i,t}$ is the load of prosumer i in per unit during t. The load is fixed. E_{pv_t} is the amount of energy in per unit produced from community solar farm. E_{npv_t} is the amount of energy produced from the community solar farm that is not used by the community.

3.2   VPP Profit

The VPP profit Vpp_{profit}, at each time interval t over the day's total number of time interval (T) is calculated as follows.

$$\sum_{t=1}^{T} Vpp_{profit_t} = \sum_{t=1}^{T} \left(Vpp_{rev_t} - Vpp_{cost_t} \right) \tag{2}$$

Where Vpp_{rev_t} and Vpp_{cost_t} are the VPP revenue and cost respectively during the time interval t. T is the day's total number of time interval. Both VPP revenue and cost are calculated based on the amount of energy imported and exported. This is because it does not cost the VPP to get energy from the solar farm, also the prosumers only sells excess energy to the VPP for export after their load demand have been met. VPP revenue and cost are calculated in (3) and (4) respectively as follows.

$$\sum_{t=1}^{T} Vpp_{rev_t} = \sum_{t=1}^{T} Pp_{buy_t} \cdot E_{imp_t} + Pv_{exp_t} \cdot E_{exp_t} \tag{3}$$

$$\sum_{t=1}^{T} Vpp_{cost_t} = \sum_{t=1}^{T} Pv_{imp_t} \cdot E_{imp_t} + Pp_{sell_t} \cdot E_{exp_t} \tag{4}$$

Where Pp_{sell_t}, Pp_{buy_t}, Pv_{imp_t}, and Pv_{exp_t} are the prosumer selling price of energy, prosumer buy price of energy, the VPP import price of energy, and the VPP export price of energy respectively during t. All measured in pence/per unit.

3.3 Prosumer Net Cost

The prosumer net cost is calculated using both the import and export energy. During energy import, only energy imported from the grid is paid for by the prosumer. Energy used from the community solar farm is not paid for by the prosumer. The import energy represents a deficit in energy production from the community solar farm. During energy export, the energy discharge from the prosumer battery is first used internally to meet the prosumer's load demand, only its excess is sold to the VPP for export. The prosumer's net cost Pp_{cost}, at each time interval t over T is calculated as follows.

$$\sum_{t=1}^{T} Pp_{cost_t} = \sum_{t=1}^{T} Pp_{buy_t} \cdot E_{imp_t} - Pp_{sell_t} \cdot E_{exp_t} \tag{5}$$

3.4 Battery State of Charge

The battery state of charge (SOC) gives an information on the battery energy level. In this work, the battery energy level is measured in per unit. Usually the battery SOC cannot be measured directly, but can be inferred from the battery energy level. Therefore, the battery state of charge of charge is a measure of the battery energy level in comparison to the battery actual capacity, assuming an ideal battery with no peukert effect, no losses (self-discharge) and whose actual capacity is the same as its nominal capacity. The SOC is measured in percentage. It gives an information on the battery depth of discharge. The battery energy level measured during t is calculated as follows.

$$E_{stored_{i,t}} = E_{o_i} + \sum_{t=1}^{T} Ecd_{i,t} \tag{6}$$

$$Ecd_{i,t} = \begin{cases} E_{c_{i,t}}, & \text{if battery charging occur} \\ -E_{d_{i,t}}, & \text{if battery discharging occur} \\ 0, & \text{if battery is idle} \end{cases}$$

$E_{stored_{i,t}}$ is prosumer i battery energy level in per unit measured at t. E_{o_i} is prosumer i initial battery energy level in per unit before participation in the day ahead power market. Each prosumer battery SOC at t is calculated as follows.

$$SOC_{i,t} = 100\frac{E_{stored_{i,t}}}{E_{batt_i}} \tag{7}$$

$SOC_{i,t}$ is the state of charge of prosumer i battery measured in percentage at t. E_{batt_i}, is the actual battery capacity in per unit of prosumer i.

3.5   Battery Constraints

Each prosumer battery discharge constraint is represented as follows.

$$E_{d,\min_i} \le E_{d_{i,t}} \le E_{d,\max_i} \tag{8}$$

Where $E_{d,\min_i}$ and $E_{d,\max_i}$ are the minimum and maximum discharge energy that can be allocated to prosumer i battery. Each prosumer battery charge constraint is represented as follows.

$$E_{c,\min_i} \le E_{c_{i,t}} \le E_{c,\max_i} \tag{9}$$

Where $E_{c,\min_i}$ and $E_{c,\max_i}$ are the minimum and maximum charge energy that can be allocated to prosumer i battery. Each prosumer battery state of charge constraint is represented as follows.

$$SOC_{\min_i} \le SOC_{i,t} \le SOC_{\max_i} \tag{10}$$

Where $SOC_{\min_i}$ and $SOC_{\max_i}$ are the minimum and maximum SOC limit of prosumer i battery.

4   Optimizations of the Community Virtual Power Plant

To understand the optimization problem, the number of prosumer chosen to participate in the community VPP was kept at three. The optimization problem is formulated considering both the prosumer net cost and the battery SOC. This is gotten from (5) and (7) and is represented as follows.

$$[Min]F = w1 \sum_{t=1}^{T} Pp_{cost_t} - w2 \sum_{t=1}^{T} \sum_{i=1}^{N} SOC_{i,t} \tag{11}$$

F is the objective function to be minimize. It represents both the prosumer net cost and the battery state of charge. $w1$ and $w2$ are the weighting factor. E_o was chosen to be 5.4 per unit. T was chosen to be 48. $Ebatt$ (actual battery capacity) was chosen to be 18 per unit. Given the day ahead pricing, solar generation, and prosumer's load profile, genetic algorithm was used to solve the optimization problem [11].

5   Results and Discussion

In Fig. 3, is the modified pricing scheme used by the VPP in this work [11, 13]. The modified pricing scheme was extended to 48 time intervals. It was considered to use the modified pricing scheme because its business incentives favors both the VPP and the prosumer [11, 13] while meeting the VPP objective. This is detailed in [11, 13].

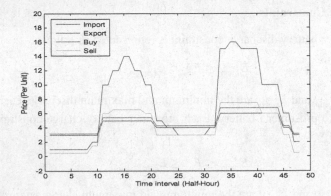

Fig. 3. Modified pricing scheme.

Figure 4, is the day ahead solar generation from the community solar farm. The data was gotten from [14], and was normalized to a peak solar generation of 3.2 per unit. This would be a more realistic value for the community considered (considering their load and charging requirements).

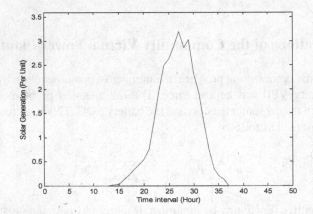

Fig. 4. Day ahead solar generation from community solar farm.

The modified pricing scheme, solar generation, and load profile were used as the input data. GA was used to perform the optimization and was initially tested by selecting $w1 = 1$ and $w2 = 0$. The simulation was done with these weighting factor, and the results are presented as follows.

In Fig. 5, the prosumer net cost decreases as the algorithm optimizes until it converges. Also, the VPP makes profit. Though the objective function with the given weighting factor purely considers the prosumers net cost minimization, the modified pricing scheme favors both the prosumer and the VPP.

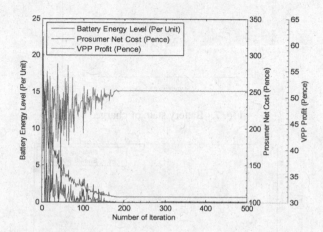

Fig. 5. Effect of optimization on community (at $w1 = 1$, $w2 = 0$).

In Fig. 6, the area above the reference point represents the charge energy while the one below the reference point represent the discharge energy. It is noticed that the batteries are charging during the period of solar generation and are discharging during the grid's peak demand. This is good, because the prosumers are actually using the energy produced from solar generation for charging of their battery, and are also discharging their battery during peak period to support their load. In Fig. 7, it is observed that the battery state of charge at the end of the day is zero percent. This is not good for the battery life and state of health. This is attributed to the optimization problem which only considers the prosumer net cost for one day period. Figure 8, is the energy exchange between the community and the grid.

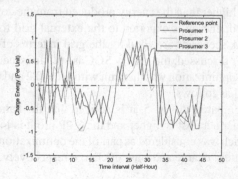

Fig. 6. Battery charge.

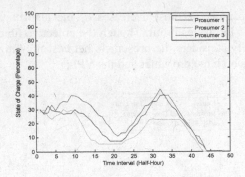

Fig. 7. Battery state of charge.

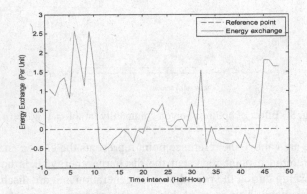

Fig. 8. Energy exchange between community and external grid.

In Fig. 8, the area above the reference point is the import energy, while below the reference point is the export energy. It is noticeable that the community is actually importing energy from the grid during off-peak period. The energy imported from the grid during the off-peak period is much lower when energy from community solar farm is available. This import is because the total load and the charging requirement of the community is slightly higher than the energy produced from the community solar farm. During the peak period, energy is exported to the external grid for grid peak support. Both peak and off-peak scenarios are good for the grid in terms of energy balancing.

However, as earlier discussed, the battery SOC is still an issue. To address this low battery SOC issue, the optimization was then run with $w1 = 0.2$ and $w2 = 0.8$. The results obtained are presented as follows.

In Fig. 9, when compared to Fig. 5, it is noticed that the battery energy level has increased. The prosumer net cost is higher and the VPP profit is lower. This is because of the battery SOC which was considered as part of the optimization function. Figure 10, and Fig. 11 are the battery charge and state of charge respectively.

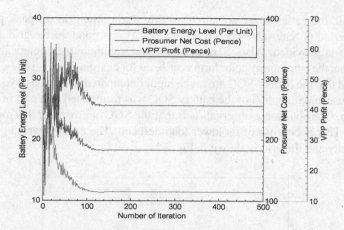

Fig. 9. Effect of optimization on community (at $w1 = 0.2$, $w2 = 0.8$).

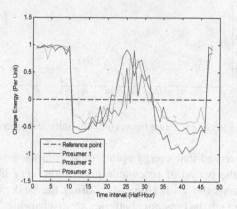

Fig. 10. Battery charge.

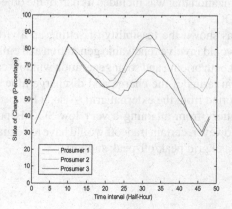

Fig. 11. Battery state of charge.

In Fig. 10, the batteries are actually charging during the grid off-peak period and during the period of renewable energy generation. This is good for the grid as grid off-peak service is provided. Also, it is good for the community as renewable energy produced from the community solar farm is utilized for charging the batteries. In Fig. 11, it is observed that the battery SOC are much higher compared to that observed in Fig. 7. This is because maximization of the battery SOC was formulated as a part of the objective function. One noticeable observation is that the SOC of prosumer 2 is much higher than others. This is because of its lower load demand. The energy exchange between the community and the grid is shown in Fig. 12.

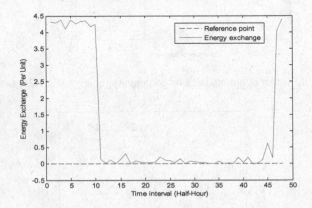

Fig. 12. Energy exchange between community and external grid.

In Fig. 12, it is observed that energy is imported from the grid during the off-peak period. Also, during the period of renewable generation, very little or no amount of energy is imported from the grid. However, during the peak period, energy is not exported to the grid, though the prosumer batteries are discharging. The discharge energy is used within the community to meet the prosumer load demand. This is attributed to the battery SOC maximization that was included as part of the objective function as well as the battery initial SOC.

This experiment has shown the feasibility of setting up a virtual power plant in a local community that would involve renewable generation and embedded storage. It has been demonstrated that both pricing and solar generation window can affect the technical operation of the VPP in terms of the charge and discharge time period as well as the amount of energy imported from the external grid. Also, it has been shown with clarity that preventing the battery from attaining a very low SOC is possible for a one-day optimization period. However, certain tradeoff would have to be made on the prosumer's incentive, VPP profit, and grid peak/off-peak support.

6   Conclusion

In this paper, it has been demonstrated that it is possible to have a virtual power plant set up that involves the use of embedded energy storage and renewable generation at a community level. It has been demonstrated that both pricing and solar generation window can affect the technical operation of the VPP in terms of the charge and discharge time period as well as the amount of energy imported from the external grid. It has been shown that battery state of charge should be accounted for in an optimization algorithm particularly for day ahead market. However, in considering battery state of charge as part of an optimization problem, certain tradeoffs in terms of provision of grid peak/off-peak support and incentives for the prosumer and the virtual power plant would have to be made.

References

1. Carvalho, M.G.: EU energy and climate change strategy. J. Energy **40**(1), 19–22 (2012)
2. Vallvé, X., Graillot, A., Gual, S., Colin, H.: Micro storage and demand side management in distributed PV grid-connected installations. In: 9th IEEE International Conference on Electrical Power Quality and Utilisation 2007, pp. 1–6 (2007)
3. Ihbal, A., Rajamani, H., Abd-Alhameed, R., Jalboub, M., Elmeshregi, A., Aljaddal, M.: Development of electricity pricing criteria at residential community level. Univers. J. Electr. Electron. Eng. **2**(2), 81–89 (2014)
4. Ferreira, H.L., Garde, R., Fulli, G., Kling, W., Lopes, J.P.: Characterisation of electrical energy storage technologies. J. Energy **53**, 288–298 (2013)
5. Boicea, V.A.: Energy storage technologies: the past and the present. Proc. IEEE **102**(11), 1777–1794 (2014)
6. IEA: Technology roadmap: energy storage, Paris (2014)
7. Kempton, W., Letendre, S.E.: Electric vehicles as a new power source for electric utilities. Transp. Res. Part D Trans. Environ. **2**(3), 157–175 (1997)
8. Wu, D., Aliprantis, D.C., Ying, L.: Load scheduling and dispatch for aggregators of plug-in electric vehicles. IEEE Trans. Smart Grid **3**(1), 368–376 (2012)
9. Pang, C., Aravinthan, V., Wang, X.: Electric vehicles as configurable distributed energy storage in the smart grid. In: Power Systems Conference (PSC) 2014, Clemson University, pp. 1–5 (2014)
10. Brooks, A., Lu, E., Reicher, D., Spirakis, C., Weihl, B.: Demand dispatch. IEEE Power Energ. Mag. **8**(3), 20–29 (2010)
11. Okpako, O., Rajamani, H., Pillai, P., Anuebunwa, U., Swarup, K.: Evaluation of community virtual power plant under various pricing schemes. In: Proceedings of 2016 IEEE Smart Energy Grid Engineering Conference, Oshawa, pp. 72–78 (2016)
12. Xcel Energy Hourly Load Profile. https://www.xcelenergy.com/staticfiles/xe/Corporate/Corporate%20PDFs/AppendixD-Hourly_Load_Profiles.pdf
13. Okpako, O., Rajamani, H., Pillai, P., Anuebunwa, U., Swarup, K.: Investigation of an optimized energy resource allocation algorithm for a community based virtual power plant. In: Proceedings of 2016 IEEE PES Power Africa Conference, Livingstone, pp. 153–157 (2016)
14. The University of Sheffield Solar. http://www.solar.sheffield.ac.uk/pvlive

Assessment of Effective Radiated Power of the Partial Discharge Emulator Source

Adel Jaber[1]([✉]), Pavlos Lazaridis[1], Bahghtar Saeed[1], Yong Zhang[1], Umar Khan[1], David Upton[1], Hamd Ahmed[1], Peter Mather[1], Robert Atkinson[2], Martin Judd[3], Maria Fatima Queiroz Vieira[4], and Ian Glover[1]

[1] Department of Engineering and Technology,
University of Huddersfield, Huddersfield HD1 3DH, UK
Adel.Jaber@hud.ac.uk
[2] Department of Electronic and Electrical Engineering,
University of Strathclyde, Glasgow G1 1XW, UK
[3] High Frequency Diagnostics and Engineering Ltd, Glasgow G3 7JT, UK
[4] Department of Electrical Engineering,
Universidade Federal de Campina, Campina Grande, Brazil

Abstract. Two effective partial discharge (PD) measurement techniques are used; a galvanic contact measurement technique similar to the IEC 60270 standard measurement and free-space radiometric (FSR) measurement. Several types of PD sources are specially constructed: two internal PD emulators and an emulator of the floating-electrode type. An AC power supply is applied to the PD source and the radiated signal is captured using a wideband biconical antenna. The calibration of PD sources is demonstrated. Effective radiated power (ERP) of the PD sources using a PD calibration device is determined.

Keywords: Absolute partial discharge intensity · Effective radiated power · Free space radiometric measurement · Galvanic contact measurement

1 Introduction

Measurement of PD activity can be used to diagnose substation insulation faults and predict the catastrophic failure of high voltage (HV) equipment. Free-space radiometric measurement has been proposed as a particularly convenient technique for PD source location and monitoring, at least in part, because it requires no physical connection to electrical components. The FSR technique uses remotely located antennas to receive the radio frequency (RF) signal radiated by transient PD pulses [1, 2]. Traditionally, it has been the temporal evolution of FSR-derived data that has been used to flag PD of immediate engineering concern since the absolute PD intensity (in pC) has been thought impractical to assess. Here, we report work in progress which targets to link FSR PD data to absolute PD intensity.

© ICST Institute for Computer Sciences, Social Informatics and Telecommunications Engineering 2017
I. Otung et al. (Eds.): WiSATS 2016, LNICST 186, pp. 108–115, 2017.
DOI: 10.1007/978-3-319-53850-1_12

2   Apparatus

The apparatus used to simultaneously capture galvanic contact, and FSR PD measurements is shown in Fig. 1. More information about PD measurements can be found in [3–6].

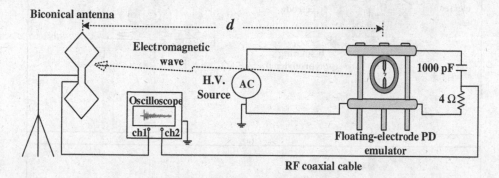

Fig. 1. Measurement apparatus.

PD is generated by applying an AC HV to the PD source. Three PD emulators have been constructed. An emulator of the floating-electrode type, an acrylic tube internal emulator (PD discharge in the air and in the oil) and an epoxy dielectric internal PD emulator, that are shown in Fig. 2. The voltage rating of the 1 nF coupling capacitor (shown in Fig. 1) used to make the galvanic PD measurements is 40 kV [5]. When the electric field is sufficiently large, PD occurs across the electrode gaps. More details about PD sources can be found in [7–10].

The radiometric measurements were made using a wideband biconical antenna connected to a 4 GHz, 20 GSa/s, digital sampling oscilloscope (DSO). The antenna was vertically polarised. The frequency range of the antenna is 20 MHz to 1 GHz and its nominal impedance is 50 ohms. The antenna gain at 100 MHz is around −9 dBi and its dimensions are 540 mm × 225 mm × 225 mm. A commercial PD calibration device has been used to assess the effective radiated power of the emulator as a function of PD apparent charge. The off-line HVPD pC calibrator is designed to provide a range of current pulses of specified charge from 1 pC up to 100 nC [11, 12].

3   Example Event

Example FSR and galvanic contact measurements for the same PD event are compared in Fig. 3(a). The PD source used for the comparison in this paper is a floating electrode PD emulator. The voltage at which this PD event occurred was 6.2 kV. The frequency spectra, obtained using an FFT, are compared in Fig. 3(b).

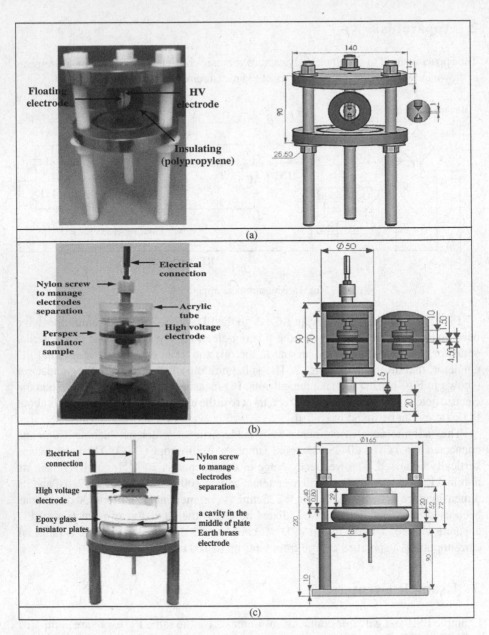

Fig. 2. (a) Floating electrode PD emulator (b) Acrylic tube internal PD emulator and (c) Epoxy dielectric internal PD emulator (dimensions in mm).

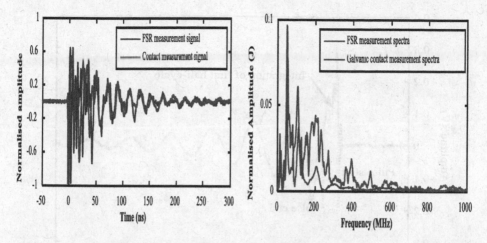

Fig. 3. (a) PD normalised time-series (b) PD spectra.

4   PD Sources Calibration

The oscillatory nature of the PD time-series makes assessing apparent charge non-trivial, even in a galvanic measurement. The example of experimental setup measuring circuit in Fig. 4 was used for calibrating PD sources. The artificial PD sources have therefore been calibrated by injecting a narrow calibration pulse of known charge. The calibration pulse emulates a PD event of a particular (known) intensity. A typical observed waveform is shown in Fig. 5. The measured charge has been estimated by integrating the first half-cycle of the PD source time-series current.

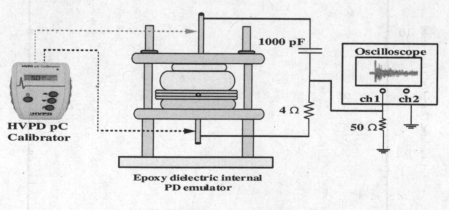

Fig. 4. PD source calibration.

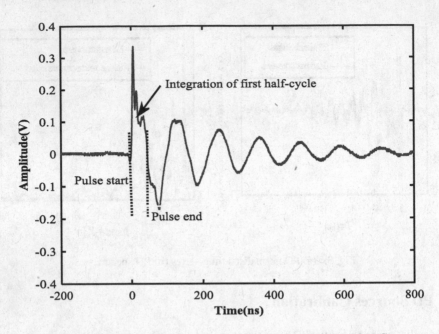

Fig. 5. Example of current waveform for an injected charge of 1 nC.

Figure 6 shows the charge calculated from the galvanic contact measurement against the specification of the charge injection device.

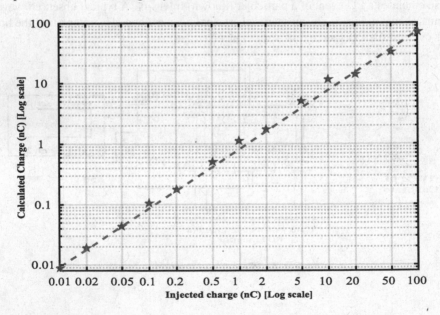

Fig. 6. Measured charge versus specified charge of charge injection device.

Regarding the Free-Space radiometric measurements, different distances were used in measurement system shown in Fig. 1 between the three PD emulators and the biconical antenna. Figure 7 shows an example of the variation with distance of received peak voltage, received field-strength and apparent effective radiated power. The radiated signal amplitude is decreasing by increasing the distance between the PD source and the biconical antenna, due to radiation losses [5]. In free-space, and in the far-field, apparent ERP would be independent of source-antenna range. The variation observed may be due to near-field and/or multipath effects. This is under investigation. The relationship between calculated charge and average ERP for different PD emulator source types is presented in Table 1. The ERP of the PD source emulator is estimated from the received electric field strength according to the formula for free space propagation formula (1) as follows [5]:

$$E(dB\mu V/m) = 107 + \text{ERP (dBm)} - 20 \, \log_{10} d(m) \tag{1}$$

where: E is the electric field strength, ERP is the effective radiated power and d is the PD source distance from the receiving antenna.

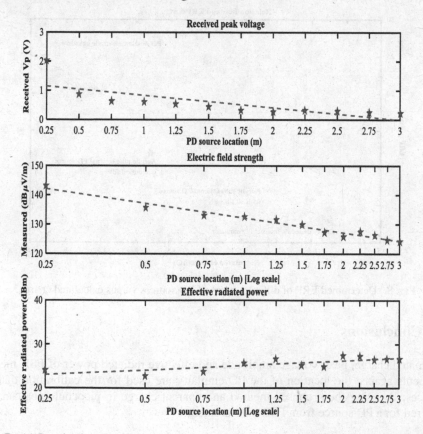

Fig. 7. (a) Received peak voltage, (b) Electric field strength and (c) ERP as a function of PD source–antenna range.

Table 1. Relationship between calculated charge and effective radiated power of PD sources.

	Floating-electrode PD source	Acrylic tube internal PD source without oil filling	Acrylic tube internal PD source with oil filling	Epoxy dielectric internal PD source
Calculated charge (nC)	5.3	3.8	2.1	0.9
Average peak ERP (dBm)	25	12	7	1.4

Figure 8 relates ERP (estimated from radiometric measurements) and absolute PD intensity (estimated from galvanic measurement of the PD current transient). The convincing nature of this relationship suggests a useful estimate of absolute PD intensity from a remote measurement of PD radiation is possible.

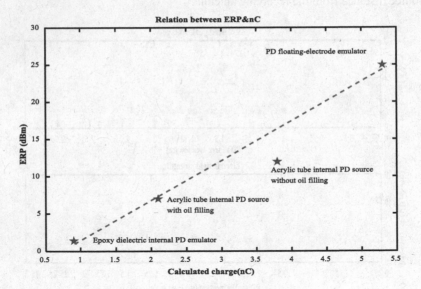

Fig. 8. Determined ERP of different types of PD sources versus calculated charge.

5   Conclusions

Estimated charge, peak voltage amplitude and effective radiated power of FSR measurements against the location of the PD emulator are used for the calibration of PD sources. By using the proposed method an apparent charge in picocoulombs can be inferred for a PD source from FSR measurements.

Acknowledgments. The authors acknowledge the Engineering and Physical Sciences Research Council for their support of this work under grant EP/J015873/1.

References

1. Zhang, Y., Upton, D., Jaber, A., Ahmed, H., Saeed, B., Mather, P., Lazaridis, P., Mopty, A., Tachtatzis, C., Atkinson, R., Judd, M., Vieira, M.F.Q., Glover, I.A.: Radiometric wireless sensor network monitoring of partial discharge sources in electrical substations. Hindawi Int. J. Distrib. Sens. Networks **2015**, 179 (2015)
2. Neto, J.M., Upton, D., Jaber, A., Ahmed, H., Saeed, B., Mather, Tachtatzis, C., Atkinson, R., Judd, M., Vieira, M.F.Q., Glover, I.A.: Radiometric location of partial discharge sources for the future smart grid. In: General Assembly and Scientific Symposium (URSI GASS), XXXIth URSI, Beijing, pp. 1–4 (2014)
3. Jaber, A., Lazaridis, P., Saeed, B., Zhang, Y., Khan, U., Upton, D., Ahmed, H., Mather, P., Vieira, M.F.Q., Atkinson, R., Judd, M., Seviour, R., Glover, I.A.: Frequency spectrum analysis of radiated partial discharge signals. In: IET EUROEM 2016 Conference (European Electromagnetics Symposium), London, pp. 1–2 (2016)
4. Reid, A.J., Judd, M.D., Fouracre, R.A., Stewart, B.G., Hepburn, D.M.: Simultaneous measurement of partial discharges using IEC60270 and radio-frequency techniques. IEEE Trans. Dielectr. Electr. Insul. **18**, 444–455 (2011)
5. Jaber, A., Lazaridis, P., Saeed, B., Zhang, Y., Khan, U., Upton, D., Ahmed, H., Mather, P., Vieira, M.F.Q., Atkinson, R., Judd, M., Glover, I.A.: Comparative study of partial discharge emulators for the calibration of free-space radiometric measurements. In: 22nd IEEE International Conference on Automation and Computing (ICAC 2016), Colchester, pp. 1–4 (2016)
6. Jaber, A., Lazaridis, P., Saeed, B., Zhang, Y., Khan, U., Upton, D., Ahmed, H., Mather, P., Vieira, M.F.Q., Atkinson, R., Judd, M., Glover, I.A.: Comparison of contact measurement and free-space radiation measurement of partial discharge signals. In: 2015 21st International Conference on Automation and Computing (ICAC), pp. 1–4. IEEE Press, Glasgow (2015)
7. Jaber, A., Lazaridis, P., Saeed, B., Zhang, Y., Khan, U., Upton, D., Ahmed, H., Mather, P., Vieira, M.F.Q., Atkinson, R., Judd, M., Glover, I.A.: Validation of partial discharge emulators simulation using free-space radiometric measurements. In: International Conference for Students on Applied Engineering (ICSAE 2016), Newcastle, pp. 1–4 (2016)
8. Hampton, B.F.: UHF diagnostics for gas insulated substations. In: Eleventh International Symposium on High Voltage Engineering (Conf. Publ. No. 467), London, pp. 6–16 (1999)
9. de Souza Neto, J.M.R., de Macedo, E.C.T., da Rocha Neto, J.S., Da Costa, E.G., Bhatti, S.A., Glover, I.A.: Partial discharge location using unsynchronized radiometer network for condition monitoring in HV substations-a proposed approach. J. Phys. Conf. Ser. **364**, 012053 (2012)
10. Niasar, M.G., Taylor, N., Janus, P., Wang, X., Edin, H., Kiiza, R.C.: Partial discharges in a cavity embedded in oil-impregnated paper: effect of electrical and thermal aging. IEEE Trans. Dielectr. Electr. Insul. **22**, 1071–1079 (2015)
11. HVPD. http://www.hvpd.co.uk
12. Jaber, A., Lazaridis, P., Zhang, Y., Saeed, B., Khan, U., Upton, D., Ahmed, H., Mather, P., Vieira, M.F.Q., Atkinson, R., Judd, M., Glover, I.A.: Assessment of absolute partial discharge intensity from a free-space radiometric measurement. In: URSI Asia-Pacific Radio Science Conference (URSI AP-RASC), Seoul, Korea, pp. 1011–1014 (2016)

Wireless, Computing and Satellite Systems Security (WCSSS) Special Session

Experimental Privacy Analysis and Characterization for Disconnected VANETs

Chibueze P. Anyigor Ogah$^{(\boxtimes)}$, Haitham Cruickshank, Philip M. Asuquo,
Ao Lei, and Zhili Sun

5G Innovation Centre (5GIC), Institute for Communication Systems,
University of Surrey, PATS Driveway, Guildford, Surrey GU2 7XS, UK
{c.anyigorogah,h.cruickshank,p.asuquo,a.lei,z.sun}@surrey.ac.uk

Abstract. Intelligent Transport Systems (ITS) are special applications of Vehicular Ad-hoc Networks (VANETs) for road safety and efficient traffic management. A major challenge for ITS and VANETs in all its flavours is ensuring the privacy of vehicle drivers and the transmitted location information. One attribute of ITS during its early roll-out stage especially in rural areas and challenged environments is low vehicle density and lack of end-to-end connectivity akin to the attribute of Vehicular Delay Tolerant Networks (VDTNs). This means that contact duration between network entities such as vehicles and road-side units (RSUs) are short-lived. Three popular solutions are the use of pseudonyms, mix-zones, and group communication. Privacy schemes based on the mix-zone technique abound for more conventional VANETs. A critical privacy analysis of such scenarios will be key to the design of privacy techniques for intermittent networks. We are not aware of any work that analyse the privacy problem in intermittent VANTEs. In this paper, we add our voice to efforts to characterize the privacy problem in disconnected VANETs.

Keywords: Anonymity · Evaluation · ITS · Privacy · VANETs · Vehicular delay tolerant networks · VDTN

1 Introduction

With the application of VANETs for Intelligent Transport Systems (ITS), enhancing road safety and traffic management becomes more effective and cost efficient. Already, there are a handful of driver-less car projects all over the world, with examples such as the Google Car project [1]. Self-driving cars have been tested in Europe when a fleet of trucks made a voyage journey across the continent from Rotterdam with no incidents [2]. Google Cars are also driving across California in pilot test-drives on a regular basis with only one incident of error on the part of the vehicles reported so far. The IEEE defines ITS as those systems utilizing synergistic technologies and systems engineering concepts to develop and improve transportation systems of all kinds. These include applications that depend on vehicle-to-vehicle (V-to-V) and vehicle-to-infrastructure

© ICST Institute for Computer Sciences, Social Informatics and Telecommunications Engineering 2017
I. Otung et al. (Eds.): WiSATS 2016, LNICST 186, pp. 119–129, 2017.
DOI: 10.1007/978-3-319-53850-1_13

(V-to-R) communication for road safety and improved traffic management [3]. A variety of ITS exist and have been well researched on. Traditional disconnected VANETs such as Delay Tolerant Networks (DTNs) do not make use of infrastructure support such as Road-Side Units (RSUs). However, recent efforts towards improving reliability and security have inspired the introduction of infrastructure [4], thereby creating such as flavors as Vehicular Delay Tolerant Networks [5].

Despite its advantages, there is yet no consensus on how to exactly address the key issues of security and privacy [6]. Privacy issues results from the fact that a malicious user can intercept the location information contained in safety messages to track a driver's location. In reality, tracking a vehicle is as good as tracking its driver or owner. Again, when these technologies are fully developed, there will be the problem of inadequate infrastructure to support thousands of vehicle in both urban and rural areas especially at the early stages of deployment. Hence, it will not be possible to conduct a thorough roll-out especially in rural areas due in part to lack of adequate infrastructure. Therefore, performance evaluation from a pilot-phase study will be compulsory to understand its viability for large-scale deployment. While a big chunk of the pilot study may concern bandwidth support for thousands of vehicle, there is also the need to understand and address security and privacy related issues. The above issues forms the crux of privacy problems in VANETs. Our focus on this paper is to add our voice towards characterizing and evaluating privacy in a disconnected VANET. This is a progressive effort towards proffering adequate solutions.

A variety of schemes have been proposed in literature to address privacy in VANETs. In the United States and Europe for instance, the Dedicated Short Range Communications/Wireless Access in Vehicular Environments (DSRC/WAVE) specifies the formats of Basic Safety Messages for ITS. Within the IEEE 802.9 family of standards, the IEEE 1609.2 makes provisions for location privacy but does not specify its modalities. Three popular Privacy-Enhancing Techniques (PETs) in VANETs include pseudonymous communication, mix-zones, and group communication [7–9]. A number of other schemes exist, most of which are indeed variants of those mentioned here; these include Silent Periods [10], Virtual Mix-Zones [11], and pseudonym management techniques such as [12]. In this work, we criticize group communication on the basis that it is difficult to easily to find group collaborators especially in light traffic situations such as in rural areas. Again, pseudonym-based privacy schemes especially in disconnected VANETs have a direct relationship with vehicle density, traffic load and generation, and mobility pattern [11,12]. The peculiar operating environment of VANETs for ITS especially in its pilot and early deployment phases can best be described as disconnected, hence even traditional PETs such as those mentioned above will fail [13]. For the same reasons, conventional mix-zones techniques are not efficient because they are limited by the number of vehicles that can potentially collaborate for pseudonym change around pseudonym changing spots [12]. While pseudonym and mix-zone techniques remains one of the most popular and documented PETs, more effort is needed in ensuring their effectiveness in disconnected environments. In order not to re-invent the wheel, we leverage these established techniques and rather focus on discussing their application in disconnected networks.

To this end, we set out to characterize and analyse the privacy behavior in a disconnected VANETs. Our research here extends our initial idea in [13] for group-based communication in VDTNs. We characterize the mobility dynamics in our network and relation to privacy. Our analysis is based on a formal model and compared with existing literature. The rest of this paper is organized as follows. We describe our scheme and it's attributes in Sect. 2. In Sect. 3, we provide a summary of the problem we set out to solve and outline key definition of terms. Our detailed simulation and system analysis is provided in Sect. 4, and finally, we conclude and present our future work in Sect. 5.

2   Model Description

In this section, we present a detailed description of our model, assumptions and the attributes of the adversary.

2.1   Network Model

We consider disconnected VANET deployment in a rural area as described in [5,14] comprised of mobile vehicles, stationery RSUs, and a central administrative authority known as the Trusted Key Manager (TKM). Our network can be modelled as a directed multi-graph, $\mathcal{G} = (\mathcal{V},\mathcal{E})$ where $\mathcal{V}$ and $\mathcal{E}$ denote some fleet of vehicles and contact edges respectively. The RSUs act as stationary relay nodes that facilitate packet routing in addition to assisting with the security and privacy administration of the TKM. We only deploy RSUs at strategic locations which we regard as density zones as in [15].

2.2   Adversary Model

We consider a global passive adversary in our model. The adversary can isolate sections of the network and monitor communication and beacon messages exchanged between vehicles within each density zone to resolve vehicle and driver identity. We assume that the RSUs are trustworthy and tamper-proof while the vehicles are not. Hence, the vehicles can deviate in behaviour and act as adversaries (e.g. by reporting wrong location information). Examples of specific location privacy related attacks the adversary can execute include tracking and packet analysis attacks. To be able to execute packet analysis attacks, the adversary can delay the message delivery for a considerable amount of time while analysing it to divulge information regarding source and destination vehicles.

3   Problem Description and Definition of Terms

Our main objective is to characterize and analyse the privacy problem in our model in relation to the disconnectedness and mobility pattern of the network. We define some terms and describe the privacy problems in the following section.

3.1   Privacy Analysis

Our analysis is based on Shanon's information theory. We take into account the fact that location privacy depends on vehicle density [16]. The relationship between vehicle density and location privacy is easily understood from the point of view of changing pseudonyms - higher vehicle density means its a higher probability for a vehicle to find potential pseudonym collaborators. Since our network is disconnected, the density and mobility pattern of vehicles in the network and around the density zones will be key to how much privacy is achieved. The following usual definitions relate to the privacy analysis of our model.

3.1.1   Anonymity, Entropy, Anonymity Set, and Anonymity Duration

Anonymity. The anonymity of a vehicle, $V_i \in \mathcal{V}$ can be defined as a state of being unidentifiable among *k-1* other vehicles. Anonymity is usually related to the *unlinkability* property. Unlinkability is a term used to describe the notion that the adversary cannot link the vehicles identity, V_i to two actions say, $Actions_1$ and $Actions_2$ executed at different times t_1 and t_2 in relation the locations l_1 and l_2 where the actions took place with ease. A typical example of an action can be a vehicle changing pseudonyms or sending a message. This means that a vehicle cannot be linked to its identity for a duration of time due to its activity on the network. The IEEE 1609.2 measures location privacy using anonymity [17,18].

Anonymity Set. The anonymity set, AS is the average number of vehicles that are indistinguishable from *k-1* other vehicles from the privacy attacker PA's point of view. Naturally, it follows that the larger the AS, the better the privacy. This also means that in a given vehicle traffic situation, heavy vehicle traffic situation tend to ensure more privacy due to the number of vehicles participating in communication and pseudonym change [16,19]. The entire AS in our case would comprise the set of all $\mathcal{V}$. However, it is not possible to have the entire vehicle population as the AS since our network is disconnected as we shall explain later.

Tracking Probability. The tracking probability, T_p of the PA over a vehicle, V_i, is the probability that the anonymity of a vehicle in a density zone is equal to 1. The tracking probability, T_p can be derived as follows, suppose we have $D_Z = \{Z_1, Z_2, Z_3, \ldots Z_n\}$ density zones, where a vehicle V_i is located in a zone Z_i during a short duration of time, $t = I_A$ where I_A is the anonymity duration (described later), then the probability of tracking by the adversary within zone D_i can be expressed as

$$T_p = Pr(|AS| = 1) \tag{1}$$

In practical terms, from the PA's point of view, this means that a vehicle has no anonymity when the system has $|AS| = 1$. Similarly, the composite anonymity of the vehicles within a zone can be calculated by the number of vehicles that meets the $|AS| = 1$ criteria. A density zone where 30% of the vehicles have an $|AS| = 1$ (i.e. $T_p = 0.30$) can be said to guarantee an anonymity of 70% (i.e. $1 - T_p = 0.70$ cannot be tracked).

Entropy. Although entropy generally means the degree of disorderliness of a system as defined in set theory. In the context of location privacy, it is a measure of anonymity according to Shanon's theory of information. Shanon's theory have been widely used in the evaluation of location privacy for vehicular networks. The uncertainty in the connection rate, the random mobility and unpredictability of our system allows us to model entropy based on Shanon's equation as [20] as follows. Let V be a discrete random variable, which is the number of vehicles, with a probability mass function $P(V = V_i)$ where $i = \{1, 2, \ldots, n\}$, then the entropy H_V of the AS can be expressed as below where p_i is the probability of each vehicle being the target of the adversary, where N represents the total number of observed vehicles by the adversary.

$$H_V = -\sum_{i=1}^{N} p_i \log_2 p_i. \tag{2}$$

Usually, the value of entropy can be normalized to have values with the domain of $[0, 1]$. This makes it possible to compare the entropy value with the maximum entropy of the system which is the uppermost limit of of H_V as follows

$$H_{max} = -\sum_{i=1}^{N} p_i \log_2 p_i = \log_2 |N| \quad \text{if } \forall i : p_i = \frac{1}{|N|} \tag{3}$$

The degree of anonymity is then

$$d_A = \frac{H_V}{H_{max}} \tag{4}$$

Anonymity Duration. In characterizing the anonymity of our system, we derive the anonymity duration, I_A as the time taken by a vehicle V_i to negotiate and change pseudonyms within a zone, Z_i. Note that our system is disconnected, hence we can only effectively evaluate the activity around each mix-zone in isolation. For this reason, we assume that the PA is running some tracking algorithm with which it tries identify target vehicles by matching their identities with different probability values.

There is an RSU located at every point-of-interest (PoI) location in our simulation area which are indeed the density zones described earlier. The connection rate is assumed to follow a Poisson process as in [12,15]. Let $T = I_A$ be the average time interval within which the RSU records vehicles connection activities to it. Again, let V be a random variable which is the number of vehicles that come in contact with RSU_i at density zone Z_i during I_A (i.e. during T),

V being the AS. Finally, let the inter-arrival time between connections have an exponential distribution with a mean value of $1/\lambda$. The anonymity interval is the time duration within which vehicles try to change pseudonym. It is also during this time that the PA monitors vehicles for tracking and possible identification. For a disconnected network, this time is not continuous but can be measured in snapshots of minutes or a few hours. Indeed, we regard (T as the anonymity interval I_A defined earlier), then the probability that ($V = V_i$) at ($T = I_A$) can be expressed as the Poisson process in (5).

$$P(V = v_i | T = T_A) = \frac{(\lambda t)^{v_i}}{v_i!} e^{-\lambda t} \tag{5}$$

The adversary's intention is to identify a target after pseudonym change in the mix-zone within the anonymity duration, I_A. However, not all vehicles within a density zone can successfully change pseudonyms. This can be attributed to such vehicles not being qualified enough to be considered pseudonym change candidates by other vehicles due to poor reputation records. Hence, we can define the expected anonymity set of vehicles, V_E as

$$P_{E_x}(V_E = V_i | T = I_A) = \sum_{i=1}^{\infty} v_i \frac{(\lambda I_A)^{v_i}}{v_i!} e^{-\lambda I_A} = \lambda I_A \tag{6}$$

V_E is essentially, the average number of vehicles expected to connect and disconnect with the RSU during I_A can be expressed as

$$E_X(V | T = I_A) = \sum_{i=1}^{\infty} v_i \frac{(\lambda I_A)^{v_i}}{v_i!} e^{-\lambda I_A} = \lambda I_A \tag{7}$$

4   Simulation and Anonymity Analysis

In this section, we describe our experiments and conduct performance evaluation of our scheme to understand its effectiveness. Our analytical model is supported by simulation results.

4.1   Simulation Setup

We implement our scheme using a popular and widely used network simulator for delay tolerant networks namely the *Opportunistic Networking Environment* (ONE) simulator [21]. The ONE simulator has been used to investigate several application scenarios for VANETs [5,22]. We evaluate the performance of our system under a specific use case of an intermittent/disconnected VANET. Our simulation runs involves 400 vehicles and 7 stationary relay nodes as RSUs. Table 1 presents a detailed summary of our key simulation parameters. The vehicles move on the map of the City of Helsinki which is the default map in the ONE simulator measuring 4500×3400 m^2. The RSUs are placed at chosen intersections which are the epicentres of density zones as shown in Fig. 1.

Fig. 1. Snapshot of the Helsinki city map

In accordance with Finnish traffic regulations, the average lower and upper speed bounds for vehicles is 30 to 60 kmh^{-1}. We set all vehicles in our experiments to drive at the uniform upper bound limit of 60 kmh^{-1} to ensure a uniform arrival rate at the density zones. Since vehicles usually follow defined routes in the form of roads, our model assumes each vehicle follows the *shortest path map-based movement* mobility model where vehicles are first situated randomly on different spots on road and then allowed to travel along predefined routes to their destinations. Different from our benchmark model, we deployed 400 vehicles and ran an extended simulation of 1 and 2 h respectively for values of the I_A. This is due to nature of our disconnected network environment that requires adequate number of vehicles to generate the desired statistics for analysis. We conduct our experiment only on top of the inbuilt PRoPHET routing protocol in the ONE simulator [23].

Table 1. Simulation settings

Simulation parameter	Settings/Description
Sim duration	1 & 2 h
Number of vehicles and RSUs	400 vehicles; 7 RSUs
Vehicle speed	30 kmh^{-1} – 60 kmh^{-1}
Transmission coverage	100 m
Mobility model	Shortest path map based movement
Packet size	500 k – 1 M
Message generation interval	25 s – 35 s

4.2 Analysis and Evaluation

The results from our experiments (marked Sim) are compared with our analytical model (marked Theory) as shown in Fig. 2 for different values of vehicle arrival rate, λ. We assumed a vehicle arrival of 5 vehicles per second up to 25 vehicles (i.e. $1/\lambda = \{5, 10, 15, 20,$ and $25\}$ with an increment of 5 and $I_A = 3600$ (1 h) and 7200 (2 h) seconds. In both Figs. 2a and b, we observe that the AS gradually depreciates as the vehicle arrival rate increases for both I_A values. This is because less frequent arrival rates means that fewer vehicles arrive at a density zone. The behavior of the graph also corroborates with the known fact that in reality, vehicles can avoid density certain zones that are notorious for low vehicular density since they have less chances of meeting pseudonym candidates in such zones compared to those known for more vehicular density. Again, we see that the values of the AS for $I_A = 7200$ is higher than that for $I_A = 3600$ which is in agreement the fact that the higher the vehicle density in a network, the higher the achievable privacy, and by extension the more chances of vehicles finding pseudonym change partners in a network. According to the work in [12], vehicles wishing to enjoy high privacy should take advantage of density zones that are notorious for high vehicle arrival rate and density to negotiate and change pseudonyms.

From existing literature, it is established that the distribution of the AS has a direct ratio to the I_A. Hence The decrease in the AS reflects the nature of our network where vehicles have temporary and intermittent connections. When compared to our baseline model [12,15] where the authors analysed pseudonym change at a small social spot, our analysis agrees with their model. A small social are temporary meeting points such as traffic intersections as against large social spots such as parking lots and shopping where vehicles meet for a longer duration of time running into hours. Note that the anonymity is based on the premise that connections can be sustained for the duration of I_A, hence the 40 s duration yields better values for the AS. This supports the notion that larger vehicle density due to a more frequent arrival rate favours a better anonymity where

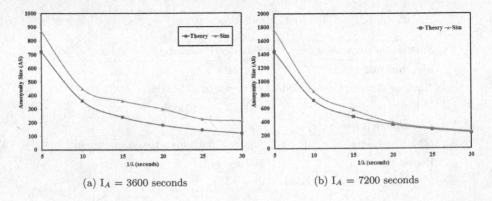

(a) $I_A = 3600$ seconds   (b) $I_A = 7200$ seconds

Fig. 2. Anonymity analysis for different anonymity intervals I_A

vehicles encounter more potential candidates with which to change pseudonyms at a density zone. Less frequent arrival rates means that fewer vehicles choose to use a density as pseudonym change points.

The use of live traffic information from navigation platforms such as Google Map for travel route planning is quite popular these days through which vehicle drivers can avoid certain routes based on the estimated traffic delay. Again, this suggests that higher arrival rate and more waiting time yields less anonymity. As we can see from both figures of the anonymity curve, the simulation results agree with previous work where longer (infrequent) arrival rates reduces the number of vehicles that aggregate at a zone. This leads to a situation where vehicles are discouraged from using a density that is prone to low vehicle density.

5   Conclusion and Future Work

In this paper, we added our voice to efforts to characterize and analyse privacy for a disconnected VANET using the use-case of a ventricular delay tolerant network. Our analysis follows established schemes for anonymity analysis in VANETs with varying vehicular density. We validate our analytical model with experimental results. Different from other schemes, to the best of our knowledge, this is the first attempt to analyse the privacy in a disconnected VANET. We note that our work is in progress, albeit has provided a new scope for further research in this area. In the light of this, in our future work, we are interested in developing a scheme to validate and analyse the anonymity of vehicles users using empirical data to compare with our experimental results. We also intend to develop a privacy solution more suited for disconnected network environments. Our experiments can also be performed on more robust and heterogeneous mobility scenarios such as those combining vehicles and pedestrians.

Acknowledgement. The funding for this work is from the Overseas Scholarship Scheme (OSS) of the Petroleum Technology Development Fund (PTDF) of the Federal Government of Nigeria with support from the PETRAS Project (in conjunction with IoTUK) and the Institute for Communication Systems, home of The 5G Innovation Center (5GIC), University of Surrey, Guildford, United Kingdom.

References

1. Greenblatt, N.A.: Self-driving cars and the law. IEEE Spectr. **53**(2), 46–51 (2016)
2. Ryan, P.: The driverless truck is coming, and its going to automate millions of jobs (2016). https://techcrunch.com/2016/04/25/the-driverless-truck-is-coming-and-its-going-to-automate-millions-of-jobs/
3. Raya, M., Papadimitratos, P., Hubaux, J.-P.: Securing vehicular communications. IEEE Wirel. Commun. Mag. **13**, 8–15 (2006). Special Issue on Inter-Vehicular Communications
4. Banerjee, N., Corner, M.D., Towsley, D., Levine, B.N.: Relays, base stations, and meshes: enhancing mobile networks with infrastructure. In: Proceedings of the 14th ACM International Conference on Mobile Computing and Networking, San Francisco, California, USA, pp. 81–91. ACM, New York (2008)

5. Pereira, P.R., Casaca, A., Rodrigues, J.J.P.C., Soares, V.N.G.J., Triay, J., Cervello-Pastor, C.: From delay-tolerant networks to vehicular delay-tolerant networks. IEEE Commun. Surv. Tutorials 14(4), 1166–1182 (2012). IEEE Press, New York
6. Mohamed, N.M., Jalel, B.-O., Mohamed, H.: Survey on VANET security challenges and possible cryptographic solutions. Veh. Commun. 1(2), 53–66 (2014)
7. Freudiger, J., Raya, M., Félegyházi, M., Papadimitratos, P.: Mix-Zones for location privacy in vehicular networks. In: Proceedings of the First International Workshop on Wireless Networking for Intelligent Transportation Systems (Win-ITS) (2007)
8. Verma, M., Dijiang, H.: SeGCom: secure group communication in VANETs. In: 6th IEEE Consumer Communications and Networking Conference (CCNC), pp. 1–5 (2009)
9. Beresford, A.R., Stajano, F.: Location privacy in pervasive computing. IEEE Pervasive Comput. 2(1), 46–55 (2003). IEEE Educational Activities Department, Piscataway, NJ, USA, ISSN: 1536-1268
10. Leping, H., Matsuura, K., Yamane, H., Sezaki, K.: Enhancing wireless location privacy using silent period. In: IEEE Wireless Communications and Networking Conference (WCNC), vol. 2, pp. 1187–1192 (2005). ISSN: 1525-3511
11. Suguo, D., Haojin, Z., Xiaolong, L., Ota, K., Mianxiong, D.: MixZone in motion: achieving dynamically cooperative location privacy protection in delay-tolerant networks. IEEE Trans. Veh. Technol. 62(9), 4565–4575 (2013). ISSN
12. Rongxing, L., Xiaodong, L., Luan, T.H., Xiaohui, L., Xuemin, S.: Pseudonym changing at social spots an effective strategy for location privacy in VANETs. IEEE Trans. Veh. Technol. 61(1), 86–96 (2012). ISSN: 0018-9545
13. Chibueze, P.A.O., Haitham, C., Zhili, G., Ganesh, C., Yue, C., Philip, M.A., Masoud, A.T.: Privacy-enhanced group communication for vehicular delay tolerant networks. In: 9th International Conference on Next Generation Mobile Applications, Services and Technologies (NGMAST), pp. 193–198 (2015)
14. Soares, V.N.G.J., Farahmand, F., Rodrigues, J.J.P.C.: A layered architecture for vehicular delay-tolerant networks. In: IEEE Symposium on Computers and Communications (ISCC), pp. 122–127 (2009)
15. Rongxing, L., Xiaodong, L., Luan, T.H., Xiaohui, L., Xuemin, S.: Anonymity analysis on social spot based pseudonym changing for location privacy in VANETs. In: IEEE International Conference on Communications (ICC), pp. 1–5 (2011). ISSN: 1550-3607
16. Tomandl, A., Scheuer, F., Federrath, H.: Simulation-based evaluation of techniques for privacy protection in VANETs. In: IEEE 8th International Conference on Wireless and Mobile Computing, Networking and Communications (WiMob), pp. 165–172 (2012). ISSN: 2160-4886
17. George, P.C., Huirong, F., Abdelnasser, B.: Evaluating location privacy in vehicular communications and applications. IEEE Trans. Intel. Transp. Syst. 9(17) (2016). ISSN: 2658-2667
18. IEEE Standard for Wireless Access in Vehicular Environments Security Services for Applications, Management Messages. In: IEEE Std 1609.2-2013 (Revision of IEEE Std 1609.2-2006), pp. 1–289 (2013)
19. Hassan, A., Noor, A.: A pseudonym management system to achieve anonymity in vehicular ad hoc networks. IEEE Trans. Dependable Secure Comput. 13, 106–119 (2016). ISSN: 1545-5971
20. Claude, E.S.: A mathematical theory of communication. Bell Syst. Tech. J. 27(3), 379–423 (1948). ISSN: 0005-8580

21. Ari, K., Jörg, O., Teemu, K.: The ONE simulator for DTN protocol evaluation. In: SIMUTools 2009: Proceedings of the 2nd International Conference on Simulation Tools and Techniques, New York, NY, USA. ICST, Rome (2009). ISBN: 978-963-9799-45-5
22. Rongxing, L., Xiaodong, L., Xuemin, S.: SPRING: A social-based privacy-preserving packet forwarding protocol for vehicular delay tolerant networks. In: Proceedings of the 29th Conference on Information Communications, pp. 1–9 (2010). ISSN: 0743-166X
23. Lindgren, A., Doria, A., Schelén, O.: Probabilistic routing in intermittently connected networks. SIGMOBILE Mob. Comput. Commun. Rev. **7**(3), 19–20 (2003). New York, USA, ISSN: 1559-1662

A Mobility-Aware Trust Management Scheme for Emergency Communication Networks Using DTN

Philip Asuquo[1,2(✉)], Haitham Cruickshank[1,2], Chibueze P. Anyigor Ogah[1,2], Ao Lei[1,2], and Kunle Olutomilayo[1,2]

[1] 5G Innovation Centre, Institute for Communication Systems, University of Surrey, Guildford, UK
p.asuquo@surrey.ac.uk
[2] Department of Electrical/Electronics and Computer Engineering, University of Uyo, Akwa Ibom, Nigeria

Abstract. In the aftermath of a disaster, collecting and disseminating critical information is very challenging. The damage to telecommunication infrastructures makes its extremely difficult to have an effective recovery and relief operation. In this paper, we consider the use of DTN as an alternative measure to temporarily disseminate emergency information in a post disaster scenario using the Post Disaster Model recommended by IETF. We consider internally motivated attacks where responder nodes are compromised thereby dropping packets forwarded to them. We design a Mobility-Aware Trust Management Scheme (MATMS) to mitigate this routing misbehaviour. We evaluate our proposed scheme through extensive simulations and compare our results with existing benchmarks schemes. Our results show that the use of adequate collaborative strategies can improve the performance of DTNs under attack taking into consideration the delivery probability and message delay from source node to the destination node.

Keywords: Disaster · Trust · Subjective logic · DTN

1 Introduction

Public safety organizations increasingly rely on wireless technology to provide effective communications during emergency operations such as earthquake relief, fire rescue or traffic accidents [1]. This natural or man-made disaster demands an efficient communication and coordination among first responders to save lives and other community resources which requires the generation and exchange of current information among first responders and emergency management centres in real time for making life saving decisions. Traditional communication infrastructures such as landlines or cellular networks are damaged and do not provide adequate services to support first responders for exchanging emergency

© ICST Institute for Computer Sciences, Social Informatics and Telecommunications Engineering 2017
I. Otung et al. (Eds.): WiSATS 2016, LNICST 186, pp. 130–141, 2017.
DOI: 10.1007/978-3-319-53850-1_14

related information during large scale disaster scenarios such as earthquakes [2]. Certain factors such as power outages and infrastructure collapse can affect emergency communications. Power outage has been pointed out as a commonplace consequence during and after disaster which often result in the inability to use communication systems. In RFC 7476 − 2.72 [3], the disaster rescue and relief operation is clearly described under baseline scenarios for Information-Centric Networks. Apart from emergency scenarios, DTN has a wide range of applications including Inter-Planetary Network (IPN), Pocket Switched Networks (PSN), Under Water Networks (UWN), Vehicular Ad-hoc Networks now known as Intelligent Transportation System (ITS) [4].

Previous works done using DTNs show that when there is a breakdown in communication infrastructure, DTN can provide an alternative solution for emergency communication. A disaster map generator DTN-MapEx which operates over a DTN with emergency responders and other emergency site actors carrying mobile devices has been shown to effectively enable information availability in disaster stricken areas [5]. Another strategy which uses distributed computing over DTN has been proposed. This strategy uses a task algorithm technique which is based on different connectivity scenarios where nodes collaborate for task allocation and task monitoring functions [6]. Similar to the approach by [6], a decision method using a DTN-based message relay has been proposed by [7] for disaster scenarios with unreliable wireless communication links. This technique is based on the relay sequence and has been shown to reduce redundant transmission and increase the delivery probability of emergency information propagated in DTN-based emergency communication network. The remainder of this work is organised as follows. In Sect. 2, we provide a background and related work on various mitigating schemes for routing misbehaviour in DTN. We present our proposed model in Sect. 3 and evaluate the performance of our proposed scheme compared to other existing schemes in Sect. 4. We conclude the paper and present our future work in Sect. 5.

2   Related Work

There has been a lot of trust management schemes proposed for peer-to-peer and ad hoc networks including [8–11]. A few authors [12–14], have proposed trust and reputation models to enhance security in DTNs to enable nodes to assess their neighbours directly and indirectly through recommendations from other nodes.

A Cooperative Watchdog Scheme (CWS) proposed by [12] for VDTNs assigns a reputation score to each node in the network. When a node comes in contact with another node based on the evaluation of three modules (classification, neighbour's evaluation and decision), the classification module categorises the nodes into different groups based on their reputation score and calculates the cooperative value of each node. The cooperative value is sent to decision module for punishment or reward while the neighbour's evaluation module determines how the reputation of a node is evaluated on the network.

A dynamic trust management for DTN is proposed by [13] to deal with blackhole attacks. This protocol uses a novel methodology based on Stochastic Petri Net (SPN) for the analysis and validation of trust protocol. The authors aim at designing and validating a dynamic trust management protocol to optimise the routing performance of DTN. In a comparative analysis with PROPHET, Epidemic and Bayesian trust-based routing, their simulation results show that the dynamic trust management protocol outperforms Bayesian trust based routing and PROPHET routing protocols without incurring a high message overhead. As pointed out in a comprehensive survey [15] that trust metrics must reflect unique properties of trust for building trust management systems, the proposed scheme uses a synthetic model which does not reflect mission context scenarios which are typical applications of DTNs.

A probabilistic misbehaviour detection scheme [14] is proposed to establish trust in DTNs which is inspired by the inspection game in [16]. In this scheme, a misbehaviour detection framework is used based on series of newly introduced data forwarding evidences called iTrust to establish trust management in DTN, simulation results from this research work shows that iTrust reduces the transmission cost that is incurred by the misbehaviour detection scheme and effectively detects the malicious nodes in single and multi-copy routing protocols in DTN. The proposed scheme is a reputation-based detection technique, however authors have not compared the proposed scheme with any existing detection scheme and the performance metrics does not reflect if the scheme has improved delivery probability in the network.

A novel approach in opportunistic data forwarding proposed by [17] uses encounter tickets which are generated when two nodes come in contact. However, malicious nodes can still boost its time of interaction through collecting redundant encounter tickets from a one-time tailgate attack. In such attacks, malicious nodes tailgate the destination once and move around the data source to intercept the data. Encounter tickets that are redundant with similar generation time can be removed by this approach, there is a risk of uncertainty in a non-controlled mobility pattern as an adversary can perform a non location-dependent attack where it frequently moves in and out of communication range to collect encounter records that are not redundant and wanders around the destination node to intercept data by multi-tailgating.

3 Proposed Trust Management Scheme

In this section, we describe the network deployment of an intermittently connected network with no end-to-end connectivity using a DTN scenario, we assume the DTN Gateway provides communication support via a geo-stationary satellite that connects to a ground station as shown in Fig. 1. We also describe the behaviour of normal nodes and misbehaving nodes.

3.1   System Model

In this paper, we adopt a system model proposed by [2] which is a community based mobilty model for Post Disaster Scenarios recommended by IETF
for ICN baseline scenarios for disaster recovery operations [18] and the Working Day Map-Based Movement model which captures reliably the properties
of movement in the real life scenarios [19]. We consider a DTN deployed in
mission context scenario as shown in Fig. 1. We assume that the DTN consist
of a group of nodes deployed in an open and hostile environment such as the
Great East Earthquake where over 375 base stations were destroyed, over 90
routes were disconnected from the relay transmission lines and the traditional
telecommunication services were unavailable [20,21]. In our scenario, we consider a community of interest where there is a DTN with several wireless devices
(i.e. nodes) moving in a community which are either held by people or fixed on
vehicles. To protect a network from a wide range of attacks, traditional security
mechanisms are not robust enough especially with networks that lack end-to-end
connectivity and a pre-defined network architecture. In DTNs, malicious nodes
aim to break routing capabilities in addition to dropping packets and exhibiting
selfish behaviours. A malicious node can be an internal attacker with the aim of
disrupting the operation of a mission such as disaster recovery operations and
in tactical warfare operations. In addition to packet dropping attacks (blackhole
and grayhole), other related attacks that can be performed by malicious nodes in
a DTN environment include location-dependent attacks, time-dependent attacks
as well as ballot- stuffing and bad-mouthing attacks.

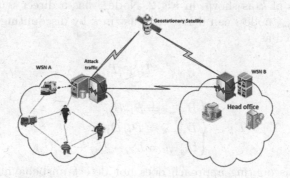

Fig. 1. An emergency communication network

3.2   Trust Computation

The trust computation is based on the history of encounters known as the
Encounter Record (ER). Suppose two nodes i and j come in contact with
each other, ER generated by node i about node j is denoted by $ER_{i \rightarrow j} =
(ER_1, ER_2, \ldots .ER_n)$ where ER_1 is a single interaction record with node j. We

describe how trust can be derived with the belief of subjective logic which uses opinion as a belief metric.

Subjective logic is suitable for the analysis of trust networks as trust relationships can be expressed as opinions with degrees of uncertainties to monitor the behaviour of responder nodes. To establish trust using subjective logic, we express binomial opinions as trust $T = (B, D, U)$ where B,D and U represent belief, disbelief and uncertainty. With accumulated forwarding evidences from encounter records, malicious nodes may provide computed trust values that does not reflect the node's behaviour if each record is treated equally regardless of the time of encounter. We express the probability density over binary event as a Beta Probability Density Function (PDF) denoted by (α, β) which is expressed as:

$$\alpha = s + 2a \quad \text{and} \quad \beta = f + 2(1 - a) \tag{1}$$

where s and f represent positive and negative observations and a is the relative atomicity. We adopt [22] to bijectively map between the opinion parameters and the beta PDF given in (2)

$$\begin{cases} B = \frac{s}{s+f+2} \\ D = \frac{f}{s+f+2} \\ U = \frac{2}{s+f+2} \end{cases} \Longleftrightarrow \begin{cases} s = \frac{2B}{U} \\ f = \frac{2D}{U} \\ 1 = B + D + U \end{cases} \tag{2}$$

Transitivity is used to compute trust along a chain of trust edges, for example two nodes i and j where i's trust towards j is denoted by T_{ij} for evaluating the trust worthiness of k as shown in Fig. 2. Node j has a direct trust in k which is denoted by T_{jk}, node i can derive its trust in k by discounting j's trust in k which is expressed as

$$T_{ij \to k} = T_{ij} \oplus T_{jk} \tag{3}$$

where

$$T_{ij} \oplus T_{jk} = \begin{cases} B_{ij \to k} = B_{ij} B_{jk} \\ D_{ij \to k} = D_{ij} D_{jk} \\ U_{ij \to k} = D_{ij} + U_{ij} + B_{ij} U_{jk} \end{cases}$$

The belief discounting approach does not detect misbehaving nodes effectively, the effect of transitivity is a general increase in the number of uncertainty and not necessarily an increase in disbelief. We adopt the cumulative fusion which is equivalent to Bayesian updating in statistics which reflects conflicting opinions in an equal and fair strategy. Let T_{ik} and T_{jk} be node i and j's trust in k respectively. The fused trust between $T_{ik} = [B_{ik}, D_{ik} U_{ik}]$ and $T_{jk} = [B_{jk}, D_{jk}, U_{jk}]$ can be expressed as:

$$T_{ij \to k} = T_{ik} \oplus T_{jk} \tag{4}$$

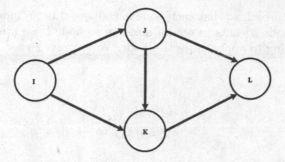

Fig. 2. An emergency communication network

where

$$B_{ij \to k} = \frac{(B_{ik}U_{jk} + B_{jk}U_{ik})}{(U_{ik} + U_{jk} - U_{ik}U_{jk})}$$

$$D_{ij \to k} = \frac{(D_{ik}U_{jk} + B_{jk}U_{ik})}{(U_{ik} + U_{jk} - U_{ik}U_{jk})}$$

$$U_{ik \to k} = \frac{(U_{ik}U_{jk}}{(U_{ik} + U_{jk} - U_{ik}U_{jk})} \tag{5}$$

Here we express the trust value as subjective opinions instead of using one integrated trust value to depict the overall trustworthiness of a node which includes the recommended trust as described in [17]. The generated trust opinions are stored locally in the buffer. Upon an encounter, a node generates its trust opinion about an encountered node based on the cumulative fission. The generated trust opinions are combined trust opinions at different time intervals, for instance for every encounter $ER_1, ER_2, ER_3....ER_n$ node i generates trust metric at $T_{ij}^{t_1}, T_{ij}^{t_2}, T_{ij}^{t_3}, T_{ij}^{t_n}$ about node j so that at $t_1, t_2, t_3...t_n$, the opinions are stored as;

$$T_{ij} = T_{ij}^{\triangle t} = T_{ij}^{t_1, t_2, t_3...t_n} \tag{6}$$

3.3 Trust in Mobility Aware Scenario

In a Post disaster response scenario, rescue workers are the main moving agents as well as the vehicles running between centres and camps for transportation of supplies or evacuation of victims from incident area to the temporary care centre or casualty collection point as described by [2,23,24]. We establish a trust transitive path with the mobility pattern undertaken by emergency responders and data mules such as centre to centre, centre to events, convergence move and the cyclic route as explained in [2] in form of trust arcs from the ERs generated. In RFC 4838 [25], a DTN network is described abstractly as a multi-graph where vertices may be connected to more than one edge. Although these edges are time varying with respect to their delay and buffer space, we introduce an edge splitting approach so that each node is connected to an independent edge. From Fig. 2, if node i wants to send a message to node l, we use edge splitting as opinion splitting to apply subjective logic. We express T_{il} as;

$$
\begin{aligned}
T_{il} = [i, l] &= ([i, j] : [j, l]) \\
&= ([i, k] : [k, l]) \\
&= ([i, j] : [j, k] : [k, l])
\end{aligned}
\tag{7}
$$

To produce independent paths by edge splitting in 7, we express T_{il} as;

$$
\begin{aligned}
T_{il} = [i, l] &= ([i, j_1] : [j_1, l]) \\
&= ([i, k_1] : [k_1, l]) \\
&= ([i, j_2] : [j_2, k_2] : [k_2, l])
\end{aligned}
\tag{8}
$$

We use edge splitting to produce independent paths so that each opinion can be expressed exclusively as shown in 8 which can be used further to derive the uncertainty for the independent paths as;

$$
\begin{aligned}
U_{ij_1} &\rightarrow l = B_{ij_1} U_{j_1 l} + D_{ij_1} + U_{ij_1} \\
U_{ik_1} &\rightarrow l = B_{ik_1} U_{k_1 l} + D_{ik_1} + U_{ik_1} \\
U_{ij_2 k_2} &\rightarrow l = B_{ij_2} D_{j_2 k_2} + D_{ij_2} + U_{ij_2} + B_{ij_2} U_{j_2 l} + B_{ij_2} B_{j_2 k_2} U_{k_2 l}
\end{aligned}
\tag{9}
$$

We refer readers to the early works of [22] on fission of opinion where an opinion can be bijectively mapped into probability density function and used as a function of the fission factor ϕ. This enables the trust transitivity to be computed as two simplified graphs as shown in 10:

$$
\begin{aligned}
T_{il} &= (T_{ij} \otimes T_{jl}) \oplus (T_{ik} \otimes T_{kl}) \\
&= T_{ij} \otimes T_{jk} \otimes T_{kl}
\end{aligned}
\tag{10}
$$

Given the ERs from historical opinion of node i about l, the base rate which is the relative atomicity a can be expressed as

$$
T_{il} = b_{il}^{\backslash} + a U_{il}^{\backslash}
\tag{11}
$$

where $T_{il}^{\backslash}$, $b_{il}^{\backslash}$ and $U_{il}^{\backslash}$ represent the independent path produced by opinion splitting.

4   Performance Evaluation

To demonstrate the performance of DTN in a disaster scenario, we implemented our scheme on the Post Disaster Mobility model proposed by Uddin et al. [2] using the ONE simulator which is specifically developed for evaluating DTN application protocols and routing [26]. In our experimental methodology, we consider 4 neighbourhoods, 2 main centres, 10 relief and evacuation camps, 20 supply vehicles, 200 rescue workers, 10 police patrol and 20 emergency vehicles. The communication messages have an average of 500 KB to 2 MB and are generated every 2 min. For our scheme, we use a message delivery time-out of 360 min with each node having a buffer size of 50 MB. Given the same simulation time and fixed message generation rate, the total messages created remains the same for all experiments. In our scenario, Malicious responders launch black hole attacks randomly by intercepting data from other nodes and dropping them.

4.1 Performance Metrics

1. Delivery Probability: This is the ratio of the total number of delivered messages to the total number of messages created.

$$D_P = \frac{M_D}{M_C} \tag{12}$$

where D_P is the delivery probability, M_D is the total number of messages delivered and M_C is the total number of created messages.

2. Latency: This is the average delivery delay which is measured as the average period of time that a message needs to travel from the source node to the destination node.

$$L = \frac{\sum_{i=1}^{M_D}(T_{M_n} - T_{C_i})}{M_D} \tag{13}$$

In the equation above, T_{M_n} is the time when the message reached its final destination node n, T_{C_i} is the time when the message was created by the source node i and M_D is the total number of messages delivered.

4.2 Result Analysis

Impact of Blackhole Attacks on Message Delivery: To evaluate the efficiency of our proposed trust-based scheme, we compare its performance with MaxProp, Spray-and-Wait and Prophet schemes with respect to the delivery probability and message delay from source node to the destination. We analyse the impacts of the blackhole attacks by evaluating the percentage of the delivered messages in the different mobility patterns including the Responder-Centre movement (R-C), Centre-Centre movement(C-C) which is mainly made up of movement of rescue vehicles and police patrol, Responder-Responder movement (R-R). The MATMS proposed reduces the negative impact of malicious nodes and performs better than other benchmark schemes as shown in Fig. 3(a), (b) and (c). It can also be seen that in our worst case scenario with 50% of malicious responders, MATMS outperforms the other schemes considered in the evaluation.

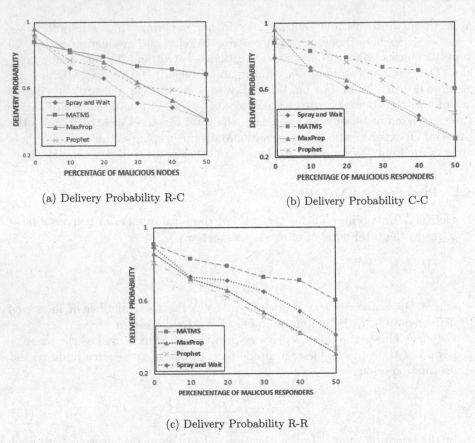

(a) Delivery Probability R-C

(b) Delivery Probability C-C

(c) Delivery Probability R-R

Fig. 3. Delivery Probability for movement models under blackhole attack in PDM

Impact of Blackhole Attacks on Message Delay: In Fig. 4(a), (b) and (c), we compare the delay in message delivery of our proposed scheme with existing benchmark schemes. In evaluating the message delivery delay, our results show that MATMS reduces delivery delay as result of the mobility pattern of the nodes which enables them to have more inter-contact times in the movement models. Since nodes consider the reputation value of encountered nodes to relay packets, only nodes with reputation values above the predefined threshold are considered cooperative nodes hence packets are forwarded to them. In our future work, we will carry out a performance comparison on subjective logic and beta distribution under best trust formation and evaluate their impact on power consumption of responder nodes.

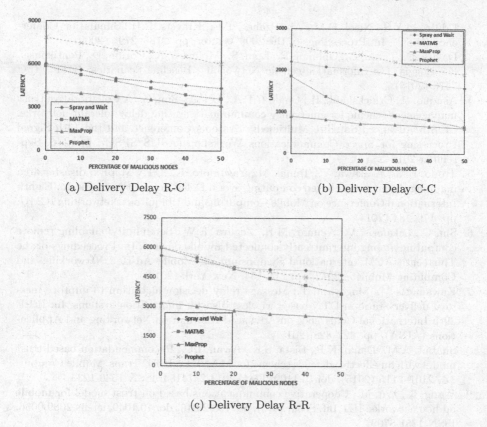

(a) Delivery Delay R-C

(b) Delivery Delay C-C

(c) Delivery Delay R-R

Fig. 4. Delivery Delay for movement models under blackhole attack in PDM

5   Conclusion

In this work, we have proposed the use of a mobility-aware trust management scheme for disaster scenarios. Simulation results show that our proposed scheme can mitigate routing misbehaviour such as packet dropping. We investigated the use of DTN in disaster relief operations using the PDM model recommended by IETF (RFC 7476) for baseline scenarios on disaster recovery and emergency support. We evaluated existing benchmark routing schemes together with our proposed scheme under blackhole attacks. Our results show that our proposed scheme can mitigate blackhole attacks when compared to the other schemes considered in this analysis.

References

1. Han, B., Li, J., Su, J., Cao, J.: Self-supported cooperative networking for emergency services in multi-hop wireless networks. IEEE J. Selected Areas Commun. **30**(2), 450–457 (2012)

2. Uddin, M.Y.S., Nicol, D.M., Abdelzaher, T.F., Kravets, R.H.: Simulation Conference (WSC). In: Proceedings of the 2009 Winter, pp. 2785–2796 (2009)

3. Davies, E., Tyson, G., Ohlman, B., Eum, S., Molinaro, A., Corujo, D., Pentikousis, K., Boggia, G.: Information-centric Networking Baseline Scenarios, IETF, RFC 7476 (2015)

4. Asuquo, P., Cruickshank, H., Ogah, C.P.A., Lei, A., Sun, Z.: A Collaborative trust management scheme for emergency communication using delay tolerant networks. In: 8th Advanced Satellite Multimedia Systems Conference and the 14th Signal Processing for Space Communications Workshop (ASMS/SPSC), pp. 1–6, September 2016

5. Trono, E.M., Arakawa, Y., Tamai, M., Yasumoto, K.: DTN MapEx: disaster area mapping through distributed computing over a Delay Tolerant Network, In: Eighth International Conference on Mobile Computing and Ubiquitous Networking ICMU, pp. 179–184 (2015)

6. Shi, C., Lakafosis, V., Ammar, M.H., Zegura, E.W.: Serendipity: enabling remote computing among intermittently connected mobile devices. In: Proceedings of the Thirteenth ACM International Symposium on Mobile Ad-Hoc Networking and Computing MobiHoc 2012, pp. 145–154, New York (2012)

7. Kawamoto, M., Shigeyasu, T.: Message relay decision algorithm to improve message delivery ratio in DTN-based wireless disaster information systems. In: IEEE 29th International Conference on Advanced Information Networking and Applications (AINA), pp. 822–828 (2015)

8. Shabut, A.M., Dahal, K.P., Bista, S.K., Awan, I.U.: Recommendation based trust model with an effective defence scheme for MANETs. IEEE Trans. Mobile Comput. **14**, 2101–2115 (2015). doi:10.1109/TMC.2014.2374154. ISSN 1536-1233

9. Wang, K., Wu, M.: Cooperative communications based on trust model for mobile ad hoc networks. IET Inf. Secur. **4**(2), 68–79 (2010). doi:10.1049/iet-ifs.2009.0056. ISSN 1751-8709

10. Chatterjee, P., Ghosh, U., Sengupta, I., Ghosh, I.S.K.: Approach for modelling trust in cluster-based wireless ad hoc networks. IET Networks **3**(3), 187–192 (2014). doi:10.1049/iet-net.2012.0212. ISSN 2047-4954

11. Can, A.B., Bhargava, B.: SORT: a self-organizing trust model for peer-to-peer systems. IEEE Trans. Dependable Secure Comput. **10**(1), 14–27 (2013). doi:10.1109/TDSC.2012.74. ISSN 1545-5971

12. Dias, J., Rodrigues, J., Mavromoustakis, C., Xia, F.: A cooperative watchdog system to detect misbehavior nodes in vehicular delay-tolerant networks. IEEE Trans. Ind. Electron. **PP**(99), 1 (2015)

13. Chen, I., Bao, F., Chang, M., Cho, J.: Dynamic trust management for delay tolerant networks and its application to secure routing. IEEE Trans. Parallel Distrib. Syst. **25**(5), 1200–1210 (2014)

14. Zhu, H., Du, S., Gao, Z., Dong, M., Cao, Z.: A probabilistic misbehavior detection scheme toward efficient trust establishment in delay-tolerant networks. IEEE Trans. Parallel Distrib. Syst. **25**(1), 22–32 (2014)

15. Cho, J.H., Swami, A., Chen, I.R.: A survey on trust management for mobile ad hoc networks. IEEE Commun. Surv. TUTORIALS **13**(4), 562–583 (2011). doi:10.1109/SURV.2011.092110.00088. ISSN 1553-877X

16. Fudenberg, D., Tirole, J.T.: Game Theory. MIT Press, Cambridge (1991)

17. Li, F., Wu, J., Srinivasan, A.: Thwarting blackhole attacks in disruption-tolerant networks using encounter tickets. IEEE INFOCOM 2009, 2428–2436 (2009)

18. Davies, E., Tyson, G., Ohlman, B., Eum, S., Molinaro, A., Corujo, D., Pentikousis, K., Boggia, G.: Information-centric Networking: Baseline Scenarios, ICNRG, Internet Draft, RFC 7476 (2015)

19. Ekman, F., Keränen, A., Karvo, J., Ott, J.: Working day movement model. In: Proceedings of the 1st ACM SIGMOBILE Workshop on Mobility Models, Mobility Models 2008, pp. 33–40. ACM, New York (2008). acmid. 1374695, doi:10.1145/1374688.1374695, ISBN 978-1-60558-111-8

20. Umeda, S.: Japan: Legal Responses to the Great East Japan Earthquake of 2011 (2013). http://www.loc.gov/law/help/japan-earthquake/

21. Yamashita, R., Takami, K.: Safety information gathering via information carriers through a DTN in a disaster-stricken area, In: International Conference on ICT Convergence (ICTC), pp. 429–434 (2013)

22. Jsang, A., Bhuiyan, T.: Optimal trust network analysis with subjective logic. In: Second International Conference on Emerging Security Information, Systems and Technologies, pp. 179–184 (2008). doi:10.1109/SECURWARE.64, ISSN 2162-2108

23. Aschenbruck, N., Gerhards-Padilla, E., Martini, P.: Modeling mobility in disaster area scenarios. J. Perform. Eval. **66**(12), 773–790 (2009)

24. ETSI TS. 103 260.: Satellite Earth Stations and Systems (SES); Satellite Emergency Communications (SatEC); Emergency Communication Cell over Satellite (ECCS), ETSI, Technical Specification ETSI TR 103 166, F-06921 Sophia Antipolis Cedex - FRANCE (2015)

25. Cerf, V., Burleigh, S., Hooke, A., Torgerson, l., Durst R., Scott K., Fall K., Weiss, H.: Delay Tolerant Networking Architecture, Internet Engineering Task Force, Internet Draft, RFC 4838 (2007)

26. Kernen, A., Ott, J., Krkkinen, T.: The ONE simulator for DTN protocol evaluation. In: Proceedings of the 2nd International Conference on Simulation Tools and Techniques, ICST, Brussels, Belgium, pp. 55:1–55:10. ICST (Institute for Computer Sciences, Social-Informatics and Telecommunications Engineering, Simutools 2009 (2009)

Technical Session 3

Technical Session 3

Effective Doppler Mitigation in Critical Satellite Communications

Alessio Fanfani, Simone Morosi[✉], Luca Simone Ronga, and Enrico Del Re

Information Engineering Department (DINFO), University of Florence,
Via S. Marta 3, 50139 Florence, Italy
{alessio.fanfani,simone.morosi,enrico.delre}@unifi.it,
luca.ronga@cnit.it

Abstract. The modems for telemetry and telecommand applications
are a key component in each satellite system: they shall guarantee reliable and effective performance during every mission phases including also
critical scenarios such as the control operation of the satellite while it
is placed into its orbit, the disposal of a satellite at the end of its life
or the deep-space missions. In these scenarios, the link could be unstable and with a rapid variability and the communication become bursty
and be characterized by poor performance. This paper introduces an all-
digital implementation of a receiver, which is based on the Differential
PSK (D-PSK) modulation and an enhanced version of the Digital Delay
and Multiplier frequency estimator and compensator for mitigating the
Doppler effect, and that results to be perfectly compliant with the aforementioned requirements. The performance of the proposed receiver is
extensively studied and compared with an incoherent technique which
is based on the Double Differential PSK (DD-PSK) modulation and is
known to be suitable for sat-com in critical scenarios.

1 Introduction

The goal of the development of advanced heterogeneous satellite systems [1,2]
requires innovative and robust technological solutions. Telemetry and telecommand (TM/TC) systems along with electrical power, on-board data handling
and attitude and determination control modules are essential for a spacecraft.
The reliability and robustness are key features for a satellite communication
system, particularly during critical satellite mission phases, like the early operations after separation from upper launcher stages or the end of life manoeuvres
[3,4]. In these scenarios, the spacecraft may have reduced functionalities and
uncontrolled attitude and consequently, the communication link could be weak,
unstable and with a rapid variability e.g., signal's amplitude could drop down
or go up according to satellite tumbling rate [5,6]. In this context, the communication becomes bursty and the link reliability harms the bit rate performance.

This paper proposes an advanced radio receiver for Low Earth Orbit (LEO)
satellite communication system. The proposed modem is based on a robust and
efficient frequency compensator to mitigate the Doppler effect, which is one of
the main channel impairments in a LEO mission.

© ICST Institute for Computer Sciences, Social Informatics and Telecommunications Engineering 2017
I. Otung et al. (Eds.): WiSATS 2016, LNICST 186, pp. 145–155, 2017.
DOI: 10.1007/978-3-319-53850-1_15

The problem of Doppler compensation has been deeply discussed in literature [8,16]. Non coherent techniques are attractive due to their simple architecture; an example is the differential PSK (DD-PSK) that does not require a reference carrier since it performs the demodulation by processing the phase of the received signal in two successive intervals and estimating the relative difference [9,10].

On the contrary, coherent techniques guarantee a better performance but are based on complex architectures because all the communication channel parameters (channel delay, frequency offset and phase) must be evaluated before the bit decision [11]. For instance, a receiver for LEO mission needs a frequency recovery circuit to reduce the frequency offset due to Doppler within the acquisition range of the carrier recovery. A typical frequency recovery system performs two functionalities, namely the estimate of the carrier frequency offset and the compensation by counter-rotating.

In the case of large frequency shift, an open-loop maximum likelihood (ML) scheme which is called the Delay and Multiply Method has been proposed in [7]. This method is suitable for burst communications thanks to the very short acquisition time; moreover, it is characterized by a mean square error that is comparable with the one of the closed-loop techniques [8]. Open-loop ML schemes only need one observation time to get the estimation whereas closed-loop require up to 5 observation times to complete the acquisition [12,13].

Because of these interesting features, the Delay and Multiply estimator has been selected for our receiver. The proposed solution is also influenced by the idea of using a coarse and a fine estimation sequentially as used in the receiver realization described in [14].

The features of a receiver which is based on Delay and Multiply (D&M) estimator will be compared with a receiver implementing an incoherent Double Differential PSK whose performance and implementation have been described in a previous contribution [5].

The paper is organized as follows: Sect. 2 provides an overview of the application's scenario including a characterization of the Doppler shift and of the link budget in a critical scenario. Section 3 proposes a complete description of the modem architecture and an analytical analysis of its operative principles Sect. 4 compares the performance of the whole receiver architecture with the one proposed in [5]. Finally, conclusive remarks are given in Sect. 5.

2   Channel Characterization

2.1   Doppler Effect

One of the main channel impairments in TM/TC link for a satellite placed in non-geostationary orbit is the large and time-variant Doppler shift within a visibility window of satellite.

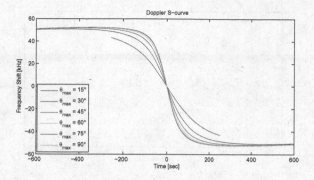

Fig. 1. Doppler shift S-curve

The Doppler Effect is caused by the relative motion of the satellite with respect to the ground station. It mainly depends on satellite orbit, ground station position (latitude) and the frequency value of the link.

The characterization of Doppler shift is a well debated argument in literature. In [15] I. Ali et al. show an exhaustive explanation of Doppler equations that are used in next sections to compare the performance of different receivers in the case of variable Doppler shift.

The frequency shift is represented by the S-curve, which is shown in Fig. 1. The shift is function of the time and of the maximum elevation angle θ_{max}. The shift is equal to zero in the middle of the visibility window when the elevation angle has the maximum value. The maximum shift is within ± 60 kHz and it occurs when the elevation angle approaches the minimum elevation angle which is evaluated equal to $10°$.

2.2   Link-Budget

A communication system for satellite TM/TC applications usually requires low or medium channel capacity. A bit rate of about 32 kbps is enough for a Satellite Ground Operator to control and monitor the satellite within a visibility window. The operative frequency is in S-Band: in particular ITU radio regulation and satellite standard [17] reserves the following sub-ranges:

– Frequency range: 2025–2110 MHz for Earth to space link;
– Frequency range: 2200–2290 MHz for space to Earth link.

The satellite is usually equipped with a hemispherical patch antenna that is dedicated to the TM/TC link and placed on yaw satellite's face. When the satellite correctly points to Ground, the received power is easily computed by means the link budget equation; a detailed case study is described in [5].

An example of signal to noise ratio E_b/N_0 for a TM/TC link within a visibility window is represented by the curves in Fig. 2. The minimum $E_b/N_0 \simeq 14$ dB is in the downlink curve at the beginning and end of each visibility window,

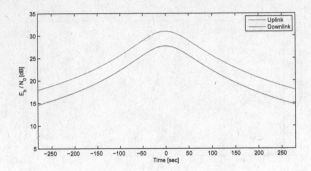

Fig. 2. Link budget curve in stable attitude condition

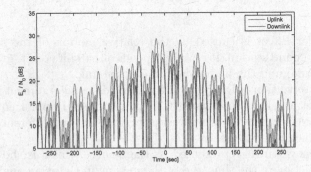

Fig. 3. Link budget curve at the satellite's end of life

when the satellite is closer to the horizon. Nevertheless, in a scenario with damaged attitude control system, the channel results becomes extremely unstable and the signal strength would follow the antenna radiation pattern dropping out completely when the antenna rotates away from ground station [6]. Figure 3 reports the values of the previously considered curves as given by the link budget curves in a possible critical scenario. A high tumble rate has been supposed around all satellite's axes. The presumed angular rotation velocities are 4 deg/s around Pitch axis, 14 deg/s around Roll axis and 10 deg/s around Yaw axis. A sequence of impulses underline the signal instability and an adequate signal power is obtained only in short burst intervals whose duration is often less than few seconds.

3   Receiver Architectures

The following section introduces the receiver architecture, that is oriented to a Software-Defined Radio (SDR) realization. A simulated implementation and a performance evaluation of the architecture have been performed in Simulink.

The receiver that is based on the use of the Digital D&M estimator and compensator is a direct-conversion receiver [7], also known as zero-Intermediate

Frequency (zero-IF) receiver: as it is known, it allows the Radio Frequency (RF) signal to be demodulated by a local oscillator whose frequency is as close as possible to the carrier frequency f_c, of the received signal.

The strategy which is pursued by the receiver is to estimate the Doppler frequency shift by evaluating the average frequency of the zero-IF input signal. In fact, that signal is frequency shifted away from zero hertz by the Doppler effect.

The implementation and the simulations that are described in this paper are based on the following assumptions:

- the signal delay and the clock recovery are performed before the carrier synchronization. The symbol delay is assumed zero;
- the pulse shape is an ideal rect and satisfies the Nyquist criterion for zero interference;
- the carrier f_c is a deterministic parameter;
- the arbitrary phase shift is a uniformly distributed random variable;
- the channel is non frequency selective and has a flat frequency response.

3.1 D&M Estimator and Compensator

The D&M Estimator, that is represented in Fig. 4, matches to the phase variation to determine the instantaneous frequency of the input signal. The rate of change is computed by using the Euler's method of approximating differential equations. The instantaneous phase is generated by the arctangent function (arg) of the complex-valued input signal $x(t)$. The delay block ΔT which is used to compute the discrete differential is equal to the sampling time and T_0 is the symbol period. The block indicated with the ()* symbol represent the complex conjugate operator.

The analytical operating principle of the D&M Estimator is defined by the following equations:

$$\widehat{\Delta f} = \frac{1}{2\pi\Delta T} arg\{\int_0^{T_0} z(t)dt\} \tag{1}$$

where:

$$z(t) = x(t)x^*(t - \Delta T) \tag{2}$$

The output signal $w(t)$ which is produced by the Direct Digital Synthesizer (DDS) has the form:

$$w(t) = A\exp(-j(2\pi\widehat{\Delta f}t)) \tag{3}$$

and the acquisition range of the estimator is equal to $\frac{1}{2\Delta T}$ [7].

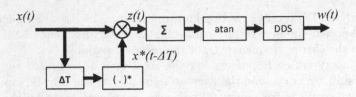

Fig. 4. D&M estimator and compensator

3.2 Baseband Decoder Block

The base band section is based on the scheme of the D-BPSK demodulator that is depicted in Fig. 5.

The performance of the Delay and Multiply scheme depends on the Frequency value of the input signal: the greater the Frequency, the greater the variance of the estimation. For this reason, the receiver uses two Delay and Multiply estimators: The first D&M is indicated as A and is a "coarse" estimator working on $r(t)$ signal: it performs a rough estimation of the frequency shift $\widehat{\Delta f}_A$. The second one is defined as D&M B: it is a "fine" estimator working on $e(t)$ signal, that is the signal with a frequency shift which is equal to the estimation error of D&M A. Thanks to this mechanism the total estimator has a good performance also with large frequency shift of the input signal.

The $r(t)$ signal, that is affected by the Doppler shift is mixed with the compensation signals in order to translate the baseband message signal spectrum closer to the zero hertz value. After the Frequency compensation, an Integrate and Dump and a D-BPSK decision complete the receiving chain. The receiver doesn't need phase recovery scheme before the bit decision because the transmitted signal $r(t)$ is D-PSK modulated.

The input signal is defined by the following equation:

$$r(t) = A \exp(j(2\pi \Delta f t + \theta_n + \varphi_n) + n(t)) \tag{4}$$

where:

- φ_n is the differentially coded modulation information;
- Δf_{D_n} is the Doppler shift on n-th symbol;
- θ_n is the phase error on n-th symbol.
- φ_n is the phase contribution associated to the transmitted data, $\varphi_n = nk\pi \rightarrow$ $n \in Z, k = [0,1]$;

The $x(t)$ signal, that is obtained after frequency compensation and filtering, is equal to:

$$x(t) = A \exp(j(2\pi(\Delta f - \widehat{\Delta f}_A - \widehat{\Delta f}_B)t + \theta_n + \varphi_n) + n(t)$$
$$= A \exp(j(2\pi(\theta_n + \varphi_n) + n(t)) \tag{5}$$

The performance of the Digital Delay-and-Multiply estimator is demonstrated through a complete simulation of the receiver performed in Simulink.

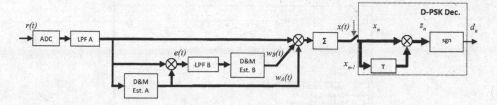

Fig. 5. Baseband decoder block diagram

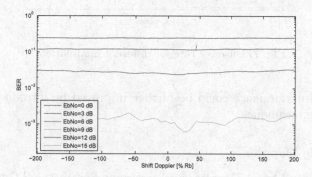

Fig. 6. Digital D&M receiver performance

The curves in Fig. 6 show the bit error rate value as a function of the Doppler shift. The results show a constant BER and proves the effectiveness of the proposed solution. When the E_b/N_0 is greater than 12 dB the Bit Error Rate is lower than 10^{-4}.

4 Performance Comparison

The previous section has shown the reason why a receiver that is based on the D&M estimator is robust against the Doppler shift. In this section the performance of the proposed receiver will be compared with those obtained by DD-PSK [5]. The performance are evaluated in three different scenarios. The first one, which is called fixed Doppler, is an ideal scenario with constant frequency Doppler shift, i.e., no time variation is assumed. The second scenario simulates a link that is affected by a real Doppler shift as defined in Sect. 2.1. Finally, the last scenario takes into account, in addition to the Doppler shift, an extremely variable Signal to Noise ratio due to the satellite tumbling as depicted in Fig. 3.

4.1 Fixed Doppler

The bit errors rate curves are nearly constant for different Doppler conditions but the DD-PSK Bit Error Probability is much higher than the other. The Fig. 7 clearly highlights a better performance of the receiver based on Delay and Multiply estimation within the assumption of time-invariant frequency Doppler shift.

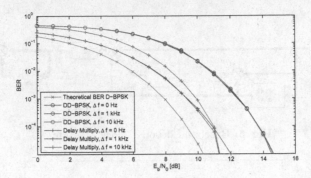

Fig. 7. Bit error rate for different modulation

The presented performance could be further improved by introducing efficient channel coding techniques.

4.2 Variable Doppler

This scenario considers a Doppler shift corresponding to the S-Curve in Fig. 1 with a maximum elevation angle θ_{max} equal to 90° and a minimum elevation angle equal to 20°. The visibility windows duration is 560 s during which are transmitted about 18350080 bit.

The selected S-curve is the worst operative case because it is characterized by the greatest Doppler shift Rate in the centre of the visibility windows.

The performance of both the receiving schemes is measured in terms of number of bit errors during a satellite visibility window. The curves in Fig. 8 shows the cumulative distribution of bit errors for different values of Signal to Noise ratio. The graphs confirms that the receiver based on Delay and Multiply frequency compensator has a very robust performance. That receiver has a constant bit error rate during all the visibility time; otherwise the DD-PSK has performance that depends on the Doppler shift Rate. Indeed, the greater growing rate

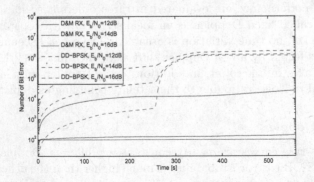

Fig. 8. Cumulative bit error for different modulation

Table 1. Bit error rate with time variant Doppler shift

E_b/N_0, dB	BER of D&M receiver	BER of DD-PSK receiver
12	$1.40 \cdot 10^{-3}$	$12 \cdot 10^{-2}$
14	$9.43 \cdot 10^{-6}$	$7.9 \cdot 10^{-2}$
16	$5.61 \cdot 10^{-6}$	$6.98 \cdot 10^{-2}$

of the cumulative distribution is obtained for the maximum value of Doppler Rate. In Table 1 the average bit error rates are summarized for different values of Signal to Noise ratios that are computed at the end of a satellite visibility windows. In the case of receiver based on Delay and Multiply frequency compensator the BER performance that is obtained for the variable Doppler shift are similar to the ones of the constant Doppler scenario. The D&M BER curves show an initial step due to the wrong bit decoding during the first observation time of the D&M estimator.

4.3   Tumbling Scenario

In order to complete the comparison, the scenario with a tumbling satellite has to be considered. The results that are shown in Fig. 9 still prove the effectiveness of the receiver based on the D&M. The curves represent the Bit Error Rate over the visibility windows for both the receivers. As expected, the BER is very high when the E_b/N_0 is poor, but as soon as the signal quality increases, the performance of D&M is better than the one of the DD-PSK.

Also this graph confirms that the DD-PSK solution is weak when the Doppler rate is high: particularly, in the center of the visibility windows, the DD-PSK BER values are about 50%.

The results of the simulation become clearer if, in the BER evaluation, only the bits with an acceptable signal to noise ratio are considered, i.e. when E_b/N_0 is greater than 12 dB. In this case, the simulation shows that the BER of the

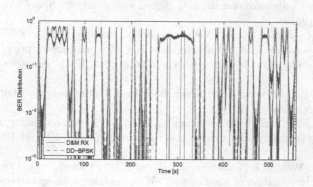

Fig. 9. Bit error rate over the time for different modulation

receiver which is based on D&M is equal to $8 \cdot 10^{-5}$ against a BER of the DD-PSK equal to 0.1.

5   Conclusion

Space applications, such as the satellite decommission, have recently requested reliable and robust telecommunication systems in order to guarantee TM/TC communications also in emergency scenarios. This paper provides a possible channel model and proposes a possible transceiver implementation for these applications that is compared to different solutions.

The solution which is based on a frequency estimator and compensator named D&M has a more complex architecture than the DD-PSK receiver but allows a very good performance. The results shows that D&M receiver guarantees a reliable link also with fast channel variations and strong Doppler shift as shown in the paper. Therefore, the proposed D&M receiver is a suitable implementation for communication in emergency scenario as the TM/TC for decommissioning device.

References

1. Del Re, E., Morosi, S., Ronga, L.S., Jayousi, S., Martinelli, A.: Flexible heterogeneous satellite-based architecture for enhanced quality of life applications. IEEE Commun. Magaz. **53**(5), 186–193 (2015)
2. Del Re, E., Morosi, S., Jayousi, S., Sacchi, C.: Salice satellite-assisted localization and communication systems for emergency services. In: Proceedings of the 1st International Conference on Wireless Communications, Vehicular Technology, Information Theory, Aerospace and Electronic Systems (WVITAE), Aalborg, Denmark (2009)
3. IADC Space Debris Mitigation Guidelines (2002)
4. European Code of Conduct for Space Debris Mitigation: Issue 1.0 (2004)
5. Del Re, E., Fanfani, A., Morosi, S., Ronga, L.S.: Robust modem design for satellite communications in emergency scenarios. In: 2014 7th Advanced Satellite Multimedia Systems Conference and the 13th Signal Processing for Space Communications Workshop (2014)
6. Bruzzi, J.R., Jensen, J.R., Fielhauer, K.B., Royster, D.W., Srinivasan, D.K.: Telemetry recovery and uplink commanding of a spacecraft prior to three-axis attitude stabilization. In: Proceedings of the 2006 IEEE Aerospace Conference (2006)
7. Mengali, U., D'Andrea, A.N.: Synchronization Techniques for Digital Receivers. Springer, Heidelberg (1997)
8. Classen, F., Meyr, H.: Two frequency estimation schemes operating independently of timing information. In: Conference Recreation (GLOBECOM 1993), Houston, TX (1993)
9. Yuce, M.R., Wentai, L., Damiano, J., Bharath, B., Franzon, P.D., Dogan, N.S.: SOI CMOS implementation of a multirate PSK demodulator for space communications. IEEE Trans. Circ. Syst. I Regul. Papers **54**(2), 420–431 (2007)

10. Ma, C., Wang, D.: The performance of DDPSK over LEO mobile satellite channels. In: Proceedings of the 2000 Asia-Pacific Microwave Conference (2000)
11. Gardner, F.: Hangup in phase-lock loops. IEEE Trans. Commun. **25**, 1210–1214 (1977)
12. Mengali, U., Morelli, M.: Data-aided frequency estimation for burst digital transmission. IEEE Trans. Commun. **45**(1), 23–25 (1997)
13. Fitz, M., Lindsey, W.: Decision-directed burst-mode carrier synchronization techniques. IEEE Trans. Commun. **40**, 1644–1653 (1992)
14. van der Westhuizen, E., van Rooyen, G.: Baseband Carrier Recovery and Phase Tracking as a Doppler Compensation Technique for a zero-IF SDR (2009)
15. Ali, I., Bonanni, P.G., Al-Dhahir, N., Hershey, J.E.: Doppler Application In LEO Satellite Communication Systems. Springer, Heidelberg (2002)
16. Ah-Thew, G.P.: Doppler Compensation for LEO Satellite Communication Systems (1998)
17. ECSS-E-ST-50-05C Rev. 2: Radio Frequency and Modulation, ESA-ESTEC, October 2011

Interference Mitigation for Multi Spot Beam Satellite Communication Systems Incorporating Spread Spectrum

Abdulkareem Karasuwa[1(✉)], Jon Eastment[2], and Ifiok Otung[1]

[1] Mobile and Satellite Communications Research Group,
University of South Wales, Pontypridd CF37 1DL, UK
{abdulkareem.karasuwa,ifiok.otung}@southwales.ac.uk
[2] STFC Rutherford Appleton Laboratory, Harwell Oxford, Didcot OX11 0QX, UK
jon.eastment@stfc.ac.uk

Abstract. Nonlinear precoding techniques have robust transmit power stability and achieve superior interference suppression when compared to their linear counterparts. Tomlinson-Harashima Precoding (THP) is a suboptimal version of Costa's well-known work on writing on dirty paper (DPC). Implementing these precoding techniques in a multi spot beam satellite communications system that employs frequency reuse can significantly reduce co-channel interference (CCI). In this paper, we investigate and compare the performance of linear and nonlinear precoding techniques on the forward link of a multiple spot beam satellite link. In addition, we examine the potential benefits of integrating the novel spread spectrum (SS) technique with the existing precoding techniques. The new system's performance is evaluated and compared with that of standard precoding techniques, and the benefits of incorporating SS are weighed against the extra bandwidth requirements.

Keywords: High throughput satellite · Frequency reuse · Multi spot beam · Co-channel interference · Precoding · Spread spectrum

1 Introduction

The desire to support increasing growth in multimedia applications and services poses a challenge to satellite communication operators to find solutions to the scarcity of bandwidth resources in the legacy frequency bands allocated for satellite services. Options considered include transition to higher frequency bands, such as *Ka* and above, and adoption of advanced signal processing techniques, such as Digital Video Broadcasting second generation (DVB-S2) adaptive modulation and coding (MODCOD), for efficient spectrum utilisation. Systems operating at higher frequencies have to contend with atmospherically-induced propagation perturbations by using fade mitigation techniques [1]. A promising strategy to increase the capacity of satellite systems is the multiple spot beam transmission scheme, which reuses the available spectrum resources, thereby expanding the system's capacity by up to an order of magnitude [2]. This has led to the emergence of so-called high throughput satellite (HTS) systems, deploying large numbers of spot beams (for example, *Ka-Sat* and *ViaSat-1*) [3]. The number of

© ICST Institute for Computer Sciences, Social Informatics and Telecommunications Engineering 2017
I. Otung et al. (Eds.): WiSATS 2016, LNICST 186, pp. 156–166, 2017.
DOI: 10.1007/978-3-319-53850-1_16

spot beams and frequency reuse factor (N_{reuse}) dictates the level of co-channel interference (CCI) amongst beams reusing the same colour (i.e. portion of the bandwidth). The highest capacity can be achieved when neighbouring spot beams share the same colour; however, the level of CCI may be severe and can limit system performance [4]. There is, therefore, a compromise between CCI level and system capacity.

Multiple spot beam satellite systems are considered as multiple-input multiple-output (MIMO) systems, with the forward link (for example, gateway via satellite to the user terminal) as a broadcast channel (BC) and the return link (for example, user terminal via satellite to the gateway) as a multiple access channel (MAC) [5]. In order to reduce the impact of CCI in the forward link, precoding can be implemented at the transmitter (gateway or satellite). The benefits of this approach are to relieve the receiver from processing burden, computational complexity and power constraints, leading to simpler, power-efficient and cheaper end-user receivers [6]. On the other hand, for the reverse link, it is well known that multi-user detection (MUDs) techniques, such as successive interference cancellation (SIC), can be used to suppress the effect of CCI [5].

This paper focuses on precoding techniques, which are broadly classified into linear and nonlinear approaches. Linear precoding includes the zero-forcing (ZF) and the minimum mean squared error (MMSE) schemes. They are less complex than nonlinear precoding but offer inferior performance. This is due to the adverse effect of channel matrix inversion, which causes the precoded signal's average energy to exceed that of the original transmitted signal [7]. Alternatively, nonlinear precoding techniques, based on Costa's optimal dirty paper method (DPC) [8], offer superior performance at the expense of extra computational complexity. A simple approach is the Tomlinson-Harashima precoding (THP) [9, 10] which delivers a performance close to that of DPC with moderate computational complexity. An important feature of the nonlinear scheme is that the energy of the precoded signal is approximately the same as that of the original transmitted signal, due to the modulo arithmetic operation introduced by the THP.

The use of linear precoding in the forward link of a broadband multiple spot beam satellite system to curb the effect of CCI has been presented in [11], and shows a significant improvement in system capacity. On the other hand, some popular THP approaches [12, 13] have their implementations extended to multiple spot beam satellite system in [14].

The technical considerations and implications of spread spectrum (SS) techniques over satellite, like multiplexing, coding, and transmission of direct-sequence SS (DS-SS), have been described in detail in [15]. In SS systems, information symbols are encoded using different spreading codes (known as signatures) at the transmitters, the chip-rate of which is significantly higher than that of the information stream. The same bandwidth resource is used by multiple users to simultaneously transmit their SS signals, while the receiver recovers the desired transmitted data by correlating the incoming SS signal with the appropriate user's signature.

In this work, the various implementations of linear and nonlinear precoding are discussed, and an implementation of THP on a multiple spot beam satellite system, based on combining the well-known precoding techniques with SS, is proposed. To the best of our knowledge, the incorporation of SS with THP over multiple spot beam satellite systems is a novel approach. While the method requires increased system complexity and higher bandwidth utilisation, enhanced overall performance is the goal. The performance of the new system is analysed via extensive simulations on a MATLAB platform, and results are compared with the performance of existing methods that are based on precoding alone.

2   The Multiple Spot Beam Satellite Channel

In this case, the satellite antenna feeds (spot beams) represents the transmit antenna elements and the user terminals' antennas can be considered as the elements of the receive antennas of a virtual MIMO system. The MIMO channel, with number of transmit antennas, N_T, and number of receive antennas, N_R, is modelled as [16]:

$$\mathbf{y} = \mathbf{Hb} + \mathbf{n}. \tag{1}$$

where $\mathbf{b}$ is the transmitted signal column vector of size N_T, $\mathbf{b} = \left[b_1, b_2, b_3, \dots, b_T\right]^T$ each with variance $\mathrm{E}\left\{|\mathbf{b}_i|^2\right\} = \sigma_b^2$, $\mathbf{y}$ is the received signal symbols column vector of size N_R, $\mathbf{y} = \left[y_1, y_2, y_3, \dots, y_R\right]^T$, and $\mathbf{n}$ is additive white zero-mean complex noise (AWGN) column vector of size N_R, $\mathbf{n} = \left[n_1, n_2, n_3, \dots, n_R\right]^T$ with variance $\mathrm{E}\left\{|\mathbf{nn}|^H\right\} = \sigma_n^2\mathbf{I}$. (where $(\cdot)^T$ and $(\cdot)^H$ stand for transpose and conjugate transpose (Hermitian) operations, respectively). The channel matrix $\mathbf{H}$ has dimension N_T by N_R and its h_{ij} elements represents the complex attenuations from the j-th beam to the i-th receiving terminal, with $i = 1, 2, \dots, N_R$ and $j = 1, 2, \dots, N_T$. For example, consider the i-th element of $\mathbf{y}$ which is given by:

$$\mathbf{y}_i = \sum_{j=1}^{N_T} h_{ij}\mathbf{b}_j + \mathbf{n}_i. \tag{2}$$

The channel delivers the interfering signal emanating from the spot beams into each of the user terminals via the side-lobe. Note that when $N_T = N_R = N_{SB}$, (N_{SB} is the number of spot beams), $\mathbf{H}$ is an $N_{SB} \times N_{SB}$ invertible square matrix. Therefore,

$$\mathbf{y}_i = h_{ii}\mathbf{b}_i + \sum_{\substack{j=1 \\ j \neq i}}^{N_{SB}} h_{ij}\mathbf{b}_j + \mathbf{n}_i. \tag{3}$$

The wanted user signal is modified by the gain h_{ii}, and distorted by the combined effect of all interference power from co-channel beams which are the off-diagonal elements of $\mathbf{H}$, and the AWGN.

CCI in multiple spot beam systems is influenced by the number of reuse colours, inter-beam spacing and the taper values of the satellite transmit antenna side-lobe levels. The interference decreases with increasing reuse number and decreasing antenna side-lobe level. The total CCI power on the forward link, I_f, in dBW, is given by

$$\sum_{k=1}^{N_{CC}} I_f = EIRP_{SAT} + G_{ES,max} - P_{BO} - L_{ATM} - L_M - L_{FS} + X. \tag{4}$$

Where,

$$X = 10\log_{10} \sum_{k=1}^{N_{CC}} \frac{\left|f_R(\theta_k)^2\right|}{L_S}. \tag{5}$$

In (4) and (5), $EIRP_{SAT}$ is the effective isotropically radiated power of the satellite in dBW, $G_{ES,max}$ is the earth station antenna maximum gain (dBi), P_{BO} is the transmitter power amplifier back-off (dB), L_{ATM} is the atmospheric losses (dB), L_M is the miscellaneous losses (dB), L_S is the antenna scan losses (dB), L_{FS} is the free-space path loss (dB), $f_R(\theta_k)$ is the normalised antenna pattern with taper and N_{CC} is the number of neighbouring co-channel cells.

The forward link of a typical Geostationary (GEO) satellite located at $19.2°$ East longitude covering Europe with a total of 96 spot beams is used for this analysis, as detailed in [5]. The half-beam width, θ_{3dB} is $0.2°$, and a frequency of 20 GHz is used with seven beams ($N_{SB} = 7$) with universal frequency reuse adopted ($N_{reuse} = 1$) so that the six neighbouring co-channel spot beams can contribute maximum interference power possible to the user in the centre of the wanted beam, as indicated in Fig. 1.

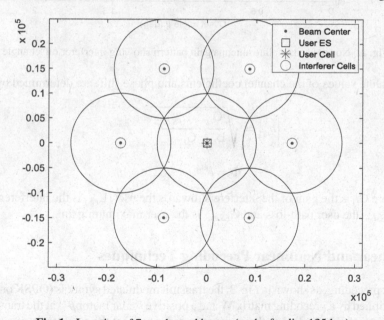

Fig. 1. Location of 7 co-channel beams (each of radius 125 km)

The interferers here are the static co-channel spot beams. Therefore, the distance between each interfering source and the user is the same. This gives rise to the same path loss and off-axis interfering antenna gain towards the user earth station. The antenna pattern, and interferer angular-offset position, is shown in Fig. 2. In addition, this means the phase shift between the beams is constant for each realisation of **H**. The coefficients of **H** and phase shift are obtained using [5]:

$$\mathbf{H} = \left| h_{i,j} \right| \mathbf{\Phi}. \tag{6}$$

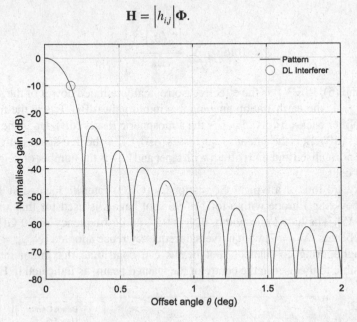

Fig. 2. Normalised satellite antenna gain pattern showing interferer offset angle

Absolute values of the channel coefficients and phase shift are determined by:

$$\left| h_{i,j} \right| = \sqrt{\frac{G_{i,j}}{L_{FS,j}} \cdot \frac{L_{FS,u}}{G_{ES,max}}}. \tag{7}$$

$$\mathbf{\Phi} = e^{j\theta_{i,j}}. \tag{8}$$

Where $G_{i,j}$ is the gain of the interferers towards the user, $L_{FS,j}$ is the interferers path-loss, $L_{FS,u}$ is the user path-loss and $G_{ES,max}$ is the user maximum gain.

3   Linear and Nonlinear Precoding Techniques

In linear precoding, as shown in Fig. 3, the transmit modulated symbols (QPSK or QAM) are multiplied by a precoding matrix **W** and a positive scalar factor β^{-1} at the transmitter. The inverse of β is applied at the receiver in order to meet the total transmitted power constraint after precoding, E_{TX}.

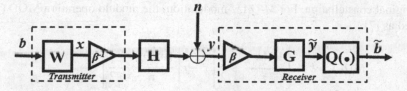

Fig. 3. Block diagram of linear precoding transmitter and receiver

The precoding matrix **W** and its transmit power constraint factor β can be expressed as follows, with subscripts ZF denoting zero-forcing [13]:

$$\mathbf{W}_{ZF} = \frac{1}{\beta}\mathbf{H}^{+} = \frac{1}{\beta}\mathbf{H}^{\mathbf{H}}(\mathbf{H}\mathbf{H}^{\mathbf{H}})^{-1}. \tag{9}$$

$$\beta_{ZF} = \sqrt{\frac{Tr\left((\mathbf{H}\mathbf{H}^{H})^{-1}\sigma_b^2\right)}{E_{TX}}}. \tag{10}$$

where $Tr(\cdot)$ means trace operation and E_{TX} is the transmit energy.

The MMSE precoding matrix $\mathbf{W}_{MMSE}$ and its transmit power constraint factor β_{MMSE} are given by:

$$\mathbf{W}_{MMSE} = \frac{1}{\beta}\left(\mathbf{H}^{H}\mathbf{H} + \xi\mathbf{I}\right)^{-1}\mathbf{H}^{H}. \tag{11}$$

$$\beta_{MMSE} = \sqrt{\frac{Tr\left((\mathbf{H}^{H}\mathbf{H} + \xi\mathbf{I})^{-2}\mathbf{H}^{H}\mathbf{H}\sigma_b^2\right)}{E_{TX}}}. \tag{12}$$

Where $\xi = N_{SB}\sigma_n^2 / \sigma_b^2$.

The MMSE precoding takes into consideration the noise variance, σ_n^2, to improve performance in the low-SNR region.

The block diagram depicting a THP nonlinear precoding system is shown in Fig. 4.

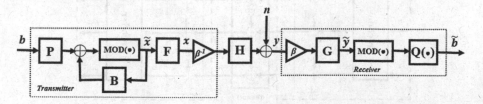

Fig. 4. Block diagram of THP precoding transmitter and receiver

The insertion of the modulo operation into the linear precoding scheme provides the nonlinearity that ensures the amplitude of signal b_i is maintained within the bounds of

the original constellation. For *M-QAM* modulation, the modulo operation MOD (·) is
defined as [7]:

$$M(b_i) = b - \left\lfloor \frac{\mathbf{Re}(b_i)}{\tau} + \frac{1}{2} \right\rfloor \tau - j \left\lfloor \frac{\mathbf{Im}(b_i)}{\tau} + \frac{1}{2} \right\rfloor \tau. \tag{13}$$

where τ is a constant for the periodic extension of the constellation, depending on the
modulation scheme employed. However, the modulo operation causes a small increase
in transmit energy, known as precoding loss, γ_p, which is given by [7]:

$$\gamma_p = \frac{M}{M-1}. \tag{14}$$

In this case, the output of the modulo operation $\tilde{x}$ is fed into the feed-forward matrix
F yielding the precoded signal **x**. An extra gain, represented by a diagonal matrix **G**, is
then applied to the rescaled received signal. Finally, the modulo operation is applied to
the signal $\tilde{y}$ and then the estimate $\tilde{b}$ of the original signal is computed by the decision
device Q(•).

4   The Proposed System

The proposed system incorporates spread spectrum with precoding (see Fig. 5). The
modulated symbols b_i are precoded as described in Sect. 3. The output x_i of the precoder
is then multiplied by a spreading code c_i to yield the spread signal s_i, which is then
transmitted via the satellite antenna spot beams and encounters additive white Gaussian
noise (AWGN) n_i in the channel. There is no cooperation amongst the user terminals,
so each sees only its own channel and is affected by CCI due to side-lobe radiation from
co-channel spot beams. The received signal ss_i is de-spread by the dc_i of each receiver
yielding xx_i, which is then decoded, reversing the precoding (plus modulo operation –
in the case of nonlinear), to give an estimate bb_i of the original transmit symbols.

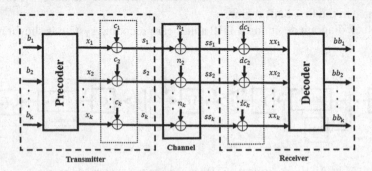

Fig. 5. Block diagram of Precoding plus SS

The advantage of the spreading techniques comes as a processing gain G_p which can be seen as the ratio of the spreading chip's rate R_c over the transmit information rate R_b. This implies the use of significantly wider bandwidth, far more than the usual amount conventionally employed for regular transmission. Higher processing gain also means that lower power is needed for the transmission of information. In essence, bandwidth is traded-off for power - as proposed by Shannon's law. Spreading the information signal with a pseudo-noise (PN) code, which is known to have good auto- and cross-correlation properties [17], can be used to provide interference mitigation. The G_p tends to improve the carrier-to-noise-plus-interference ratio (CNIR) in such a way that will strengthen the diagonal elements and lower the off-diagonal elements of the channel matrix **H**. If we define CNR as the carrier-to-noise ratio, and CIR as the carrier-to-interference ratio, then:

$$CNIR = \left((CNR)^{-1} + G_P(CIR)^{-1}\right)^{-1}. \tag{15}$$

$$G_p = \frac{R_c}{R_b}. \tag{16}$$

With modern HTS systems such as *Hylas* 2 [18] employing transponder bandwidth up to 230 MHz, there is ample scope for SS processing gains in excess of 10 dB to be realised. This translates into significant CCI mitigation that can offset the deficiencies in precoding performance due to an imperfect knowledge of the channel state information (CSI). Therefore, assuming an information bit rate of 40 Mb/s in 20 MHz (QPSK), with this available transponder bandwidth, a chip rate that could offer up to a 7 dB processing gain can be achieved.

5 Results and Discussion

Computer simulations of linear and non-linear precoding were implemented for the satellite system described earlier in this paper. The results shown in Fig. 6 indicate that, where no precoding has been employed, the BER curve exhibits a floor which shows that the system is interference-limited. This is not unexpected, due to the fact that the six neighbouring cells reuse the same frequency spectrum as the wanted user's earth station. It is also clear from the results that the linear precoding techniques improve the system's performance in a manner consistent with the findings of other workers, as reported in the existing literature. The MMSE approach slightly outperformed the ZF approach, with about 1.5 dB additional improvement in the high-SNR region.

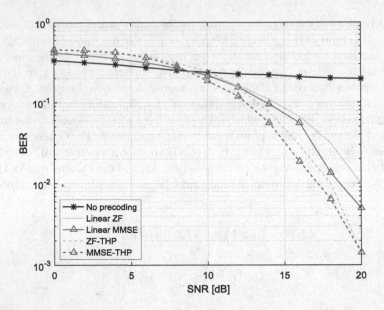

Fig. 6. Comparison of linear and non-linear ZF and MMSE – for QPSK modulation

The non-linear techniques introduce further improvement compared to that offered by the linear approach. The ZF-THP and MMSE-THP are almost 2 dB better than their linear counterparts in the high-SNR region. At lower SNRs, performance of the linear techniques is slightly better than the non-linear techniques; this is, however, not unconnected to the impact of the precoding loss prevalent in the non-linear approach, especially for lower-order modulation schemes like QPSK. This loss is expected to be negligible for higher-order modulation schemes, such as 16-QAM. The no-precoding curve shows better performance at low SNRs, due to the absence of both energy enhancement (for the case of the linear approach) and precoding loss (for the non-linear approach).

Figure 7 shows the results of the impact of the spreading processing gain, G_p on the system performance for the non-linear precoding approach. Due to the reduction of transmit power, there is no significant change in performance between the system with and without spreading for the ZF-THP approach. This is not unconnected with the peculiar effect of the increase in average transmit power, which leads to relatively poor performance. However, for the MMSE-THP approach, the performance improvement due to spreading processing gain is significant. For a BER of 10^{-2}, there is a 4 dB gain in favour of the system that incorporates spread spectrum.

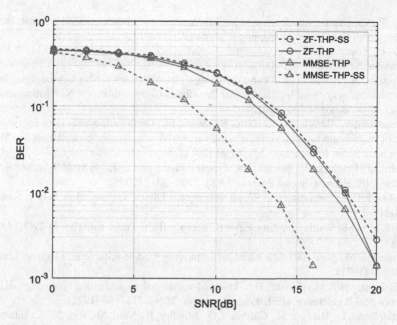

Fig. 7. Comparison of non-linear ZF and MMSE, with and without SS – for QPSK modulation

6   Conclusion

In this work, the impact of co-channel interference on multiple spot beam satellite systems employing extensive frequency reuse has been presented and some methods of mitigating the interference effects have been reviewed and implemented. A new method of improving the performance of precoding techniques has been proposed, and the expected benefits have been discussed. The preliminary results show that incorporating spread spectrum techniques with precoding has the potential to improve interference mitigation performance. It is recognised, however, that this improved performance comes at the expense of both increased complexity and extra bandwidth utilisation. Our future work will concentrate on investigating the system configurations and operational parameters under which the combination of spread spectrum with the various precoding techniques provides maximum scope for improved overall satellite communications system performance.

Acknowledgments. The Authors would like to acknowledge the Petroleum Technology Development Fund (PTDF), Abuja Nigeria which has supported this work.

References

1. Panagopoulos, A.D., Arapoglou, P.M., Cottis, P.G.: Satellite communications at KU, KA, and V bands: propagation impairments and mitigation techniques. IEEE Commun. Surv. Tutorials **6**(3), 2–14 (2004)

2. Lutz, E.: Co-channel interference in high-throughput multibeam satellite systems. In: IEEE International Conference on Communications (ICC) (2015)
3. Lutz, E.: Towards the Terabit/s satellite – interference issues in the user link. Int. J. Satellite Commun. Netw. **34**(4), 461–482 (2015)
4. Karasuwa, A., Eastment, J., Otung, I.: Design considerations for high throughput satellite communication systems. In: 21st Ka and Broadband Communications, Navigation and Earth Observation, Bologna, Italy (2015)
5. Boussemart, V., Berioli, M., Rossetto, F., Joham, M.: On the achievable rates for the return-link of multi-beam satellite systems using successive interference cancellation. In: Military Communications Conference - MILCOM (2011)
6. Joham, M., Utschick, W., Nossek, J.A.: Linear transmit processing in MIMO communications systems. IEEE Trans. Signal Process. **53**(8), 2700–2712 (2005)
7. Fischer, R.F.H.: Precoding and Signal Shaping for Digital Transmission. Wiley, New York (2002)
8. Costa, M.H.M.: Writing on dirty paper (Corresp.). IEEE Trans. Inf. Theory **29**(3), 439–441 (1983)
9. Tomlinson, M.: New automatic equaliser employing modulo arithmetic. Electron. Lett. **7**(5), 138–139 (1971)
10. Harashima, H., Miyakawa, H.: Matched-transmission technique for channels with intersymbol interference. IEEE Trans. Commun. **20**(4), 774–780 (1972)
11. Cottatellucci, L., Debbah, M., Gallinaro, G., Mueller, R., Neiri, M., Rinado, R.: Interference mitigation techniques for broadband satellite systems. In: 24th Proceedings of AIAA International Communication Satellite Systems Conference (ICSSC), San Diego, CA, vol. 1, pp. 1–13 (2006)
12. Fischer, R.F.H., Windpassingre, C., Lampe, A., Huber, J.B.: MIMO precoding for decentralized receivers. In: Proceedings of the IEEE International Symposium on Information Theory (2002)
13. Joham, M., Brehmer, J., Utschick, W.: MMSE approaches to multiuser spatio-temporal Tomlinson-harashima precoding. In: 5th International Conference on Source and Channel Coding (SCC 2004), Erlange, Germany (2004)
14. Diaz, M.A., Courville, N., Mosquera, C., Gianluigi, L., Corazza, G.E.: Non-linear interference mitigation for broadband multimedia satellite systems. In: International Workshop on Satellite and Space Communications (IWSSC 2007) (2007)
15. Gaudenzi, R.D., Giannetti, F., Luise, M.: Advances in satellite CDMA transmission for mobile and personal communications. Proc. IEEE **84**(1), 18–39 (1996)
16. Cho, Y.S., Kim, J., Yang, W.Y., Kang, C.G.: MIMO-OFDM Wireless Communications with MATLAB. Wiley, Singapore (2010)
17. Fazel, K., Kaiser, S.: Multi-carrier Spread Spectrum Systems: From OFDM and MC-CDMA to LTE and WiMAX, 2nd edn. John Wiley and Sons Ltd., Chichester (2008)
18. Avanti Communications Group plc. http://www.avantiplc.com/sites/default/files/hylas-2-tech-sheet.pdf

Specific Rain Attenuation Derived from a Gaussian Mixture Model for Rainfall Drop Size Distribution

K'ufre-Mfon E. Ekerete[1], Francis H. Hunt[1]([⊠]), Judith L. Jeffery[2], and Ifiok E. Otung[1]

[1] Mobile and Satellite Communications Research Group,
University of South Wales, Pontypridd CF37 1DL, UK
{kufre-mfon.ekerete,francis.hunt,ifiok.otung}@southwales.ac.uk
[2] STFC Rutherford Appleton Laboratory, Harwell Oxford, Didcot OX11 0QX, UK
judith.jeffery@stfc.ac.uk

Abstract. Precipitation, particularly rain affects the millimetre and sub-millimetre frequencies more severely than it does for lower frequencies in the Earth-space path. There is therefore a need for accurate models that will enable the rainfall drop size distribution (DSD) to be better predicted for better planning and improved service delivery. Using data captured at Chilbolton Observatory, this paper looks at modelling the DSD using the Gaussian Mixture Model (GMM), and attempts to predict the specific attenuation due to rain based on this model and compares the result with other well-established statistical models (lognormal and gamma). Results show that specific attenuation tends to increase with the drop sizes, and the smaller drops contribute little to the overall attenuation experienced by signals. Specific attenuation was computed based on several standard statistical distributions, and compared with that derived from the ITU recommendation.

Keywords: Theoretical modelling · Space and satellite communications · Estimation and forecasting · Probability distributions · Rainfall drop size distribution (DSD) · Gaussian Mixture Model (GMM) · Specific attenuation

1 Introduction

Modernity requires vast exchange of information, mostly digital. Information service providers constantly seek new ways and methods to transmit these information efficiently and reliably. In the search for the better transmission of these information, the lower frequency bands are congested, and providers now seek to transmit information using increasingly higher frequencies, where more data can be transmitted more economically.

In the higher frequencies, precipitation, particularly rain plays a great role in the dispersion of transmitted signals, causing attenuation in the received signals. Signals are scattered by raindrops since the transmitted wavelengths are much smaller than the raindrop sizes. There have been several studies [1–3] showing how signals are affected by different sizes of raindrops, and a thorough understanding of the distribution of these

© ICST Institute for Computer Sciences, Social Informatics and Telecommunications Engineering 2017
I. Otung et al. (Eds.): WiSATS 2016, LNICST 186, pp. 167–177, 2017.
DOI: 10.1007/978-3-319-53850-1_17

raindrops enables the systems designer to design mitigation plans to ensure a better quality of service delivery.

Kumar *et al.* [1] discusses the effect of ignoring the smaller drop bin sizes, and reaches the conclusion that since the smaller drops contributes little to the overall DSD, hence the attenuation and the removal of the smaller-sized bins have little impact on attenuation. Thurai *et al.* [2] suggests that even with the more sophisticated 2D Video Disdrometer, the readings of the smaller drops are still not good enough to be considered reliable, as it under-estimates the drop densities. Åsen and Gibbins [3] while suggesting that the disdrometer is not sensitive to small drop diameters, and thus mis-estimates the attenuation, goes on to suggest that the difference between measured and modelled attenuation may be due to wind drafts.

Rainfall data collected from the disdrometer located at the Chilbolton Observatory, is analysed and the rainfall drop size distribution (DSD) is determined. The data sometimes suggests the presence of underlying multimodal distribution [4–7]. As well as standard statistical distributions like the lognormal and gamma, the Gaussian Mixture Model (GMM) is used to model the rainfall data.

This work attempts to compute the specific attenuation based on the ITU P R 838 model, and compares the specific attenuation derived from the GMM as well as the other statistical models aforementioned. Section 2 discusses the statistical modelling of rainfall DSDs, looking at the commonly used statistical models for the derivation of the DSDs, and introduces the Gaussian Mixture Model (GMM) as a solution to model multimodal distributions encountered in the data. Section 3 discusses specific attenuation – how the ITU recommendation derives specific attenuation for a given rain rate, as well the derivation of specific attenuation from the distributions by integrating the DSD and the extinction cross section of the drops over the entire bin. Section 4 deals with the data collection and procedures, giving insight into the experimentation and the analyses carried out. Section 5 presents and discusses the results, with Sect. 6 concluding the report.

2 Rainfall DSDs

2.1 Statistical Modelling of DSDs

The rainfall DSD, $N(D)$ is taken as the number of raindrops per unit volume per unit diameter centered on D the drop diameter (in mm), measured in $m^{-3} mm^{-1}$, where $N(D)$ dD, (in m^{-3}), is the number of such drops per unit volume having diameters in the infinitesimal range $(D - dD/2, D + dD/2)$ [7]. The DSD is significant in the computation of rain rates and signal attenuation. The DSD may vary significantly, yet result in the same rain rate given that a large number of small drops may yield the same rain volume (rain rate) as a small number of large drops. And this may explain why two different DSDs with the same rain rate may give two different attenuation values.

Given that D is a continuous and non-negative, various statistical distributions have been used to model $N(D)$. Marshall and Palmer [8] suggested that DSD is distributed exponentially, and can be represented as

$$N(D) = N_0\, exp(-\Lambda D), 0 < D \leq D_{max} \tag{1}$$

and

$$\Lambda = \alpha R^\beta \tag{2}$$

with D_{max} being the biggest drop diameter measured, where N_0 and Λ (in mm^{-1}) are the intercept and slope parameters respectively, and Λ is dependent on the rainfall rate R (in mm/h). This relationship is however valid for $D < 1.5$ mm [8].

Other studies [9–12] modelled the DSD using the lognormal distribution, given as

$$N(D) = \frac{N_T}{\sqrt{2\pi}\sigma_g(D - \theta)} \exp\left[-\frac{\left(\ln(D - \theta) - \mu_g\right)^2}{2\sigma_g^2}\right] \tag{3}$$

with σ_g and μ_g being the geometric standard deviation and geometric mean respectively, and θ, the offset value.

The gamma distribution yields more accurate rainfall rate computations than the exponential distribution, especially when combined with radar data [13]. The gamma distribution is given as

$$N(D) = N_T D^\mu \exp\left(-\Lambda D\right), \quad 0 \leq D \leq D_{max} \tag{4}$$

with Λ, μ, and N_T as the slope, shape and scaling parameters respectively, and these allow for the characterisation of a wide range of rainfall scenarios. The exponential distribution is a special case of the gamma distribution with $\mu = 0$.

However, these distributions do not describe all DSDs, as it has been suggested that different rain types [14, 15] and regions [13, 16, 17] may be described by different statistical models. Previous works [5–7, 18–20] present cases where these unimodal distributions do not adequately describe distributions that are distributed multimodally. Ekerete, *et al.* [6] proposes that these distributions be modelled with a Gaussian Mixture Model (GMM) in the log domain.

The GMM probability density function is given as [7]

$$p(D) = \sum_{i=1}^{k} w_i \cdot \frac{1}{D} \exp\left[-\frac{\left(\ln(D) - \mu_i\right)^2}{2\sigma_i^2}\right] \tag{5}$$

where μ_i and σ_i are the mean and standard deviation of the ith mode respectively and the weights w_i have the property $\sum_{i=1}^{k} w_i = 1$.

3   Attenuation Due to Rain

3.1   Specific Attenuation

Radio signals travelling through the earth-space paths are attenuated, the severity depending on many factors; frequency, temperature, pressure, as well as the presence of precipitation, chiefly raindrops. The higher the frequency, the higher the signal impairment as the wavelength to raindrop diameter ratio becomes smaller.

Specific rain attenuation, measured in dB/km, is the attenuation of the signal due to rain per unit distance. At any given point in the earth-space path, the specific attenuation is largely dependent on the rain rate at that point. Integrating the specific attenuation along the path gives the total attenuation [21]. The specific attenuation can be estimated by assuming spherical raindrops and using Mie's scattering theory [22].

The received power, P_r, on a uniformly distributed spherical water drop of radius r with transmitted power, P_t, over length L is given as

$$P_r = P_t \cdot \exp(-kL) \tag{6}$$

where k is the attenuation coefficient for the rain volume expressed in units of reciprocal length.

The attenuation, A (in dB) will be given as

$$A = 10 \cdot log_{10}(P_t/P_r) = 10 \cdot log_{10} \exp(kL) = 4.343 \cdot kL \tag{7}$$

where the attenuation coefficient, k, is

$$k = N(D) \cdot Q_t \tag{8}$$

and $N(D)$ is the drop density, and Q_t is the extinction cross section of the drop with diameter D [23].

An alternative approach to estimating the specific attenuation is given by the ITU-R P.838-3 [24], where the specific attenuation, γ in (dB/km), is given as a power law relationship dependent on the rain rate, R.

$$\gamma = a \cdot R^b \tag{9}$$

where the coefficients a and b are dependent on the frequency, f (GHz), and given in [24].

3.2   Extinction Cross Section

The extinction (or attenuation) cross section, Q_t, is dependent on the wavelength, λ, the complex refractive index of water, $m = p + iq$ and the drop diameter, D. $Q_t = Q_t(\lambda, m, D)$. A deeper treatment of the extinction cross section is given by [25].

The attenuation coefficient is determined by integration over all the drop sizes since the drop sizes are not all equal, the attenuation coefficient is given as

$$k = \int_0^\infty Q_t(\lambda, m, D)\, N(D)\, dD \tag{10}$$

The specific attenuation is then given as [14]

$$\gamma = 4.343 \int_0^\infty Q_t(\lambda, m, D)\, N(D)\, dD \; \text{dB/km} \tag{11}$$

According to Mie's theory for a plane wave radiation on an absorbing sphere, the wave number $x = \pi D/\lambda$.

The complex forward scattering amplitude for the spherical raindrop function is given as [26]

$$S(0) = \frac{1}{2} \sum_{n=1}^\infty (2n + 1)(a_n + b_n) \tag{12}$$

This gives the extinction cross section as

$$Q_t = \frac{4\pi}{k^2} Re\, S(0) = \frac{2}{x^2} \sum_{n=1}^\infty (2n + 1)\, Re(a_n + b_n) \tag{13}$$

where a_n and b_n are the Mie scattering coefficients, complex functions of λ, m and D.

3.3 How Specific Attenuation Scales with Drop Size

It is interesting to see how the ITU specific attenuation scales theoretically as drop size varies, whilst keeping rain rate constant. To do this, it is assumed the drops are all identically sized spheres of diameter D. Then the number of drops falling on a plane surface at a constant rain rate R scales proportional to D^{-3}. The specific attenuation depends on the spatial distribution of drops in the atmosphere, which is the number of drops per unit volume. This depends on the fall speed of drops. A common approximation to this is that the terminal velocity of drop is proportional to $D^{0.67}$ [27]. Thus the number of rain drops per unit volume scales as $D^{-3.67}$. Mie scattering theory says that the specific attenuation is proportional to the number of drops multiplied by the extinction cross section Q_t. At 20 GHz, Q_t can be approximated as proportional to D^4 [28]. Hence the specific attenuation at constant rain rate scales approximately as $D^{1/3}$, i.e. attenuation at constant R increases with drop size. This suggests that the attenuation predicted by the ITU-R model, which is of the form kR^α (for constants k and α), will be high for small drop sizes and low for large drop sizes.

4　Data and Procedures Used in the Study

4.1　Data Collection and Processing

Data from the Chilbolton Observatory (51.14° N, 1.44° W) were collected and analysed. This data is from a RD69 JWD impact disdrometer, and a co-located rain gauge's data from 2010 to 2013.

The JWD impact disdrometer, with a sampling cross-sectional area of 50 cm^2 measures the size of raindrops falling on its top Styrofoam® cup by converting the impact into electrical pulses, and the amplitude of the impulse is then used to determine the diameter of the drops. The measurements are sorted into 127 increasingly non-uniform groupings termed channels or bins depending on the amplitude of the impacting rainfall. Algorithms convert the recorded amplitude to drop diameters. This is accurate to ±5% [29].

The disdrometer and the rain gauge collects data at 10 s interval, but this study merges this into 1 min samples with the assumption that the underlying distribution does not change radically over the 1 min period considered. This study only considered rain events with rates greater than 0.1 mm/h.

The drop velocities for rain with diameter D_i, was taken to be [30]:

$$v_i = 9.65 - 10.3 \cdot \exp(-0.6 D_i) \tag{14}$$

The rain rate (in mm/h) at time instant t, (in seconds) was derived as:

$$R_t = \frac{3600 \cdot \sum V_i \cdot n_i(t)}{\Delta t \cdot A} \tag{15}$$

where V_i is the drop volume, n_i is the drop counts, Δt is the integration time and A is the disdrometers's cross section.

The parameters for the disdrometer at Chilbolton are as follows (Table 1):

Table 1.　Parameters for the disdrometer at Chilbolton Observatory for ITU-R P.838

Parameter	Value
Latitude	51.14°N
Longitude	357.74°E
Frequency	19.7 GHz
Elevation angle	29.9°
Tilt angle	13°
Height above sea level	84 m

Given the above, the a and b, as derived from the suggestions of ITU-R P.838-3 are 0.0907 and 1.0229 respectively.

4.2   Procedures

Six consecutive 10 s samples were merged. This was done to achieve a larger sample size, with the implicit assumption that the underlying distribution is approximately stationary over the one minute period under consideration. This is similar to the approaches adopted by Montopoli *et al.* [31], Townsend *et al.* [32] and Islam *et al.* [33].

Given the doubt about the reliability of the smaller drops measurements [1, 34, 35], especially in the JWD, this work considered only bins with drop diameters greater 0.6 mm. This consideration resulted in a sample of 93 super bins, with the boundaries determined by the ETH re-calibration given in McFarquhar and List [36].

Based on the rain rates computed from Eq. (16) and the k and α determined, the specific attenuation based on the ITU-R P. 838-3 recommendation was computed using the relationship $\gamma = a\,R^b$ (Eq. 9).

The method of Mätzler [37] was used to determine the extinction cross section, Q_t, from the Mie's coefficients at 19.7 GHz (the radio wave frequency), with the refractive index of water taken as $m = 6.867 + 2.630i$ [38].

For each 1 min sample above the rainfall threshold, (taken here to be 0.1 mm/h), the DSD was computed from the disdrometer's rain drop counts, and each was compared to a co-located rain gauge to ensure accuracy.

The lognormal and gamma (using the method of moments, MoM) were fitted to the 1 min spatial drop density data. Equally, the GMM, using the number of modes specified in Ekerete *et al.* [6] were fitted for the observed number of modes.

For each of these distributions (spatial drop densities, lognormal, gamma (MoM), and the GMMs based on the observed number of modes), the specific attenuation were computed for each one minute sample, showing how each drop diameter volume affects the signals. The results were compared with that derived from the ITU-recommended specific attenuation calculations.

5   Results and Interpretations

Based on the methodology described in 4.2 above, the rainfall DSD (shown in the upper panels of Figs. 1 and 2) were used to derive the specific attenuation for a 1-minute time slice. The specific attenuation was derived from the drop densities, shown as bars in the lower panel and the computed specific attenuation for 1st May, 2012 at 0037 and 0053 gave the following:

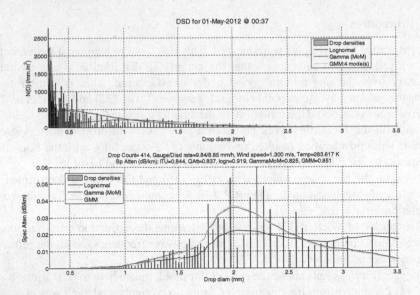

Fig. 1. DSD and specific attenuation, with corresponding meteorological readings for 1-May-2012/0037

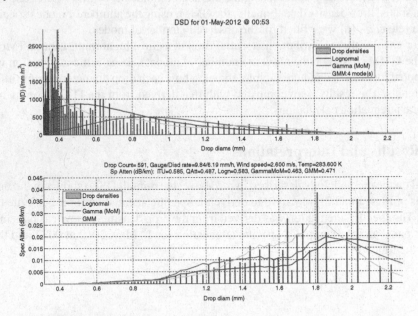

Fig. 2. DSD and specific attenuation, with corresponding meteorological readings for 1-May-2012/0053

Results show that the small-sized drops contribute little to the overall attenuation, as seen by the near flat curve in the graphs. The larger drops contribute more to the overall attenuation, even when the number of drops are small. This is shown clearly in Fig. 2, where attenuation is high (right side lower panel) even with very few drops.

Using the specific attenuation drawn from the drop densities, it can be seen (from Table 2) that specific attenuation computed from the GMM may be better than those derived from other statistical models. This may be explained from the fact that the GMM models the multimodality present in the data better than the other unimodal distributions.

Table 2. Summary of results for the specific attenuation

Date	01-May-2012	01-May-2012	
Time	00:37	00:53	
Drop count	414	591	
Disdrometer rain rate	8.85	6.19	mm/h
Rain gauge rain rate	9.84	9.84	mm/h
Specific attenuation			
ITU	0.844	0.585	dB/km
Drop density	0.837	0.487	dB/km
Lognormal	0.919	0.583	dB/km
Gamma (MoM)	0.825	0.663	dB/km
GMM	0.851	0.471	dB/km

6 Conclusions

This work has shown that the small drops in the DSD contribute little to the overall attenuation of signals as it passes through the earth-space path. It also demonstrated that larger drops, even in small numbers contribute greatly to the overall attenuation of signals. Results equally suggest that the Gaussian Mixture Model may sometimes model specific attenuation better than unimodal statistical models, as the GMM gives a better fit to multimodality encountered in rainfall DSD data.

While the data set used in this work is small, there is a need to investigate further the seasonal variation of the fit of the attenuation, as well as the variation of the specific attenuation in different rain regimes. The authors are working on realizing the above in the next phase of the research.

References

1. Kumar, L.S., Lee, Y.H., Ong, J.T.: Truncated gamma drop size distribution models for rain attenuation in Singapore. IEEE Trans. Antennas Propag. **58**(4), 1325–1335 (2010)
2. Thurai, M., Bringi, V.N., Shimomai, T.: 20 GHz Specific attenuation calculations using drop size distributions and drop shape measurements from 2D video disdrometer data in different rain climates. In: 6th International Conference on Information, Communications & Signal Processing. IEEE, Singapore (2007)
3. Åsen, W., Gibbins, C.J.: A comparison of rain attenuation and drop size distributions measured in Chilbolton and Singapore. Radio Sci. **37**(3), 6-1–6-15 (2002)

4. Ekerete, K.-M.E., Hunt, F.H., Otung, I.E., Jeffery, J.L.: Multimodality in the rainfall drop size distribution in southern England. In: Pillai, P., Hu, Y.F., Otung, I., Giambene, G. (eds.) WiSATS 2015. LNICSSITE, vol. 154, pp. 177–184. Springer, Heidelberg (2015). doi: 10.1007/978-3-319-25479-1_13

5. Ekerete, K.E., et al.: Experimental study and modelling of rain drop size distribution in southern England. In: IET Colloquium on Antennas, Wireless and Electromagnetics, London (2014)

6. Ekerete, K.E., et al.: Variation of multimodality in rainfall drop size distribution with wind speeds and rain rates. J. Eng. (2016)

7. Ekerete, K.E., et al.: Modeling rainfall drop size distribution in southern England using a Gaussian Mixture Model. Radio Sci. (2015)

8. Marshall, J.S., Palmer, W.M.K.: The distribution of raindrops with size. J. Meteorol. 5(4), 165–166 (1948)

9. Levin, L.M.: The distribution function of cloud and rain drops by sizes. Dokl. Akad. Nauk SSSR 94(6), 1045–1048 (1954)

10. Markowitz, A.H.: Raindrop size distribution expressions. J. Appl. Meteorol. 15(9), 1029–1031 (1976)

11. Feingold, G., Levin, Z.: The lognormal fit to raindrop spectra from frontal convective clouds in Israel. J. Appl. Meteorol. 25(10), 1346–1363 (1986)

12. Owolawi, P.: Raindrop size distribution model for the prediction of rain attenuation in Durban. PIERS Online 7(6), 516–523 (2011)

13. Ulbrich, C.W., Atlas, D.: Assessment of the contribution of differential polarization to improved rainfall measurements. Radio Sci. 19(1), 49–57 (1984)

14. Adimula, I.A., Ajayi, G.O.: Variations in raindrop size distribution and specific attenuation due to rain in Nigeria. Ann. Telecommun. 51(1–2), 87–93 (1996)

15. Maitra, A., Chakravarty, K.: Raindrop size distribution measurements and associated rain parameters at a tropical location in the Indian region (2005)

16. Ajayi, G.O., Olsen, R.L.: Modeling of a tropical raindrop size distribution for microwave and millimetre wave applications. Radio Sci. 20(2), 193–202 (1985)

17. Maciel, L.R., Assis, M.S.: Tropical rainfall drop-size distribution. Int. J. Satell. Commun. 8, 181–186 (1990)

18. McFarquhar, G.M.: Raindrop size distribution and evolution. In: Rainfall: State of the Science, Geophysical Monograph Series, vol. 191, pp. 49–60 (2010)

19. Radhakrishna, B., Rao, T.N.: Multipeak raindrop size distribution observed by UHF/VHF wind profilers during the passage of a mesoscale convective system. Mon. Weather Rev. 137(3), 976–990 (2009)

20. Sauvageot, H., Koffi, M.: Multimodal raindrop size distribution. J. Atmos. Sci. 57, 2480–2492 (2000)

21. Olsen, R.L., Rogers, D.V., Hodge, D.B.: The aRb relation in the calculation of rain attenuation. IEEE Trans. Antennas Propag. AP-26(2), 318–329 (1978)

22. Mie, G.: Beiträge zur Optik trüber Medien, speziell kolloidaler Metallösungen. Ann. Phys. 330, 377–445 (1908)

23. Ippolito, L.J.: Satellite Communications Systems Engineering: Atmospheric Effects, Satellite Link Design and System Performance. Wiley, Washington, DC (2008)

24. ITU-R: R-REC-P.838-3 - Specific attenuation model for rain for use in prediction methods (2005)

25. Mishchenko, M.I., et al.: On definition and measurement of extinction cross section. J. Quant. Spectrosc. Radiat. Transfer 110, 323–327 (2009)

26. van de Hulst, H.C.: Light Scattering by Small Particles. Wiley, New York (1957)

27. Ulbrich, C.W.: Natural variations in the analytical form of the raindrop size distribution. J. Clim. Appl. Meteorol. **22**, 1764–1775 (1983)
28. Odedina, M.O., Afullo, T.J.: Determination of rain attenuation from electromagnetic scattering by spherical raindrops: theory and experiment. Radio Sci. **45**(1) (2010)
29. Distromet: Disdrometer RD-80, D. Ltd, Editor, Switzerland (2002)
30. Atas, D., Srivastava, R.C., Sekhon, R.S.: Doppler radar characteristics of precipitation at vertical incidence. Rev. Geophys. Space Phys. **11**, 1–35 (1973)
31. Montopoli, M., et al., Statistical characterization and modeling of raindrop spectra time series for different climatological regions. IEEE Trans. Geosci. Remote Sens. **46**(10) (2008)
32. Townsend, A.J., Watson, R.J.: The linear relationship between attenuation and average rainfall rate for terrestrial links. IEEE Trans. Antennas Propag. **59**(3), 994–1002 (2011)
33. Islam, T., et al.: Characteristics of raindrop spectra as normalized gamma distribution from a Joss-Waldvogel disdrometer. Atmos. Res. **108**, 57–73 (2012)
34. Thurai, M., et al.: Towards completing the rain drop size distribution spectrum: a case study involving 2D video disdrometer, droplet spectrometer, and polarimetic radar measurements in Greely, Colorado. In: AMS Conference on Radar Meteorology, Norman, Oklahoma, USA (2015)
35. Tokay, A., Kruger, A., Krajewski, W.F.: Comparison of drop size distribution measurements by impact and optical disdrometers. J. Appl. Meteorol. **40**, 2083–2097 (2001)
36. McFarquhar, G.M., List, R.: The effect of curve fits for the disdrometer calibration on raindrop spectra, rainfall rate, and radar reflectivity. J. Appl. Meteorol. **32**, 774–782 (1993)
37. Mätzler, C.: MATLAB Functions for Mie Scattering and Absorption. Institut für Angewandte Physik (2002)
38. Segelstein, D.: The Complex Refractive Index of Water, University of Missouri, Kansas City, USA (1981)

Cognitive Interference Management Techniques for the Spectral Co-existence of GSO and NGSO Satellites

Ameneh Pourmoghadas[✉], Shree Krishna Sharma,
Symeon Chatzinotas, and Björn Ottersten

SnT - Securityandtrust.lu, University of Luxembourg,
Luxembourg, Luxembourg
ameneh.pourmoghaddaslangroudi@uni.lu

Abstract. One of the main challenges in the co-existence of geostationary satellite orbit (GSO) and non-geostationary satellite orbit (NGSO) satellite networks is to mitigate the in-line interference caused by an NGSO satellite to the GSO earth terminal, while the NGSO satellite is crossing the GSO satellite's illumination zone. The method recommended in ITU-R S.1325-3 involves utilizing a range-based power control on the NGSO satellite for downlink communication to the NGSO earth terminals. In this paper, we investigate a cognitive range-based power control algorithm while taking into account the imposed interference level to the GSO fixed satellite service (FSS) system. Results show that the proposed cognitive power control algorithm can mitigate the harmful in-line interference on the GSO terminal receiver, while also providing the desired link quality for the NGSO system. More importantly, we formulate and solve an optimization problem with the objective of minimizing the inter-site distance (ISD) of the GSO-NGSO earth user-terminals. Finally, we develop an analytical method to calculate the ISD between GSO and NGSO earth terminals and validate this with the help of simulation results.

1 Introduction

Satellites communications today provide many possibilities and opportunities to achieve better quality of service and extend backhaul services to anywhere and any-time [1]. However, fixed satellite service (FSS) involves deployment of a large number of user terminals on the earth. Further study on uncoordinated techniques for satellite systems is required to mitigate the interference caused by an adjacent satellite network to FSS systems. In general, the main contribution of the networking solutions for satellite networks are involved in techniques for satellite energy saving [2], efficient resource allocation [3], and FSS system interference mitigation [1,4]. Studies on efficient usage of satellite resources and their co-existence with either terrestrial systems or other satellite networks exist in the literature [5,6]. The co-existence of satellite systems with either other satellite systems or terrestrial networks can be achieved by employing suitable resource

© ICST Institute for Computer Sciences, Social Informatics and Telecommunications Engineering 2017
I. Otung et al. (Eds.): WiSATS 2016, LNICST 186, pp. 178–190, 2017.
DOI: 10.1007/978-3-319-53850-1_18

allocation and interference mitigation techniques [7,8]. Apart from the requirement of finding intelligent (or cognitive) resource allocation, it is important to ensure that the co-existence of multi-satellite systems does not cause interference to other co-channel systems such as FSS systems, mobile satellite services (MSS), or terrestrial systems. In particular, the interference mitigation is more complicated considering a practical dual satellite system (DSS) scenario, in which two satellites (e.g., GSO-NGSO satellites) operate over the same coverage area while sharing the spectrum bands [9]. In the co-existence scenarios of GSO-NGSO networks, *in-line* interference arises whenever an NGSO satellite passes through a line of sight path between an earth station and a GSO satellite [10]. It occurs due to the fact that an NGSO satellite may create/receive interference through its sidelobe or mainlobe to the GSO system (please see Fig. 1). To understand this scenario better, we can consider the co-existence of O3b satellites within $\pm 5°$ latitude from the equator and GSO Eutelsat KA-SAT satellite [longitude: 9.0°, inclination: 0.01°]. The O3b satellite which uses the medium earth orbit (MEO) constellation and shares the frequency 18.8–19.3 GHz in downlink communication with the GSO system, has a high potential to cause interference to the GSO FSS system. In this context, one of the key challenges that has been identified in ITU Radio Regulations and European Space Agency is the need to explore efficient techniques to mitigate the in-line interference for the spectral co-existence of GSO-NGSO satellite networks.

1.1   Related Literature

Various studies have been conducted to address challenges in interference mitigation in the literature and ITU-R reports [5–10]. Concerning the uncoordinated (cognitive) techniques some of these approaches are: satellite selection strategies with the largest angular discrimination [11]; spot turnoff method [12,13]; and power control technique [10]. In the last technique, a cognitive transmission power algorithm is used to provide the required signal to noise ratio (SNR) at the receiver and maintain the interference level at the victim receiver. Most of the studies on dynamic transmission power controls on satellite stations involves on-board energy saving, without attention to investigations on controlling the imposed interferences on the victim receiver [17,18]. Besides, majority of the research works in the literature have been carried out for individual satellite systems. Wherein, the integration between different satellite constellations plays a key role in moving towards the next generation of the satellite networks. A more related work to the objective of current paper can be found in [10,19].

Authors in [19] find the minimum separation distance between terrestrial base station (BS) and FSS earth station by considering the interference caused from terrestrial BS to the FSS earth station. In [10] a cognitive transmission power algorithm is used to provide the required signal to noise ratio (SNR) at the receiver and maintain the interference level at the victim receiver. Nevertheless, the impact of the inter-site distance (ISD) between GSO-NGSO earth terminals on the interference level of the victim GSO earth receiver is not studied.

1.2   Motivation and Contributions

According to the ITU-R S.1325-3 recommendation, adaptive power control on range in the downlink is one of the useful interference mitigation techniques in facilitating spectrum sharing between GSO and NGSO networks. This technique is left for further investigation in ITU-R S.1325-3. Besides, studies on earth terminal deployment strategies (such as inter-site distance among terminals) is one of the possible approaches for the efficient use of limited spectrum bands and network's capacity improvement [19]. In this context, the main contributions of this paper are as follows: (1) We utilize the cognitive power control in [10] based on the range (distance between NGSO satellite and NGSO earth terminal) in the co-existence scenario of GSO and NGSO FSS systems. (2) We analyse the feasibility of the cognitive range-based power control method in terms of GSO-NGSO geometry. (3) More importantly, we develop a theoretical model for minimum possible between the GSO and NGSO FSS earth terminals through analysis. (4) We present the improvements on the minimum ISD between FSS earth terminals using the proposed model, in which the NGSO satellite does not utilize any dynamic power control method on-board.

The rest of the paper is as follows: Sect. 2 provides the system model and the in-line interference scenario. The cognitive range-based power control is defined in Sect. 3. We propose a method to determine the minimum ISD between FSS earth terminals in Sect. 4. Section 5 provides the analysis and simulation results. Finally, we draw the conclusion in Sect. 6.

2   System Model and Interference Scenario

In accordance with the co-existence of GSO-NGSO FSS systems while sharing spectrum on downlink[1] and uplink, the following in-line interference scenarios are probable to occur [10]: (1) Interference from the NGSO satellite to the GSO earth terminal in the downlink. (2) Interference from the GSO earth terminal to the NGSO satellite in the uplink. (3) Interference from the GSO satellite to the NGSO earth terminal in the downlink. (4) Interference from the NGSO earth terminal to the GSO satellite in the uplink. In this paper, we consider the GEO and MEO constellations, where an O3b satellite in MEO orbit is chosen as the use case scenario causing harmful in-line interference to the GSO earth terminal. Earth terminals are the user terminals operating in Ka-band in the FSS system such as VSAT. Reports in ITU-R S.1325-3 indicate that the number of interference events from NGSO satellite on GSO earth terminals observed more in downlink communication. Therefore, in this work, we focus on the downlink in-line interference from NGSO satellite to the GSO earth terminal (item (1) from the above listed bullets, please see Fig. 1), and we leave the rest of the scenarios for future work. Throughout this paper, we have assumed that the transmitters of the NGSO satellite communicate with their wanted receivers

---

[1] Throughout this article, the interference in downlink refers to the user-link interference.

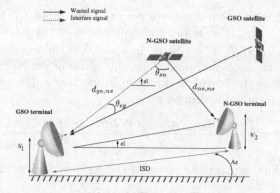

Fig. 1. The interference scenario between GSO and NGSO FSS systems.

(NGSO earth terminal) along the boresight direction (i.e., off-axis angle = 0°); which means that the antenna gain of the NGSO satellite and the NGSO earth terminal remains fixed in the downlink communication. In our system model, we have assumed free space loss (FSL) on the direct or interference channels, and fading phenomena such as diffraction or tropospheric propagation effects etc., are not taken into account.

3 Cognitive and Range-Based Power Control Algorithms

According to the ITU-R S.1325-3 recommendation, NGSO satellite can decrease or increase the transmission power based on the range, while providing the desired SNR level to the NGSO earth terminal. This is known as a range-based power control method. To enhance this method, we propose a cognitive range-based power control algorithm at the NGSO satellite. In the proposed algorithm, the NGSO satellite will decrease or increase its transmission power while its distance to the NGSO earth terminal is getting shorter or longer accordingly. We have considered two threshold values for optimizing the transmission power of the NGSO satellite. The minimum SNR level at the wanted receiver, SNR_{min}, and the tolerable interference threshold at the victim receiver, I_{th}. We define two power control methods in the following subsections. In the rest of this work, the following subscripts are used: e for the earth system, s for the satellite, n for the NGSO system, and g for the GSO system.

3.1 Range-Based Power Control Method

To compute the transmission power on the NGSO satellite as a function of range, $d_{ne,ns}$ (see Fig. 1), we first need to find the SNR level at the NGSO earth terminal. Using the FSL model, the received power at the NGSO earth terminal from the NGSO satellite can be computed as:

$$Prx_{ne} = Ptx_{ns}(d_{ne,ns})Gtx_{ns}(0)Grx_{ne}(0)FSL(\lambda, d_{ne,ns}), \qquad (1)$$

where Prx_{ne} [W] is the desired receive power at the input to the NGSO earth terminal antenna, Ptx_{ns} [W] is the transmit power of the NGSO satellite station, and function $FSL(\lambda, d) = \left(\frac{\lambda}{4\pi d}\right)^2$, in which λ is the wavelength. $Gtx_{ns}(0)$, $Grx_{ne}(0)$ are the transmit and receive antenna gains of the NGSO satellite and earth terminal along the boresight direction, respectively. The received SNR at the NGSO earth terminal is defined as:

$$SNR = \frac{Ptx_{ns}(d_{ne,ns})Gtx_{ns}(0)Grx_{ne}(0)}{N} \left(\frac{\lambda}{4\pi d_{ne,ns}}\right)^2, \tag{2}$$

where N [W] is the thermal noise power at the receiver and can be expressed as:

$$N = k \times T_{ne} \times BW, \tag{3}$$

where k is the Boltzmann's constant (1.38×10^{-23} [J/K]), and T_{ne} [K] is the noise temperature at the NGSO earth terminal, and BW [Hz] is the receiver bandwidth. In order to guarantee SNR_{min} at the NGSO earth terminal the transmit power on the NGSO satellite as a function of range can be computed as follows.

$$Ptx_{ns}(d_{ne,ns}) = \frac{SNR_{min} \times N}{Grx_{ne}(0) \times Gtx_{ns}(0)} \left(\frac{4\pi d_{ne,ns}}{\lambda}\right)^2. \tag{4}$$

3.2 Cognitive Range-Based Power Control Method

The range-based power control technique in Eq. (4) satisfies the required SNR_{min} at the NGSO earth terminal receiver to close the link. To apply the range-based power control in the considered coexistence scenario, we re-write this technique by taking into account the interference threshold level (I_{th}) of the GSO earth terminal as following optimization problem[2].

$$\begin{aligned}
&\text{minimize} \quad Ptx(d_{ne,ns}) \\
&\text{C.1.} \qquad\quad SNR \geq SNR_{min} \\
&\text{C.2.} \qquad\quad I \leq I_{th} \\
&\text{C.3.} \qquad\quad Ptx(d_{ne,ns}) \leq Ptx_{max},
\end{aligned} \tag{5}$$

where Ptx_{max} is the available maximum transmission power on NGSO satellite board. In Eq. (5), conditions $C.1$ is to take care of the NGSO FSS QoS requirement, $C.2$ is to avoid harmful interference on the GSO earth terminal, and $C.3$ is to make sure the range-based transmission power allocation does not exceed Ptx_{max}. I is the interference ratio with respect to the wanted signal SNR at the GSO earth terminal as follows.

$$I = \frac{Ptx(d_{ne,ns})Gtx_{ns}(\theta_{ns})Grx_{ge}(\theta_{ge})}{FSL(\lambda, d_{ge,ns})}, \tag{6}$$

---

[2] In this technique we have assumed that I_{th} level at the victim GSO earth termianl is known in public domain.

where $Ptx(d_{ne,ns})$ [W] is the available transmit power at the NGSO satellite computed in Eq. (4), $d_{ge,ns}$ [m] is the distance between the GSO earth terminal and NGSO satellite, and $Gtx_{ns}(\theta_{ns})$, $Grx_{ge}(\theta_{ge})$ are the transmit and receive antenna gains at the off-axis angles of the NGSO satellite and GSO earth terminal respectively. The values of the parameters are given in the Table 1. Depending, on the geometry of the considered earth stations and satellites, it is obvious that the optimization problem in Eq. (5) may not be feasible when NGSO satellite is closer to the GSO earth station and far from the NGSO earth station. In this case, although the NGSO satellite can use the maximum power for its transmission to close the link with the NGSO earth station receiver, it may not satisfy the interference threshold level at the GSO earth station. Therefore, it is better to handover the transmission to the next NGSO satellite that has better link conditions. This challenge motivates us to find the possible minimum ISD between the GSO-NGSO earth terminals such that the threshold constraints (in Eq. (5)) are satisfied.

In following, we first discuss the geometry determination of ISD between earth stations; then we follow the optimization problem for computing the minimum distance, ISD_{min}, between GSO and NGSO earth terminals.

4   Proposed ISD Determination Method

In this section, we develop an analytical method for finding the minimum ISD between the GSO and NGSO earth terminals by formulating an optimization problem. Our optimization problem will take into account the interference level from NGSO satellite to the GSO earth terminal in downlink communication. We have assumed that the position of GSO earth terminal is fixed, and we can only control the repositioning of the NGSO earth terminal. In this analysis it is assumed that satellite communication system operators have complete freedom in determining the geographical location of ground stations. First, let's find a relation between the ISD and the wanted range between NGSO satellite and

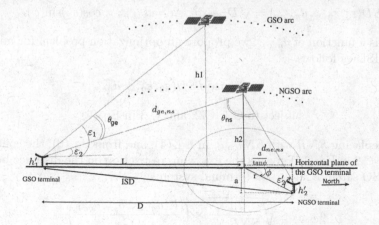

Fig. 2. Geometry of GSO and NGSO FSS systems with respect to the ISD.

earth terminal, $d_{ne,ns}$ (please see Fig. 2). Having the altitude, longitude and latitude of each earth terminal and satellite we can compute distance between any earth terminal to any given satellite $(d_{*e,*s})$, as follows.

$$d_{*e,*s} = r_{sat}\sqrt{1 + \left(\frac{R_E^2}{r_{sat}}\right)^2 - 2\left(\frac{R_E^2}{r_{sat}}\right)\cos\omega\cos\Gamma}, \tag{7}$$

where r_{sat} is the satellite radius, R_E is the earth radius, ω is the difference in longitude, in degrees, between the earth station and the satellite, and Γ is the earth station latitude in degrees. Let's denote local heights of the GSO and NGSO earth terminals as h_1' and h_2' respectively. Then, we have:

$$L = \frac{h_2}{\tan(\varepsilon_2)}, \ h_2 = d_{ne,ns} \times \sin(\varepsilon_2') + H, \ H = |h_1' - h_2'|, \tag{8}$$

where L is the horizontal distance of the NGSO satellite from the GSO earth terminal, h_1 and h_2 are the altitudes of the GSO and NGSO satellites from the horizontal plane of the GSO terminal. ε_2 is the elevation angle of the NGSO satellite from the GSO earth terminal, and, ε_2' is the elevation angle of the NGSO satellite from the NGSO earth terminal. From Eq. (8), we can compute L as:

$$L = \frac{d_{ne,ns} \times \sin(\varepsilon_2') + H}{\tan(\varepsilon_2)}. \tag{9}$$

Since L is known, we can compute the horizontal distance between NGSO and GSO earth terminals, D, as follows.

$$D = \frac{d_{ne,ns} + \sin(\varepsilon_2') + H}{\tan(\varepsilon_2)} + d_{ne,ns} \times \cos(\phi)\cos(\varepsilon_2'). \tag{10}$$

where ϕ is the azimuth angle of the NGSO earth terminal from the GSO earth horizon in degrees. ISD can be computed as

$$ISD(\varepsilon_2, \varepsilon_2', \phi, d_{ne,ns}) = \sqrt{D^2 + a^2}; \quad a = d_{ne,ns} \times \cos(\varepsilon_2')\sin(\phi). \tag{11}$$

As ISD is a function of $d_{ne,ns}$, we propose an optimization problem for minimizing the ISD as follows.

$$\operatorname*{minimize}_{d_{ne,ns}} ISD(\varepsilon_2, \varepsilon_2', \phi, d_{ne,ns}) \tag{12}$$

subject to C.1, C.2, and C.3 in Eq. (5)

By replacing SNR with SNR_{min} in Eq. (4), and from Eq. (6), the conditions $C.1$ and $C.2$ in Eq. (12) give us the following restriction on the distance between the NGSO satellite and earth terminal systems.

$$d_{ne,ns} \le \sqrt{\frac{I_{th}}{SNR_{min}}} \times \left(\frac{F(d_{ge,ns}, \theta_{sn}, \theta_{ge})}{C}\right). \tag{13}$$

Table 1. System parameters

Parameter	Value
Downlink frequency channel	18.8 GHz
BW	125 MHz
$Grx_{en}(\theta)$, $Grx_{eg}(\theta)$	ITU-R S.1428
$Gtx_{sn}(\theta)$, $Gtx_{sg}(\theta)$	ITU-R S.1528, ITU-R S.672-4
h'_1, h'_2	7 m, 12 m
GSO earth antenna diameter	0.9 m
NGSO earth antenna diameter	1.2 m
NGSO satellite antenna diameter	0.361 m
T_{ne}, T_{ge}	275 K
GSO (Eutelsat) satellite [lat, lon, alt]	$[0°S \pm 0.1°, 9°E \pm 0.1°, 35,794$ km]
NGSO (O3b) satellite [lat, lon, alt]	$[1.55°S, 31.1°E, 8,062$ km]
GSO terminal [lat, lon]	$[7.79°S, 24.25°E]$
NGSO satellite EIRP in the direction of the NGSO receiver earth station	10 dBW
I_{th}	−10 dB
SNR_{min}	10 dB, 15 dB

By assuming the off-axis angles (θ_{sn}, θ_{ge}), and $d_{ge,ns}$ are not changing, F can be considered as a constant term. The constant term C contains antenna gains of NGSO systems on boresight angle ($\theta = 0$). Therefore, by substituting $d_{ne,ns}$ from Eqs. (13) into (11), the minimum value for ISD can be computed.

In next section, we provide results for the cognitive and range-based mechanisms in the co-existence of GSO-NGSO FSS systems. Besides, we provide the results in terms of the link (SNR) outage probability for the NGSO link. We also compare the results for ISD_{min}, using the analytical model in Eq. (11), and the simulation results.

5   Numerical and Simulation Results

In this section, first, we compare results of the range-based power control with the cognitive range-based power control method. Then, we explain a Monte Carlo technique, which is conducted for computing the ISD_{min} in our simulation, and we compare this result with the analytical model provided in Sect. 4. We have assumed that the traffic statistics do not vary with geographic location or service type. Throughout our numerical results, it is assumed that the NGSO earth terminal is in association with the constellation, and tracks the corresponding NGSO space station once a communication link is established. We increased the range, $d_{ne,ns}$, by moving the NGSO satellite on its longitude. The range between NGSO satellite and earth systems is in associate with the elevation

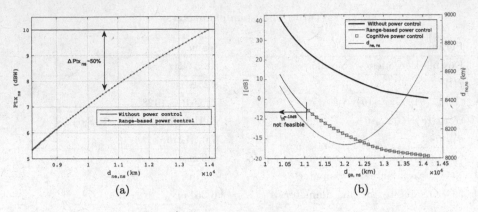

(a)   (b)

Fig. 3. (a) Comparison of the power transmission on the NGSO satellite, (b) Interference level comparison at GSO earth terminal; $SNR_{min} = 15\,\text{dB}$, $I_{th} = -10\,\text{dB}$, $EIRP = 10\,\text{dBW}$.

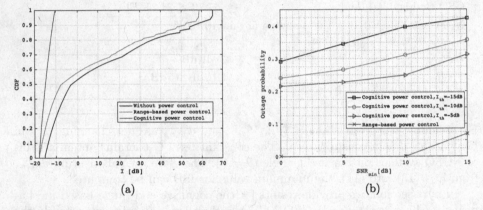

(a)   (b)

Fig. 4. (a) CDF of interference for GSO earth terminal, $SNR_{min} = 10\,\text{dB}$, (b) Probability of outage in SNR for NGSO earth terminal from single NGSO satellite, $EIRP = 10\,\text{dBW}$.

angle on the NGSO earth terminal, ε_2'. Once the elevation angle of the NGSO earth terminal is lower than the minimum elevation angle, the NGSO earth terminal communicates with the next available NGSO satellite with highest elevation angle (90°). The minimum elevation angle is considered to be 5° for NGSO earth terminal. Figure 3(a) shows the transmission power of the NGSO satellite operating with the range-based algorithm, in comparison with the NGSO satellite that does not utilize any power control mechanism. As it is depicted in Fig. 3(a), the NGSO satellite without any dynamic power control, operates with the maximum transmission power constantly[3]. Wherein, with the range-based

---

[3] Note that in our numerical calculation, we have used the effective isotropically radiated power (EIRP) of the NGSO satellite, which is calculated as $EIRP\,[\text{dBW}] = 10 \times (\log_{10} Ptx_{max}[\text{W}] + \log_{10} Gtx_{sn}(0))$.

power control, the transmission power of the NGSO satellite gradually increases with respect to the distance range, $d_{ne,ns}$. To evaluate the effect of the cognitive range-based power control on the interference level of the GSO earth terminal, please see Fig. 3(b). As it comes from the Fig. 3(b), interference level decreases when the range between NGSO satellite station and GSO earth terminal, $d_{ge,ns}$, increases. However, the range-based power control has no limit on the interference level of the GSO earth terminal, and it can reach above the I_{th} with smaller $d_{ge,ns}$. Whereas, with the cognitive range-based power control, the GSO doesn't receive harmful in-line interference above the threshold level. As it is depicted in Fig. 3(b), Eq. (5) has no-feasible solution when the NGSO satellite is getting closer to the GSO earth terminal and getting far from the NGSO earth terminal. Cumulative distribution function (CDF) of the interference level at the GSO earth terminal with respect to the same distances in Fig. 3(b), is shown in Fig. 4(a). To evaluate the effect of the no-feasible solution results on the SNR level of the NGSO earth terminal, please see Fig. 4(b). Using simulation results we have compared the probability of outage in SNR for NGSO earth terminal in this figure. The probability of outage in SNR is calculated as the ratio of the total number of no-feasible solutions and the number of the NGSO satellite movement in the arc between $[5° \leq \epsilon'_2 \leq 90°]$. As it comes from the Fig. 4(b), the outage probability on NGSO earth terminal increases for smaller I_{th} requirements, whereas, in the range-based power control method the outage probability does not vary with I_{th}.

5.1   Monte Carlo Method for Choosing ISD_{min} Between Earth Terminals and Their Associated GSO-NGSO Satellite Coverage

In this method, for N number of times, we simulate a GSO earth terminal location randomly distributed with an associated GSO satellite, which is at a fixed location. The GSO earth terminal locations are computed by choosing a random latitude from $-45°$ to $45°$ and a random longitude within $0°$ to $45°$, which is the coverage of the earth from an O3b satellite, that can be interfered with the GSO satellite coverage. The longitude of the GSO earth terminal is chosen by a uniform probability distribution within $[0°, 45°]$. Whereas, to take care of the spherical shape of the earth, the latitude distribution of the GSO earth terminal is chosen from following function

$$F(x, 45°) = (180/\pi) \arcsin(\sin(45 \times \pi/180)(2x - 1)), \qquad (14)$$

where x is an uniformly distributed variable between $[0, 1]$. Once the GSO earth terminal location is chosen, it is tested to see if the elevation angle, ε_1, is within the minimum operating elevation angle of the GSO network or not. The minimum elevation angle at the GSO earth terminal location should be greater than or equal to $10°$ (ITU-R S.1325-3). If not, this location is not included as one of the locations simulated. To find the minimum distance between the GSO and NGSO earth terminals, we locate the associated NGSO satellite in random longitudes such that it has minimum elevation angle to the NGSO earth terminal.

The minimum elevation angle defines the worst case scenario, where $d_{ne,ns}$ is at the maximum distance. Once the GSO earth terminal location is selected, then, with respect to azimuth angle of the GSO terminal, $0° \leq \phi \leq 360°$, NGSO earth terminal will be localized. For each azimuth angle, the ISD_{min} will be found such that its elevation angle with the associated NGSO satellite is $5°$, and the optimization problem in Eq. (12) is satisfied. We have assumed that the computed ISD_{min} in this worst case scenario, in which $\varepsilon'_2 = 5°$, is always greater than the minimum required distance between the two earth terminals. We have compared the result of this simulation with the results of the analysis formula for ISD, using Eqs. (11) and (13) in Fig. 5. This result is compared with when the NGSO satellite operates with the maximum transmission power in Fig. 5. As it comes from this figure, the cognitive range-based power control method can significantly reduce the ISD_{min} between FSS earth terminals.

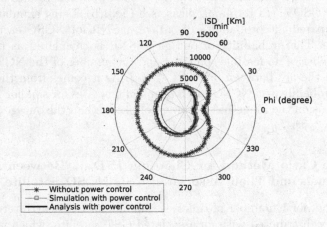

Fig. 5. ISD_{min} between GSO and NGSO earth terminals.

6   Conclusions

In this work, we proposed to employ a cognitive range-based power control mechanism for an NGSO satellite operating in the downlink mode. We have examined the proposed power control method with the range-based power control mechanism suggested by ITU-R S.1325-3. The results verify that the cognitive power control method avoids the harmful in-line interference on the victim receiver. We note that although finding the distance from the satellite to an adjacent earth terminal is not practically possible, still our optimization problem can benefit the victim receiver by maintaining I_{th} as a constant all the time. This threshold value lessens the imposed harmful interference on the adjacent earth terminals. We also proposed an optimization problem for finding the minimum inter-side distance between the FSS earth stations. The proposed ISD optimization technique can play a critical role in optimizing the network planing strategies.

Acknowledgement. This work was supported by the National Research Fund, Luxembourg under the project "HSBNet".

References

1. Evans, B., Werner, M., Lutz, E., Bousquet, M., Corazza, G.E., Maral, G.: Integration of satellite and terrestrial systems in future multimedia communications. IEEE Wirel. Commun. **12**(5), 72–80 (2005)
2. Mohammed, H., Jakllari, G., Paillassa, B.: Network pruning for extending satellite service life in LEO satellite constellations. Wirel. Netw. 1–13 (2015)
3. Kolodzy, P.: Interference avoidance spectrum policy task force. Technical report, Federal Commun 02–135 (2002)
4. Laurent, C., Alamaac, A., Bousquet, M.: Interference and fade mitigation techniques for Ka and Q/V band satellite communication systems. In: Proceedings of the 2nd International Workshop of COST Action, vol. 280 (2008)
5. Dae-Sub, O., Ku, B.J., Kim, S.: Compatibility study on terrestrial radio system operated in the coverage of multi-beam satellite system. In: 17th Asia-Pacific Conference on Communications (APCC). IEEE (2011)
6. Koletta, M., Milas, V.: Determination of the coordination area for mobile earth stations operating with geostationary space stations in the frequency band shared with the terrestrial services. In: IEEE VTC, pp. 2707–2710 (2005)
7. Chatzinotas, S., Ottersten, B., De Gaudenzi, R.: Cooperative and Cognitive Satellite Systems. Academic Press, New York (2015)
8. Sharma, S.K., et al.: Satellite cognitive communications: interference modelling and techniques selection. In: ASMS Conference and 12th SPSC Workshopp, pp. 111–118 (2012)
9. Chatzinotas, S., Sharma, S.K., Ottersten, B.: Frequency packing for interference alignment-based cognitive dual satellite systems. In: Vehicular Technology Conference (VTC Fall), pp. 1–7. IEEE (2013)
10. Sharma, S.K., Chatzinotas, S., Ottersten, B.: In-line interference mitigation techniques for spectral coexistence of GEO and NGEO satellites. Int. J. Satell. Commun. Netw. **34**(1), 11–39 (2016)
11. Wang, A.W.: Method and apparatus for providing wideband services using medium and low earth orbit satellites. US Patent No. 7,627,284 (2009)
12. Vatalaro, F., Corazza, G., Caini, C., Ferrarelli, C.: Analysis of LEO, MEO, and GEO global mobile satellite systems in the presence of interference and fading. IEEE J. Sel. Areas Commun. **13**(2), 291–300 (1995)
13. Reed, A., Posen, M.: Interference in the fixed satellite service bands between the feeder-links of networks using nongeostationary satellites and network using geostationary satellites. In: 3rd European Conference on Satellite Communications (ECSC-3), Manchester, pp. 251–256 (1993)
14. Sharma, S.K., Chatzinotas, S., Ottersten, B.: Transmit beamforming for spectral coexistence of satellite and terrestrial networks. In: 8th International Conference on CROWNCOM, pp. 275–281 (2013)
15. Lei, S., Sung, K.W., Zander, J.: Controlling aggregate interference under adjacent channel interference constraint in TV white space. In: 7th International Conference on CROWNCOM, pp. 1–6. IEEE (2012)
16. Farrokhi, R., Liu, K.J., Tassiulas, L.: Transmit beamforming and power control for cellular wireless systems. IEEE J. Sel. Areas Commun. **16**(8), 1437–1450 (1998)

17. Alvin, F., Eytan, M., Tsitsiklis, J.N.: Optimal energy allocation and admission control for communications satellites. ACM Trans. Netw. **11**(3), 488–500 (2003). IEEE
18. Ganho, F., et al.: Energy-efficient QOS provisioning in demand assigned satellite NDMA schemes. In: 21st International Conference on ICCCN, pp. 1–8. IEEE (2012)
19. Dae-Sub, O., et al.: A study on the separation distance for frequency sharing between GSO network and terrestrial network in Ka band. In: Vehicular Technology Conference, VTC Spring, pp. 2967–2971. IEEE (2008)

Technical Session 4

Technical Session 4

A 15.5 W Si-LDMOS Balanced Power Amplifier with 53% Ultimate PAE for High Speed LTE

B.A. Mohammed, N.A. Abduljabbar, M.A.G. Al-Sadoon, K. Hameed, A.S. Hussaini,
S.M.R. Jones, F. Elmegri, R.W. Clark, and R. Abd-Alhameed[(✉)]

School of Engineering, Design and Technology, University of Bradford, Bradford, UK
{mbabuba1,r.a.a.abd,nabeel}@bradford.ac.uk, ash@av.it.pt

Abstract. In this paper, a 15.5 W Si-LDMOS balanced power amplifier (PA) technique operating in the 2.620–2.690 GHz frequency band for LTE systems is presented. The amplifier was designed using large signal Si-LDMOS models, which demonstrated saturation P1dB of 41 dBm and 53% PAE. The AM-AM and AM-PM measured data of the balanced amplifier is extracted and embedded in the device under test (DUT) based on IEEE 802.16 OFDM WLAN Transceiver system. A simple linear model was design for behavioral modelling of memoryless baseband digital pre-distorter. The nonlinearity of the balanced amplifier has been compensated using the Simulink version R2011a.

Keywords: Balanced power amplifier (BPA) · Linearity · Power added efficiency (PAE) · Long term evolution (LTE) · Digital pre-distortion (DPD)

1 Introduction

A number of modern wireless communication systems, adopt highly-efficient modulation schemes to enhance spectral efficiency and increase multiple spectral user channels for a wide range of data and voice services. These include orthogonal frequency division multiplexing (OFDM) transceiver systems, such as long term evolution (LTE), wideband code division multiple access (WCDMA), IEEE 802.16 OFDM WLAN transceiver system and numerous IEEE wireless communication systems [1, 2]. These systems are highly sensitive to nonlinear distortion effects in the transmission path, due to their non-constant envelope. Such systems produce high peak-to-average-power-ratio (PAPR). Subsequently, the source of the nonlinear distortion effects in the transceiver configuration is the RF power amplifier; this research focuses on the design and modelling of a high energy-efficient power amplifier with high linearity [1–3].

The RF power amplifier is an important device not only in wireless communication systems, but also in TV transmission, radar systems and RF heating. The amplitude of radio frequency signal is increase to a certain level of amplification [4, 5]. Spectral efficiency and linearity are the main elements driving the design of power amplifier. The most challenging aspect of power amplifier concept is achieving an excellent efficiency with linearity [6]. However, the design of a power amplifier has to be accomplished in accordance with the system specifications, such as operating frequency, bandwidth, output power, gain, linearity, efficiency and return loss [7]. According to [8, 9], linearity

© ICST Institute for Computer Sciences, Social Informatics and Telecommunications Engineering 2017
I. Otung et al. (Eds.): WiSATS 2016, LNICST 186, pp. 193–201, 2017.
DOI: 10.1007/978-3-319-53850-1_19

is required to sustain information for error free transmission. Efficiency reduces power consumption and improves battery life span at the mobile terminal [5, 10].

The effect of spectral regrowth in power amplifiers has become a major concern in communication systems engineering [11]. Spectral regrowth is the result of non-linearity in the transmission path and leads to in-band and adjacent channel interference [3]. To reduce the effect of nonlinearity and achieve a state-of-the-art system, the power amplifier must be designed carefully to give high data rate and spectral efficiency for high speed broadband services. The best of these technologies embrace higher data rate and higher spectral efficiency from 20 MHz signal bandwidth, downlink data rate of 100 Mbps, with the uplink rate of 50 Mbps obtainable [5, 12] (Fig. 1).

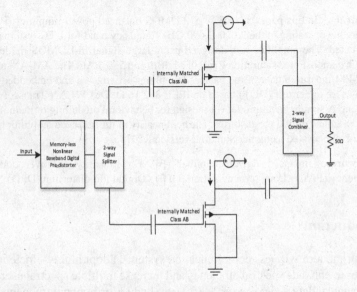

Fig. 1. Balanced power amplifier architecture.

This work is an extension of author's previous work [3] where a design of balanced RF power amplifier is discussed. The amplitude-to-amplitude and amplitude-to-phase characteristics (AM-AM/AM-PM) of the amplifier is used in the modelling of nonlinearities for a wireless metropolitan area network IEEE 802.16 OFDM transceiver. Simulink version R2011a configuration is introduced. Section 2 presents a balanced PA configuration; results will be discussed in Sect. 3. This section also covers the extraction and modelling of AM-AM and AM-PM polynomials in the pre-distorter. Conclusions from the work are drawn in Sect. 4.

2   Balanced Amplifier Design

A balanced power amplifier has been demonstrated in this paper and designed using two transistor models for high data rate, providing efficiency with dynamic range of linearity. Dynamic load adaptation is conveyed by the use of a 50 Ω, quarter wavelength transmission line impedance inverter. In the design of the balanced power amplifier, there are stages that must be followed to achieve high level performance [13, 14]. The first stage of the design is DC circuit design and simulation. Simulation of the DC circuit determines the bias point and bias network. This is according to the class of operation and power requirement. The bias condition set drain source voltage Vds = 28 V, drain source current (Ids) = 422 mA and gate source voltage Vgs = 2.7 V. The bias network is however designed based on class-AB carrier. The DC simulation results specify the class of operation. The main purpose of good biasing is to prevent signal reflection. The DC quiescent current is obtained to prevent signal distortion [5]. The radio frequency is prevented from going back to the DC source. For the matching network, this transistor requires no matching process, as indicated in the data sheet of the component, input and output impedance are internally matched. The 21 mm length of micro-strip line are connected using line-calc from Agilent advanced design system simulator (ADS) with RT 5880 substrates, parameters; ε_r = 2.2, H = 0.508 mm, z_0 = ohms, T = 3 μm and tan δ = 0.017. The 50 Ω line impedance of open and short circuit is incorporated to right angle of the RF blocking transmission lines. A class-AB power amplifier element values have been positioned using tune tool of the ADS simulator for best performance of the proposed system.

Linear and nonlinear simulation was performed for class-AB design. The design and simulation process for a class-AB amplifier is necessary in order to prepare the single stage class-AB design into a multiple stage balanced power amplifier. The linear simulation shows a good flat gain, where the S21 is almost 14 dB, the return loss, S11 and S22 are also good. The nonlinear single tone simulation result for the class-AB amplifier was obtained. However, it achieved up to 29% PAE at 39 dBm P1dB. A 3 dB 2-ways 900 hybrid splitter was designed using 100 Ω impedance for optimum resistance. This is to achieve 90° phase difference between the carrier class-AB and the peaking class-AB amplifier. For a two-stage balanced PA, the carrier and peaking bias points are in the same mode, the input-output matching circuitry and the output impedances are similar as well. For the two-way splitter, various simulation tests were performed such as isolation response over the operating bandwidth, phase difference across port 1–2 and 1–3, and insertion loss response of the splitter [3]. From the 3 dB splitter design, the insertion loss achieved is reasonably low due to the high return loss, the phase difference of two signals are parallel to each other by 100 Ω, which means they are separated by 90° and have equal magnitude, and the isolation between 2 and 3, which results in −48.56 dB at 2.655 GHz centre frequency. Consequently, these results represent a response to protect the amplifier with all the instruments connected to it and allow measurement with reasonable accuracy. At the output of the two-stage amplifier is a combiner coupling the carrier and peaking amplifier signals to the output of the balanced amplifier [3, 15].

Table 1 shows the performance of the present work in comparison with a few selected PAs reported in the literature, taking account of operating frequency, output power, efficiency and gain. In [4] a power amplifier consisting of up to 54% PAE at 2.14 GHz operating frequency is presented. The design presented a two stage line-up Doherty amplifiers, consisting of a High Voltage HBT Doherty final design is cascaded with a 20 W LDMOS Doherty driver, exhibiting up to 325 W (55 dBm) power to improve the gain to 30 dB. In the case of [10] a high power hybrid envelope elimination and restoration transmitter was design using gallium arsenide high electron mobility transistor (GaN-HEMT) at 2.655 GHz operating frequency. The design introduced a conventional hybrid switching amplifier with up to 71.2% PAE. However, the efficiency of H-EER transmitter reduced down to 37.04% at 41.18 dBm Pout. In [11] a conventional balanced amplifier with 90° branch line hybrid coupler (BLHC) was used to achieve power matching rather than maximum high gain. The impedance matching is not excellent and there is inherent out-of-phase characteristic cause from the properties of 90° BLHC. To improve the performance and correct the high signal reflection, an auxiliary amplifier was added to the conventional balanced amplifier design, only to increase the PAE to 33.4%. The design for [13] use up to 250 W output power at saturation to achieve drain efficiency of 60%. The final 40 W GaN-HEMT Doherty power amplifier design used a digital pre-distorter to enhance linearity, as a result experienced reduction in PAE to 48%. Finally, in [14] a 10 W, Si-LDMOS transistor power amplifier was presented with 50% PAE, 14.5 dB gain achieved at 41.8 dBm saturation within 1.8 to 2.0 GHz operating frequency. The drawback of [14] is that heat sink is used due to excessive heating produced by the amplifier, which extensively affect the general performance of the system.

Table 1. Performance comparisons for various power amplifiers.

Device	f_c [MHz]	PAE [%]	P_{out} [dBm]	Gain [dB]	Reference
LDMOS	2655	51	41	14.6	Balanced
LDMOS	2655	29	39	15	Class-AB
LDMOS	2140	54	48.77	30	[4]
G-HEMT	2655	37.14	41.18	12.78	[10]
G-HEMT	2125	33.4	34.9	7.7	[11]
G-HEMT	2500	48	46	13.4	[13]
LDMOS	1900	50	40	14.5	[14]

However, this work presents a simplified balanced amplifier using Si-LDMOS transistor while achieving up to 53% PAE, 14 dB gain at 41 dBm P1dB. This design is matched perfectly due to the internal input and output matching network in the transistor device. There is no evidence of leakage or signal reflection from the first stage of the design to the design of balanced amplifier. Another advantage of this design is its simplicity, requiring no auxiliary amplifier or additional cascade Doherty device to improve the efficiency. Additional circuitry accounts for extra power consumption and results in negligible impact to the overall efficiency of the amplifier [3].

3   Results and Discussion

The proposed balanced amplifier consisting of two similar class-AB amplifiers has been measured and discussed. The results show a useful extension of dynamic range with good PAE, making this approach the best choice for LTE base station applications. Figure 2 has shown the results of the balanced amplifier in comparison with conventional class-AB amplifier. The result have shown good performance from the balanced amplifier, achieving up to 53% PAE with 14 dB gain at 41 dBm P1dB, as against the conventional class-AB amplifier with 29% PAE, 39 dBm Pout and 15 dB gain.

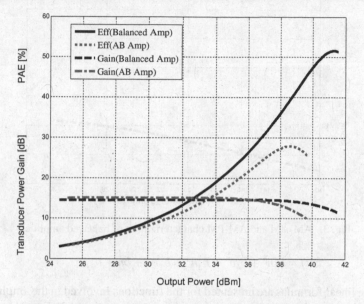

Fig. 2. PAE and gain characterization for class AB and the proposed balanced PA.

In the one-tone nonlinear simulation test, AM-AM and AM-PM characterisation parameters are also achieved as illustrated in Fig. 3. These are very important parameters in the characterisation of PA. However, the AM-AM distortion appears in a nonlinear PA, while the AM-PM distortion appears in MOSFET PAs and produce memory effects. The AM-AM and AM-PM transfer functions are used in the MATLAB curve fitting to generate coefficients. The extracted AM-AM and AM-PM data are measured in amplitude and phase in the context of normalized input voltage as a function of output voltage of the balanced amplifier. These are AM-AM extracted data, exported to the MATLAB curve fitting to generate the following coefficients: a6 = 33.066, a5 = −85.52, a4 = 82.06, a3 = −34.052, a2 = 2.85, a1 = 3.21 and a0 = −0.01. The AM-AM distortion is effected by the device reaching a saturation point. The normalized input voltage as a function of output phase of the balanced amplifier is also considered with the following AM-PM MATLAB fitted coefficients: b6 = 3.5485, b5 = −5.7836, b4 = 3.0384, b3 = −0.8434, b2 = 0.1826, b1 = −0.0225 and b0 = 0.1001. The AM-PM distortion is effected by the device reaching a saturation point. These data will be embedded in the device under test of a transmitter device, in a Simulink simulation based on IEEE 802.16 OFDM WLAN transceiver system. The polynomial functions for AM-AM and AM-PM are respectively given by the following equations:

$$y(t) = a_5 u^5 + a_4 u^4 + a_3 u^3 + a_2 u^2 + au + a_0 \tag{1}$$

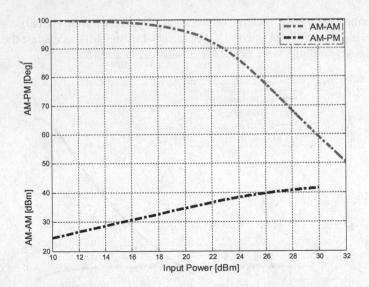

Fig. 3. AM-AM and AM-PM characterization of balanced amplifier.

$$z(t) = b_5 n^5 + b_4 n^4 + b_3 n^3 + b_2 n^2 + bn + b_0 \tag{2}$$

Simple linear formulas are presented for the functions involved in the amplitude and phase nonlinear models of the balanced amplifier, and are shown in Eqs. (1) and (2) to fit measured data very well. This model is exported to the memory-less baseband digital pre-distorter to linearize the DUT at the front-end of the OFDM transceiver system. Figure 4 illustrates results of a multiple-input-single-output (MISO) transceiver system which is set to run on simple linear model with baseband digital pre-distortion to compensate the nonlinearity of balanced power amplifier. Figure 4a and b depict AM-AM and AM-PM responses of the DUT without pre-distorter. Figure 4c and d is the same amplitude and phase results of the DUT after switching on the baseband digital pre-distorter of the transceiver system. The memory-less nonlinearity of the balanced amplifier has been compensated by the use of the digital pre-distortion mechanism. This has proven that the simple linear model used on the IEEE 802.16 OFDM WLAN transceiver system can model the AM-AM and AM-PM characteristics of the balanced amplifier.

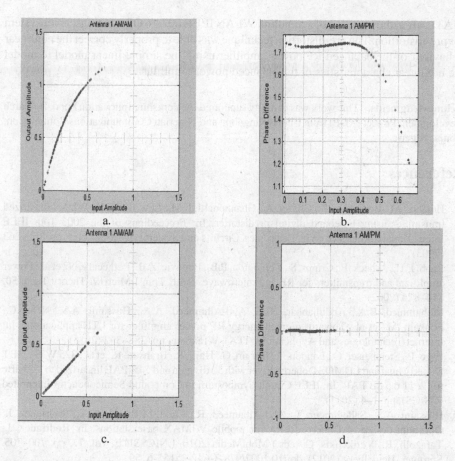

Fig. 4. a and b are the AM-AM/AM-PM responses of the DUT without pre-distortion, while c and d the pre-distortion is included.

4   Conclusion

In this paper, a balanced RF power amplifier was presented with a two class-AB amplifiers. The design used free-scale n-channel enhancement mode lateral MOSFET transistor. Linear and nonlinear simulation was achieved with ADS simulator and on the performance metric result is presented with considerable improvement. Comparison was made between the conventional class-AB amplifier and the double stage balanced RF amplifier. The balanced amplifier exhibited acceptable improvement in-terms of PAE and P1 dB by 22% and 2 dBm, with the gain decreasing by 1 dB. A relative comparison was made with power amplifiers of various types and the present work has proven a good choice of device.

This paper also conducted research on the effect of balanced amplifier AM-AM and AM-PM characteristics, when the coefficients are loaded onto the digital pre-distortion. AM-AM and AM-PM coefficients were converted to generate polynomials, using

MATLAB in the presence of a Simulink WLAN IEEE 802.16 OFDM transceiver system for pre-distortion. The pre-distortion technique was able to properly correct the nonlinear behaviour of the balanced RF power amplifier using the simple linear model to model the nonlinear characteristics of the balanced power amplifier.

Acknowledgments. This work was partially supported by Yorkshire Innovation Fund, Research Development Project (RDP) from United Kingdom; and Nigerian Communications Commission, Abuja, Nigeria.

References

1. Helaoui, M., Boumaiza, S., Ghazel, A., Ghannouchi, F.M.: Low-IF 5 GHz WLAN linearized transmitter using baseband digital predistorter. In: Proceedings of the 2003 10th IEEE International Conference on in Electronics, Circuits and Systems, ICECS, vol. 1, pp. 260–263 (2003)
2. Raab, F.H., Asbeck, P., Cripps, S., Kenington, P.B., Popovic, Z.B., Pothecary, N., et al.: Power amplifiers and transmitters for RF and microwave. IEEE Trans. Microw. Theory Tech. **50**, 814–826 (2002)
3. Mohammed, B.A., Abduljabbar, N.A., Abd-Alhameed, A.A., Hussaini, A.S., Nche, C., Fonkam, M., et al.: Towards a green energy RF power amplifier for LTE applications. In: Internet Technologies and Applications (ITA), Wrexham, pp. 388–392 (2015)
4. Page, P., Steinbeiser, C., Landon, T., Burgin, G., Hajji, R., Branson, R., et al.: 325 W HVHBT Doherty final and LDMOS Doherty driver with 30 dB gain and 54% PAE linearized to −55 dBc for 2c11 6.5 dB PAR. In: IEEE Circuit Symposium in Compound Semiconductor Integrated (CSICS), pp. 1–4 (2011)
5. Hussaini, A.S., Sadeghpour, T., Abd-Alhameed, R., Child, M.B., Ali, N.T., Rodriguez, J.: Optimum design of Doherty RFPA for mobile WiMAX base stations. In: Rodriguez, J., Tafazolli, R., Verikoukis, C. (eds.) MobiMedia 2010. LNICSSITE, vol. 77, pp. 700–705. Springer, Heidelberg (2012). doi:10.1007/978-3-642-35155-6_59
6. Deguchi, H., Ui, N., Ebihara, K., Inoue, K., Yoshimura, N., Takahashi, H.: A 33 W GaN HEMT Doherty amplifier with 55% drain efficiency for 2.6 GHz base stations. In: IEEE MTT-S International in Microwave Symposium Digest, pp. 1273–1276 (2009)
7. Wang, Z.: Demystifying envelope tracking: use for high-efficiency power amplifiers for 4G and beyond. IEEE Microwave Mag. **16**, 106–129 (2015)
8. Deguchi, H., Watanabe, N., Kawano, A., Yoshimura, N., Ui, N., Ebihara, K.: A 2.6 GHz band 537 W peak power GaN HEMT asymmetric Doherty amplifier with 48% drain efficiency at 7 dB. In: IEEE MTT-S International Microwave Symposium Digest (MTT), pp. 1–3 (2012)
9. Ismail, A.A., Younis, A.T., Abduljabbar, N.A., Mohammed, B.A., Abd-Alhameed, R.A.: A 2.45-GHz class-F power amplifier for CDMA systems. In: Internet Technologies and Applications (ITA), pp. 428–433 (2015)
10. Ildu, K., Junghwan, M., Jangheon, K., Jungjoon, K., Cheol Soo, Kae-Oh, S.S., et al.: Envelope injection consideration of high power hybrid EER transmitter for IEEE 802.16e mobile WiMAX application. In: IEEE MTT-S International Microwave Symposium Digest, pp. 411–414 (2008)
11. Jongsik, L., Chunseon, P., Jakyung, K., Hyeonwon, C., Yongchae, J., Sang-Min, H., et al.: A balanced power amplifier utilizing the reflected input power. In: IEEE International Symposium on Radio-Frequency Integration Technology (RFIT), pp. 88–91 (2009)

12. Markos, A., Bathich, K., Tanany, A., Gruner, D., Boeck, G.: Design of a 120 W balanced GaN Doherty power amplifier. In: Microwave Conference (GeMIC), German, pp. 1–4 (2011)
13. Sano, H., Ui, N., Sano, S.: A 40 W GaN HEMT Doherty power amplifier with 48% efficiency for WiMAX applications. In: IEEE Symposium in Compound Semiconductor Integrated Circuit (CSIC), pp. 1–4 (2007)
14. Dai, D., Sun, L., Wen, J., Su, G., Guo, L.: A 10 W broadband power amplifier for base station. In: 2012 International Conference on Microwave and Millimeter Wave Technology (ICMMT), pp. 1–4 (2012)
15. Kim, S., Moon, J., Lee, J., Park, Y., Minn, D., Kim, B.: Mitigating phase variation of peaking amplifier using offset line. IEEE Microwave Wirel. Compon. Lett. **2**, 1–3 (2016)

Energy Efficient Adaptive Network Coding Schemes for Satellite Communications

Ala Eddine Gharsellaoui[1]([⊠]), Samah A.M. Ghanem[2], Daniele Tarchi[1],
and Alessandro Vanelli Coralli[1]

[1] Department of Electrical, Electronic and Information Engineering,
University of Bologna, Bologna, Italy
{ala.gharsellaoui2,daniele.tarchi,alessandro.vanelli}@unibo.it
[2] Huawei R&D Labs, Stockholm, Sweden
samah.ghanem@huawei.com

Abstract. In this paper, we propose novel energy efficient adaptive network coding and modulation schemes for time variant channels. We evaluate such schemes under a realistic channel model for open area environments and Geostationary Earth Orbit (GEO) satellites. Compared to non-adaptive network coding and adaptive rate efficient network-coded schemes for time variant channels, we show that our proposed schemes, through physical layer awareness can be designed to transmit only if a target quality of service (QoS) is achieved. As a result, such schemes can provide remarkable energy savings.

Keywords: Energy efficiency · Network coding · Satellite communications

1 Introduction

Network coding is a transmission technique that, by performing algebraic operations across transmitted packets rather than relying on packet repetition or replication, allows to reliably transmit with lower end to end delays in a communication system. Additionally, network coding mechanisms are key enablers to energy efficient communications. Due to the steady increase in energy consumption and energy costs in mobile communication systems, more efficient schemes are required. In particular, with higher reliability obtained via network coding, less re-transmissions are required. Consequently, more energy savings can be achieved [1]. Moreover, when the network coded schemes are specifically designed for enhancing their awareness with respect to the system characteristics, higher performance gains can be achieved in terms of delay, throughput or energy efficiency [2,3]. One of the most important issue to be considered in satellite communications is energy efficiency. In [4], several factors that have a direct impact on energy efficiency of satellite and mobile terminals have been discussed, including dynamic spectrum access and cross layer design. In [2,5],

© ICST Institute for Computer Sciences, Social Informatics and Telecommunications Engineering 2017
I. Otung et al. (Eds.): WiSATS 2016, LNICST 186, pp. 202–212, 2017.
DOI: 10.1007/978-3-319-53850-1_20

the authors show that channel-aware transmission schemes jointly with network coding, can serve to reduce the delay and allow for energy performance gains. In [3], the authors propose novel adaptive network coding schemes and show a clear trade-off between energy-driven channel-aware schemes, that remain silent when channel encounter high erasures, and rate-driven channel-aware schemes that chose to transmit more to account for erasures.

In this work, various aspects of energy efficiency using network coding and modulation schemes are proposed. The schemes are evaluated in a realistic satellite channel model for open area environments and Geostationary Earth Orbit (GEO) satellites. Simulation results demonstrate clear trade-offs among average number of transmissions, delay, throughput and energy efficiency. We highlight that adaptation through channel-aware policies allows for silence periods or less transmissions which leads to significant energy savings compared to non-adaptive network coding or adaptive network coded schemes that are rate efficient.

2   System Model

Our focus is on a GEO satellite communications system forward link transmission, by considering a mobile terminal with constant speed in a open area environment. In such system, the transmitter performs a Random Linear Network Coding (RLNC), which is a Network Coding (NC) scheme that relies on coding across the packets using random linear coefficients in order to increase the transmission reliability mimicking the wireless diversity concept. The open area environment is modeled by resorting to the Land Mobile Satellite (LMS) model in [6], that is one of the most known in the literature. This model is based on a joint exploitation of a state based and a Loo based distribution [7] that allow to efficiently reproduce the shadowing and fading effects of a forward link satellite channel under mobile terminal assumptions. In this paper, we capitalize on the coded/uncoded packet transmission over the Markov model proposed in [2] to analyze our proposed schemes that rely mainly on channel variation awareness. Each state in the Markov model is represented by the couple (i, h_j) that stands for the number i of coded/uncoded packets to be sent and the channel state h_j, whose value varies over time. Therefore, such Markov model can be expressed by a one-step transition probability matrix P, whose size is defined by a finite number of states, and its components are defined by using two transition probability components: $p_{(i,h_j) \to (i-1,h_{j+1})} = 1 - P_e(h_j)$, and $p_{(i,h_j) \to (i,h_{j+1})} = P_e(h_j)$, where $P_e(h_j)$ is the packet erasure probability at the channel state h_j for the duration of the packet transmission, and the probability of transitioning from the channel state and back to itself equals zero due to channel variation over time. This means that for a packet of size B bits, and with bit error probability $P_b(h_j)$ at a given channel state h_j, the erasure probability is given as, $P_e(h_j) = 1 - (1 - P_b(h_j))^B$. We resort to the approximation of the delay under network-coded transmission provided in [2], where the expected time to deliver

N_i coded packets is given as:

$$T(i, h_j) = T_d(N_i, h_j) + \sum_{l=1}^{i} P_{(i,h_j) \to (l, h_{j+N_i})}^{N_i} T(l, h_{j+N_i+1}), \tag{1}$$

with $T_d(N_i, h_j) = N_i T_p + T_w$, where T_p is the duration of one packet, and T_w is the waiting time for acknowledgment. $P_{(i,h_j) \to (l, h_{j+N_i})}^{N_i}$, corresponds to the transition probability between states at the N_i^{th} transition of matrix P. Finally, in $j + N_i + 1$ the term $+1$ appears due to acknowledgment. Figure 1 illustrates the Markov chain as proposed in [2]. This model of coded and uncoded packet transmission over time varying channels assumes a finite number of time slots for sending a given number of packets. Thus, the model and the delay approximation inherently constraints the number of re-transmissions of packets, but has sufficiently large number of slots for a reliable approximation.

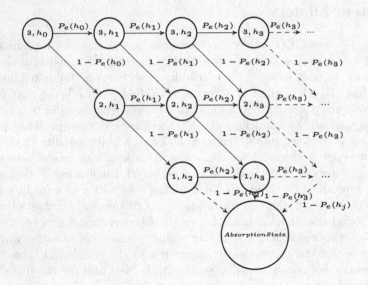

Fig. 1. Time varying channel model of 3 packets transmission in [2]

3   Energy Efficient Adaptive Network Coding Schemes

The main objective is to propose energy efficient schemes by the exploitation of the adaptation of the coded packets transmission to the channel awareness under different levels of algorithm complexities. We discuss three proposed schemes and compare them to non-adaptive network coding scheme for time varying channels and to the rate driven adaptive network coded scheme in [2].

3.1   Adaptive Network Coding with Energy Efficiency (ANCEF)

This scheme adapts the transmission for achieving the energy efficient, by following the observation of the channel erasure; the strategy is to transmit small batches of coded packets if the observation of channel erasure is high (applies to low SNR), and to transmit larger batches of coded packets if erasure is less (applies to high SNR). Through this, the system can reduce transmissions and re-transmissions and save energy. Furthermore, QoS measure has been introduced to design such algorithm. In particular, if a bit error probability P_b less than 10^{-5} is not met[1], the transmitter will choose to be silent with no transmissions. Therefore, much energy savings can be obtained. The following equation illustrates the number of coded packets N_i required to be sent at the channel state h_j when i degrees of freedom (dof)[2] are required at the receiver,

$$N_i = \sum_{s=j}^{j+i-1} (1 - P_e(h_s)). \tag{2}$$

It's worth mentioning that N_i required to be rounded to nearest decimal or integer number, because it represents the number of coded packets. Moreover, it is worth to note that the sum is expressed with a shifted start of the state of measurements. This is due to the channel evolution over time, thus, a new round of transmission/re-transmission is associated to shift in the channel window. When erasures are high (at low SNR) such sum vanishes to zero corresponding to no transmission. However, when erasures are very low (at high SNR) such sum converges to the transmission of i degrees of freedom almost surely.

3.2   Self-Tracing Adaptive Network Coding with Energy Efficiency (STANCEF)

In this scheme, we propose a self-tracing ANCEF scheme, which improves ANCEF by adding to the observation of the channel erasure the capability of looking-forward into the channel erasures if, looking-backwards, the packets at earlier transmissions are lower than the dof. Thus, the transmission strategy of such algorithm is similar to the ANCEF discussed in previous section, where less coded packets will be transmitted adaptively at high erasures, and more packets will be transmitted adaptively at low erasures. However, there is an amount of coded packets Δ_i needed to be as additional amount of future re-transmissions to establish all lost dof. Therefore, such Δ_i decreases as we move towards higher SNR, until it vanishes to zero when the transmission strategy of $N_i = i$. Once again, a certain QoS measure needs to be met, otherwise, the transmitter remains

---

[1] The acceptable bit error rate acceptable by the ITU ranges between 10^{-3} to 10^{-6} based on the rate and service expected at the mobile terminal.

[2] A degree of freedom corresponds to the number of linear combinations that are required at the receiver to allow decoding the RLNC combined packets.

silent. The following equation represents the STANCEF transmission strategy of the number of coded packets N_i required to be sent at a certain channel state h_j:

$$N_i = \sum_{s=j}^{j+i+\Delta_i-1} (1 - P_e(h_s)), \tag{3}$$

where Δ_i is the foreseen losses due to self-tracing which is the difference between i dof required at preliminary transmission at state h_{j*} and the number of coded packets N_i adapted to the channel at the same state. It is given by, $\Delta_i = i - N_i$, where Δ_i equals 0 at the initial state of first transmission. However, Δ_i is higher or equal to 0, at h_j^* corresponds to zero or more coded packets contributed at a re-transmission stage one step ahead of its previous transmission. Thus, Δ_i at h_j^* will contribute to N_i at a forward channel state $h_{j*+N_{i+1}+1}$, where the addition of one represents the one step ahead due to ACK after preliminary transmission and before re-transmission.

3.3 Adaptive Network Coding and Modulation with Energy Efficiency (ANCMEF)

In this scheme, we integrated adaptive modulation to the ANCEF scheme. The rationale behind this, is that, on the one hand, a higher modulation order m allows for transmitting the same amount of information in shorter packets due to the concatenation of more bits in the real and imaginary spaces. On the other hand, a higher modulation order is associated with higher energy per symbol, and less energy per bit, i.e. $E_b/N_0 = E_s/(N_0 * \log m)$. Thus, a higher bit error probability suggests that higher number of packets need to be sent due to adaptation. Such trade-off between the packet length and the number of coded packets for a given modulation scheme is of particular interest to address when taking into account energy efficiency. ANCMEF transmission strategy of coded packets N_{i_m} is given by,

$$N_{i_m} = \sum_{s=j}^{j+i*\log m-1} (1 - P_{e_m}(h_s)), \tag{4}$$

Resorting to the energy efficiency of the proposed scheme, the lower bound on random linear network coding, with $N_{i_m} \geq i$, i.e. with equality, is used, this was reflected in the sum range, by scaling the degrees of freedom i by a factor $\log m$ that unifies the energy per symbol for each modulation scheme. $P_{e_m}(h_s)$ is the erasure probability of that modulation which can be derived as $P_{e_m} = 1 - (1 - P_{b_m})^B$, where P_{b_m} is the bit error probability for the given modulation order m, and B is the number of bits per packet.

Indeed the aim of the scheme is to find the optimal number of coded packets N_i^m for a given modulation order m to be transmitted/re-transmitted for assuring successful reception of a given number of i dof along the way with energy efficiency; hence when P_{b_m} of m-th modulation order is derived, for fair energy comparison among the different modulation schemes, E_s is supposed to be constant for each modulation scheme.

4   Numerical Results

We shall now provide a set of illustrative results that cast further insights to the proposed schemes. Particularly, we focus on a satellite scenario and its related LMS channel considering GEO satellite with delay T_w equals 0.2388 s, open area, and a mobile terminal with speed of 10 m/s. To construct the simulation environment, we consider to transmit 4 coded packets/dof, the maximum batch length due to channel adaptation of the schemes is constrained to 16 coded packets/dof, and the number of transmission/re-transmission trials is constrained to 10. This corresponds to a transition matrix of maximum size equals 401×401 including one additional slot for absorption state, which changes entries and size according to the transmitted packets.

The performance of the proposed schemes is compared in terms of average number of sent packets, delay, throughput, and energy efficiency.

The two benchmark schemes are the non-adaptive network coding scheme for time variant channels and the adaptive rate-efficient network coding scheme, both schemes are in [2]. In the non-adaptive network coding scheme, it is clear that the number of coded packets are fixed along the transmission/re-transmission with no adaptation considered. The rate efficient adaptive network coding scheme is self explanatory, as it favors reliable transmission/reception and higher rates over energy efficiency. Contrary to the non-adaptive network coding scheme, the three proposed schemes adapt the number of coded packets for each batch of transmission based on the missing dof and on the channel erasures at a given window of estimated channel.

The modulation scheme considered is the BPSK in case of NC, ANC, ANCEF and STANCEF, while the ANCMEF exploits four possible modulation schemes, i.e., BPSK, QPSK, 8PSK and 16QAM, in order to efficiently exploit the channel behavior. The selection of modulation order is driven by the E_s/N_0 level.

The number of bits per packet is considered to be 1000, and since the maximum number of packets per batch equals 16, the maximum possible batch of packet size equals 16000 bits. This number of bits corresponds to the same, the half, the one-third, and the one-forth number of samples in BPSK, QPSK, 8PSK, and 16QAM, respectively.

First, the average number of coded packets sent back to back for the different schemes is compared; under different E_s/N_0 values and with mobility speed equals 10 m/s, this can be seen in Fig. 2. In general, we can see that the average number of packets for all the schemes at low SNR is greater than those at high SNR due to the higher probability of re-transmission at low SNR. Due to energy efficiency rule, the average number of packets will be as much small as to commensurate with the higher erasure probability at low E_s/N_0 values, since they are designed to limit the number of sent packets in case of bad channel conditions i.e., there is no need to spend more energy in such low chance of delivery. This can be emphasized looking into the low SNR, where the erasure probability is high such that energy efficient schemes favor not to send anything in order to avoid energy wasting; this is the contrary for the ANC benchmark that has been designed to achieve the highest possible rates. It is worth to note

that the average number of coded packets in ANCMEF gets larger for higher
E_s/N_0 values; this is expected since we aim to adapt the number of sent packets
for achieving target reliability, keeping into account the energy efficiency.

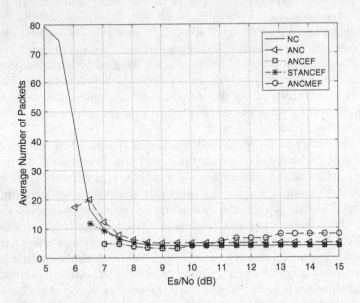

Fig. 2. Average number of sent packets for variable E_s/N_0 values and 10 m/s mobility
speed.

However, the maximum constrained batch size in ANCMEF is affected not
only by E_s/N_0 but also by modulation method and energy consumption, so at
low SNR it behaves similarly to the NC, then, going to higher SNR, it selects
a higher modulation order allowing to increase the transmission reliability by
the exploitation of higher diversity or modulation order. However, the increase
of number of packets of ANCMEF is associated to shorter size packets that
allows for equivalent energy per symbol for all modulation orders and across all
schemes.

In Fig. 3, we can see the behavior in terms of transmission delay for the
proposed schemes in a GEO satellite scenario. The proposed schemes have the
higher delay for low SNR values; this is due to the fact that the energy efficient
adaptive schemes adapt its transmission to small size batches at the low E_s/N_0
associated with high erasures. Therefore, the transmission suffers from extra
waiting times for acknowledgment at the end of each short batch. Thus, as
illustrated in Fig. 3, the time spent waiting for acknowledgment is very large
compared to the time of delivering the coded packets. After a certain E_s/N_0
value, the schemes have similar performance due to the number of packets in each
batch that has been increased and then converged to the exact dof value of the
non-adaptive NC scheme. ANCMEF is not an exception since a normalization on
the average number of packets with $\log m$ matches with the dof for such shorter

length packets. It is indeed straightforward to understand the delay saturation of all schemes to its minimal value at the high SNR.

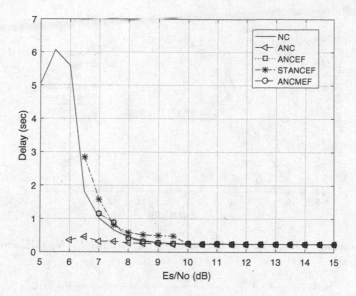

Fig. 3. Transmission delay in a GEO satellite scenario for variable E_s/N_0 values and 10 m/s mobility speed.

Figure 4 presents the throughput for the measured schemes NC and ANC with the proposed ones, i.e., ANCEF, STANCEF and ANCMEF. For low and intermediate E_s/N_0 values, the schemes show remarkable differences but all of them give less throughput than ANC and NC schemes due to the reduced number of transmitted packets. However, we emphasize that the main aim of these schemes is to avoid any source of energy consumption that rise due to bad channel conditions, hence, our schemes favors to be silent from transmission, than consuming energy by limiting the transmitted packets, and its utilization to adaptive coding techniques allows for reliable transmission and less energy due to decreased re-transmissions encountered. Thus, achieving less throughput is understandable. Furthermore, its worth to observe that at a certain E_s/N_0, all the schemes converge to maximum saturation throughput independent of mobile speed or channel variation. While, ANCEF and ANCMEF almost coincide in the performance behavior but not the reliability, we can see that STANCEF tries to build a trade-off that resonates just in a limited throughput gain due to its dof one step loss tractability. In fact, such a small gain in throughput is shown to be associated with a small cost in the energy. For medium E_s/N_0 the extra complexity due to self tractability and excess transmissions has no gains, therefore, we see that STANCEF throughput performance deteriorate with respect to the ANCEF and ANCMEF. Finally, Fig. 5 presents the most important part of this study, the total energy consumption that has been calculated using both the

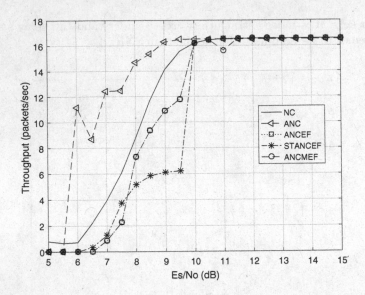

Fig. 4. Throughput in a GEO satellite scenario for variable E_s/N_0 values and $10\,\text{m/s}$ mobility speed.

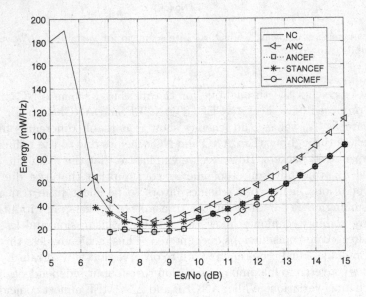

Fig. 5. Energy consumed in a GEO satellite scenario for variable E_s/N_0 values and $10\,\text{m/s}$ mobility speed.

spectral noise level as $N_0 = -107\,\text{dBm}$ and the expected time needed to send 4 coded packets/dofs for each E_s/N_0 of each scheme. It is possible to note that all the proposed schemes allow significant gains in terms of energy consumption with respect to the benchmarks. Its clear that at the low SNR we can see STANCEF gains roughly 15 mWatt/Hz with respect to the NC scheme. Moreover, it is worth to see that ANCEF and ANCMEF reduce remarkably the energy consumption by gaining up to roughly 20 mWatt/Hz with respect to the NC scheme; such an amount might seem to be small, however, this represents very high figure in a large scale system with multiple receivers. Furthermore, at the moderate E_s/N_0 we can see that due to the shorter sizes of the packets length used for higher modulation orders, the ANCMEF continues to have highest energy efficiency with further gains. Finally, at the high E_s/N_0 beyond 10 dB, is associated with an increase in the transmitted message which necessarily increases the overall system energy consumption.

5 Conclusions

This paper addresses energy efficient adaptive network coding schemes for land satellite mobile with time varying channel. We proposed three novel adaptive physical layer aware schemes for coded packet transmission over LMS channel. Those schemes compensate for the lost degrees of freedom by tracking the packet erasures over time. The novelty of such schemes is expressed by their remarkable energy savings due to adaption to a set of various factors such as channel quality, that inherently adapts to the mobile speed, and thus allows due to smart silence/transmission periods to significant energy savings. Finally, we emphasize that, at SNR values high enough for reliable transmission, the schemes can be switched off to allow for a reduction in the processing power at the transmitter side.

References

1. Fragouli, C., Widmer, J., Boudec, J.Y.L.: A network coding approach to energy efficient broadcasting: from theory to practice. In: Proceedings of 25th IEEE International Conference on Computer Communications (IEEE INFOCOM 2006), pp. 1–11, April 2006
2. Ghanem, S.A.M.: Network coding mechanisms for Ka-band satellite time varying channel. In: Proceedings of 2013 IEEE 24th Annual International Symposium on Personal, Indoor, and Mobile Radio Communications (PIMRC), London, UK, pp. 3291–3296, September 2013
3. Gharsellaoui, A., Ghanem, S.A.M., Tarchi, D., Vanelli-Coralli, A.: Adaptive network coding schemes for satellite communications. In: Proceedings of 8th Advanced Satellite Multimedia Systems Conference and the 14th Signal Processing for Space Communications Workshop (ASMS/SPSC 2016), Palma De Mallorca, Spain, September 2016
4. Alagoz, F., Gur, G.: Energy efficiency and satellite networking: a holistic overview. Proc. IEEE **99**(11), 1954–1979 (2011)
5. Lucani, D.E., Kliewer, J.: On the delay and energy performance in coded two-hop line networks with bursty erasures. In: Proceedings of 2011 8th International Symposium on Wireless Communication Systems (ISWCS), pp. 502–506, November 2011

6. Fontan, F.P., Vazquez-Castro, M., Cabado, C.E., Garcia, J.P., Kubista, E.: Statistical modeling of the LMS channel. IEEE Trans. Veh. Technol. **50**(6), 1549–1567 (2001)
7. Loo, C.: A statistical model for a land mobile satellite link. IEEE Trans. Veh. Technol. **34**(3), 122–127 (1985)

Distribution of SDTV and HDTV Using VLC Techniques for Domestic Applications

Timothy J. Amsdon, Martin J.N. Sibley$^{(\boxtimes)}$, and Peter J. Mather

School of Computing and Engineering, The University of Huddersfield, Queensgate, Huddersfield HD1 3DH, UK

{timothy.amsdon,m.j.n.sibley,p.j.mather}@hud.ac.uk

Abstract. This paper presents a visible light communication system that enables flat-panel TVs to receive DVB terrestrial, cable and satellite digital content wirelessly. The benefits of VLC over Wi-Fi and power-line networking based solutions are discussed, and the physical requirements of the system are defined. The paper also discusses how the MPEG transport stream of a set-top-box can be re-encoded for transmission over a free-space optical channel using a novel PPM modulation scheme.

Keywords: DVB-T · DVB-T2 · Digital TV · H.264 LED · MPEG · Offset PPM · VLC

1 Introduction

The International Telecommunication Union (ITU) reported in 2013 that there were over 1.4 billion households worldwide with at least one TV set, and that this represented 79% of the total worldwide households [1]. The ITU also reported that approximately 55% of these TV households are capable of receiving digital transmissions, meaning that at least 770 million TV sets are capable of receiving digital transmissions.

The deployment of consumer digital TV sets and digital broadcast services to support them is increasing. TV technology has evolved significantly over the last 20 years, and in particular, there has been a shift away from TV sets fitted with cathode-ray tube (CRT) technologies, to flat-panel, plasma, liquid crystal display (LCD), and more recently, OLED based technologies. These technologies have brought about significant reductions in power consumption, weight, bulk and the cost of TV sets, whilst increasing the reliability and the range of display screen sizes available. Flat-panel technologies have also facilitated the trend in wall-mounted sets, which has enabled consumers to reclaim floor space and enhance their viewing experience. However, in consumer premises, where solid wall construction techniques are used, routing of the signal and power cables to the rear panel of the set is problematic. In such cases, conduit or chasing is necessary to route the cables, which is potentially disruptive and expensive.

The rear panel of a modern, high-end TV sets has numerous connector interfaces, ranging from legacy analogue baseband video and audio inputs, to state-of-the-art digital HDMI interfaces. There are also RF connector inputs that feed broadcast content from terrestrial, cable and satellite services to an internal tuner/demodulator sub-system, the

© ICST Institute for Computer Sciences, Social Informatics and Telecommunications Engineering 2017
I. Otung et al. (Eds.): WiSATS 2016, LNICST 186, pp. 213–222, 2017.
DOI: 10.1007/978-3-319-53850-1_21

type and specification of which is defined by the region of the world the set operates. Furthermore, modern sets now provide access to digital content via USB, Ethernet, Wi-Fi and, in some cases, power-line networking. The inclusion of TCP/IP enables consumers to access online services such as video streaming and web-browsing.

Given modern TV sets have access to digital broadcasting and internet services, and that the support for legacy analogue baseband devices such as VCRs is declining, TV manufacturers have the opportunity to eliminate all of the connector interfaces, including the RF connectors, from the rear panel of the set and use completely all-digital, wireless based connectivity. This leads to a number of desirable benefits. Firstly, this approach benefits the consumer by simplifying wall-mount installation. Secondly, and most obviously, it reduces the cost of the TV set. Not only does the elimination of the connectors reduce cost, so too does the elimination of their associated internal support circuitry and PCB area. In addition, any software overhead associated with this circuitry is also eliminated. In particular, the elimination of the RF connectors is significant, since it leads to the removal of the tuner/demodulator sub-system that enables reception of broadcast services. As already stated, this sub-system is defined by the reception type and region of the world the set operates. By removing it and sourcing the content by alternate means, the set effectively becomes a region-less monitor, enabling TV manufacturers to produce generic TV sets that operate in any region of the world.

This paper presents a visible light communication (VLC) based system to address this opportunity, presenting the case for VLC over Wi-Fi and power-line networking based solutions. The physical requirements of the system are defined, and a novel modulation scheme for the system is also presented. The paper is primarily focused on the distribution of digital based terrestrial, cable and satellite broadcasting services wirelessly to a consumer TV set in a domestic setting.

2 DVB Standards

Digital broadcasting standards and the function of the tuner/demodulator is easily explained using the all-digital DVB broadcasting model used in Western Europe [2]. The standards applicable to terrestrial, cable and satellite services are shown in Table 1. The modulation schemes employed by each of the broadcast standards are very different, with each chosen to achieve optimal data transmission over channels with specific characteristics and impairments. However, all three DVB modulation schemes are encoded with the same underlying digital transport stream, namely the MPEG transport stream (MPEG TS). MPEG is a digital compression codec that is used to compress video and audio to facilitate transmission across band-limited channels. The key compression standards applicable to DVB are MPEG-2 for standard-definition TV (SDTV) and H. 264 for high-definition TV (HDTV). DVB standards with suffix '2' e.g. DVB-T2, are capable of receiving SDTV and HDTV, and standards without the suffix e.g. DVB-T are only capable of receiving SDTV.

Table 1. DVB standards: terrestrial, cable and satellite broadcasts

Broadcast type	Standard	Bit-rate (Mbit/s)	Modulation and conditions
Terrestrial	DVB-T	31.7	COFDM: Constellation 64-QAM, code rate 7/8, guard interval 1/32, 8 K FFT, BW 8 MHz
	DVB-T2	50.2	COFDM: Constellation 256-QAM, code rate 5/6, guard interval 1/128, 32 K FFT, BW 8 MHz
Cable	DVB-C	51.3	Constellation 256-QAM, BW 8 MHz
	DVB-C2	83.1	Constellation 4096-QAM, BW 8 MHz
Satellite	DVB-S	42.9	Constellation QPSK, BW 36 MHz
	DVB-S2	64.5	Constellation 8PSK, BW 36 MHz

A simplified block diagram of each DVB standards transmit and receive path is shown in Fig. 1. The basic principle of operation begins at the transmitter where video and audio are compressed by the MPEG encoder. The subsequent multiplexer inter-leaves multiple video, audio and data streams into a single MPEG TS. This is done by assigning programme identification (PID) sequences to the content so the receiver can reconstruct the original independent streams (demultiplexing). Scrambling (encrypting) data streams is also possible to restrict access to subscriber based services. The resultant MPEG TS is then presented at the specific modulator i.e. QPSK, QAM, COFDM, for optimal transmission over a specific channel [3].

At the TV receiver, the process of the transmitter is reversed. The desired transmission channel is first selected and isolated from other channels by the tuner. The selected channel is then presented to the demodulator where appropriate demodulation techniques recover the MPEG TS. The transport stream is then demultiplexed using PIDs, and descrambled as necessary, to recover the independent MPEG video and audio streams. The required video and audio streams are then decoded by the MPEG decoder so that the original video and audio is reproduced.

By removing the tuner/demodulator function from the TV set, and integrating it into a wireless transmitter, the most convenient place to access the digital broadcast content is at the MPEG TS interface, since the stream is highly compressed and potentially encrypted. The transport stream is available at the output of the DVB demodulator, and is configurable for either serial or parallel output mode. The former mode is preferable for transmission over a wireless channel, and is composed of a four key lines. The first is the transport streams 50% duty cycle reference clock. The second is the serial data line, which transports payloads of 188 bytes ($188 \times 8 = 1504$ bits). The third is the valid line which indicates the beginning and ending of each payload, this line remains high

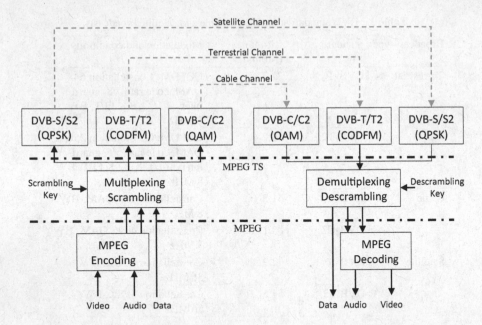

Fig. 1. DVB standards: terrestrial, cable and satellite transmit and receive paths

during the transmission of payload bytes d0 to d187. The fourth is the synchronisation line, which remains high only for the duration of d0 byte, or the first bit of the payload [4].

These lines can be combined into a single data stream using digital processing techniques and then re-encoded for transmission over a wireless channel to a TV set. The receiving TV set then only needs to decode the transmitted signal and use an MPEG decoder to reproduce the audio and video.

3 Wi-Fi and Power-Line

The superficially obvious candidate for transmitting the MPEG TS is Wi-Fi, but given that the demand placed on Wi-Fi is growing, bandwidth capacity is becoming an issue. Wi-Fi transmissions also suffer from an inherent security weakness caused by the fact that RF signals can penetrate the walls of buildings and therefore can be broadcast beyond the consumer premises. Indoor coverage ranges for Wi-Fi standards 802.11b and 802.11g are typically 50 m, and 802.11n around 100 m, meaning that transmissions can be intercepted and the content accessed by eavesdroppers. Power-line networking, although not a wireless based system, is also an attractive candidate as it provides dual purposing of the power cable to the set. This scheme enables both mains power and data transmission to coexist on the same cable, and is achieved by superimposing a digitally modulated OFDM signal onto the mains supply voltage. However, domestic power distribution systems are not designed to support data transmission, and this system is limited by multipath dispersion and the impulsive noise [5]. Wi-Fi and power-line systems are also required to meet stringent regulatory compliance due to both systems radiating RF energy which can interfere with other electrical devices.

4 VLC

A visible light based solution is compelling as it overcomes some of the problems encountered with Wi-Fi. Firstly, VLC uses a region of the electromagnetic (EM) spectrum which is unlicensed and unregulated (375 nm and 780 nm) [6]. This eliminates the regulatory compliance required by Wi-Fi and powerline solutions. Secondly, visible light has inherent security, since it cannot penetrate walls, ceilings and floors. Thirdly, VLC is immune to electrical interference, and therefore transmissions are not impaired by electrical noise or spurious signals. Finally, the alignment of a VLC transmitter and receiver is intuitive, given that the light in this range is visible, the emission can be positioned and focused onto the receiver's photodetector (PD) to achieve maximum signal to noise performance.

The first free-space optical wireless system was demonstrated in 1979 by Gfeller and Bapst [7], and operated in the near-IR (950 nm) range. The system achieved a bit-rate of 1Mbit/s using diffuse transmission and On-off keying (OOK) modulation to communicate with a cluster of computer terminals. However, it was not until 2003 that Tanaka et al. demonstrated a visible white-light LED based dual purpose illumination and communication system. This also used diffuse transmission and OOK modulation, achieving a bit-rate of 400 Mbit/s [8].

Diffuse transmission relies on the reflections from walls, ceiling, floor and other surfaces to increase the coverage area of the radiating source. Diffuse transmission is desirable for mobile applications, but results in significant multipath, and inter-symbol interference (ISI). In order to overcome this, robust modulation schemes such as direct-current-biased optical OFDM (DCO-OFDM) [9] and discrete multitones (DMT) [10] have been developed. These schemes reportedly achieve gigabits/s rates, but have complicated architectures compared to OOK and PPM schemes.

Research has demonstrated that bit-rates are limited by the power output and the bandwidth of the LED. Typical LED bandwidth is in excess of 10 MHz, but is extendable using electrical equalisation and optical filtering. Li et al. presented a system using combination of blue optical filtering, and passive and active equalisation at the receiver (post-equalisation) to achieve bandwidths in excess of 150 MHz, and enabling bit-rates of 340 Mbit/s using OOK [11]. The blue optical filtering is used to increase the bandwidth of LEDs by removing the slower yellow component introduced by LEDs that use yellow phosphor.

4.1 Directed LOS Transmission

As described, most VLC research is focused on the diffuse transmission model because it provides the widest coverage area. However, due to multipath, robust modulation schemes and complex system architectures are required. The transmission model proposed here is the directed LOS channel model, since this model assumes that there are no reflections from walls, ceiling, floor and other surfaces present at the receiver's PD, enabling a simpler OOK and PPM schemes to be used. The transmitter and receiver in this case are also assumed to be static.

The directed LOS transmission function is defined by Eq. 1.

$$H(\emptyset)_{LOS} = \begin{cases} \dfrac{A_{R_x}}{d^2} Ro(\emptyset) \cos(\psi) & \text{for } 0 \leq \psi \leq \psi_c \\ 0 & \text{for } 0 \leq \psi \leq \psi_c \end{cases} \tag{1}$$

Where A_{R_x} is defined as the PD area, d is the distance between the LED and the PD, ψ is the angle of incidence, and ψ_c is the field of view (FOV) of the PD. $Ro(\emptyset)$ is the radiant intensity of the LED which is assumed to be Lambertian [12] as shown in Eq. 2.

$$Ro(\emptyset) = \left[\frac{m+1}{2\pi}\right] \cos^m(\emptyset) \tag{2}$$

Where m is the order of the Lambertian emission, and is related to the semi-angle (half power) $\emptyset_{1/2}$ of the LED emission. Equation 3 defines m.

$$m = -\frac{ln\,2}{ln\,(cos(\emptyset_{1/2}))} \tag{3}$$

4.2 Channel Model

Figure 2 shows the basic block diagram of the transmitter and receiver elements of an optical communications system. At the transmitter a transconductance amplifier (TCA) converts the voltage levels of data stream into current changes that intensity modulates the LED. At the receiver, the PD detects these intensity changes and converts them back to current changes. A transimpedance amplifier (TIA) then converts the current back into voltage changes.

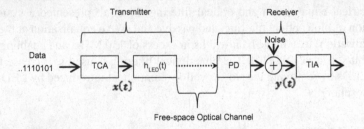

Fig. 2. Optical communications transmitter and receiver elements

The received signal $y(t)$ is a distorted and noisy representation of the intensity modulating signal $x(t)$. The transfer function [13] of the system is given by Eq. 4.

$$y(t) = R \cdot P_{LED} \cdot H(\emptyset)_{LOS} \cdot [x(t) \otimes h(t)] + n(t) \qquad (4)$$

R is the responsivity of the receiving PD, P_{LED} is the average output power of the LED, and $H(\emptyset)_{LOS}$ is the directed LOS transmission function. The symbol $\otimes$ denotes convolution, where $x(t)$ is the intensity modulating signal that is convolved with the optical impulse response $h(t)$ of the channel (Gaussian). Additive noise is represented by $n(t)$, and is the root mean square noise current introduced by the receiver.

4.3 Physical Requirements

Based on the directed LOS model, the physical requirements of the VLC system can be defined. A set-top-box (STB) capable of receiving DVB broadcasts and providing the necessary MPEG TS can be integrated with the VLC transmitter. This integrated VLC STB is then located in the plenum space above the room containing the TV set. The transmitting LED is mounted on a gimbal suspended from the ceiling, and providing 360° rotation. The wireless TV is now mountable on any wall in the room, and only the power cable needs consideration. A lens mounted on the LED, can then be used to provide focusing of the transmitted light onto TVs PD. Installation of the VLC STB in the plenum space is less disruptive, as power and RF feed cables for terrestrial, cable and satellite services are more readily accessible in this location. Figure 3 shows the physical interpretation of the system. Programme selection is possible through the TV using IR remote control. The TV is also be fitted with an IR transmitter to facilitate communication with the VLC STB.

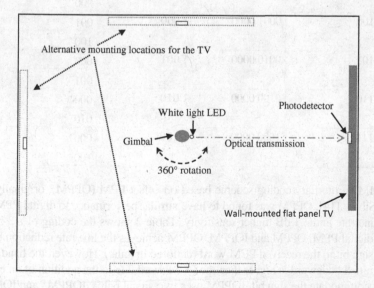

Fig. 3. Optical communications transmitter and receiver elements

5   Inversion Offset PPM Scheme

A novel PPM scheme, inverse offset PPM (IOPPM), is proposed for the system. This scheme is to be used to re-encode the serial MPEG TS, provided by a DVB STB, and then use the modified data stream to intensity modulating the LED.

As described earlier, the primary limiting factors of a VLC system are the output power and the bandwidth of the LED. Based on the DVB standards for terrestrial, cable and satellite broadcasts, the highest bit-rate is generated by the DVB-2 standard which is 83.1 Mbits/s (shown in Table 1). This is inside the bandwidth of 150 MHz achieved with electrical equalization and optical filtering. Also, the optical signal power at the PD is increased by using directed LOS transmission and lens focusing at the LED. However, the modulation scheme should maximise sensitivity and minimise bandwidth.

Table 2. 3-bit coding table: digital PPM, OPPM and IOPPM

PCM word	Digital PPM codeword	OPPM codeword	IOPPM codeword $IOPPM^+$ $IOPPM^-$
000	0000 0001	0 000	100^+
			001^-
001	0000 0010	0 001	001^+
			000^-
010	0000 0100	0 010	010^+
			000^-
011	0000 1000	0 100	100^+
			000^-
100	0001 0000	1 000	001^+
			100^-
101	0010 0000	1 001	000^+
			001^-
110	0100 0000	1 010	000^+
			010^-
111	1000 0000	1 100	000^+
			100^-

IOPMM is a tertiary coding scheme based on offset PPM (OPPM), originally developed by Sibley [14]. OPPM was found to have similar performance to digital PPM, but at half the line rate and 3.1 dB higher sensitivity. Table 2 shows the coding of a 3-bit PCM word for digital PPM, OPPM and IOPPM. OPPM achieves the line rate reduction by introducing a sign bit to the received PCM word (denoted in italic). However, the bandwidth of the transmitted codeword is higher than the PCM word due to the addition of an extra slot time to accommodate the sign bit. IOPPM uses two signal paths, IOPPM$^+$ and IOPPM$^-$ to convey the sign bit. This enables the bandwidth of the IOPPM codeword to equal that of the PCM word, but has the consequence of reducing sensitivity by 3 dB.

Figure 4 demonstrates how the IOPPM$^+$ and IOPPM$^-$ codeword paths are used to intensity modulate the LED. The LED is biased at a mid-point radiant intensity set by R1, R2 and Q1. If IOPPM$^+$ is at logic '0', as shown, Q2 is off and no increase in Q1 base bias occurs. However, if IOPPM$^-$ is at logic '1' Q3 is forward biased and Q1 base bias is reduced, resulting in a decrease in the radiant intensity of the LED. This push-pull based driver approach divides the LED radiant intensity in two, thereby enabling the transmission of the IOPPM$^+$ and IOPPM$^-$ streams.

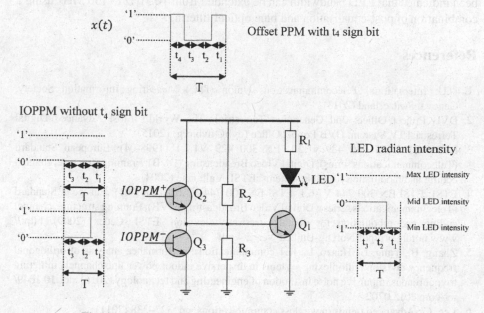

Fig. 4. Optical communications transmitter and receiver elements

6 Results

Most of the work underway on this research investigation is of a practical nature. Thus far a DVB-T/T2 tuner/demodulator reference design from Silicon Labs has been used and configured to generate a serial MPEG TS output. Off-air testing has revealed that the HDTV multiplex for C41 (634 MHz) from Emley Moor transmitter (Kirklees, England) is operating at a bit rate of 40.21 Mbits/s, and this stream is currently being used to develop an FPGA implementation of the IOPPM encoder and decoder. A DVB-T2 STB has also been successfully reverse engineered in order to access its MPEG decoder. Successful testing of the MPEG TS interface between the Silicon Labs reference board and STB MPEG decoder has been carried out. Design work is also underway on the LED drive circuitry using HEXFET devices.

7 Conclusions

A VLC system for wireless connectivity to flat-panel TVs using LOS transmission has been presented. LOS transmission was chosen as it eliminates multipath, thereby reducing ISI. The concept of a VLC STB has been presented, where DVB broadcast content for terrestrial, cable and satellite can be accessed at the MPEG TS interface and the re-encoded using a novel coding scheme (IOPPM), and then used to intensity modulate an LED. The IOPPM scheme has been shown to have a line rate equal to input word when 3-bit encoding is used, but incurs a 3 dB loss in sensitivity as a result. It has also been indicated that LED bandwidth can be extended from 10 MHz to 150 MHz using a combination of post-equalisation and blue optical filtering.

References

1. ITU: International Telecommunications Union (ITU) Measuring Information Society, Geneva, Switzerland (2013)
2. DVB Project Office: 2nd Generation Terrestrial: The World's Most Advanced Digital Terrestrial TV System. DVB Project Office (dvb@dvb.org) (2015)
3. ETSI: ETSI EN 300 429 v1.2.1. EN 300 429 V1.2.1 (1998-04); European Standard (Telecommunications series); Digital Video Broadcasting (DVB); Framing structure, channel coding and modulation for cable systems. ETSI, Valbonne (2004)
4. ETSI: ETSI EN 300 744 V1.6.1. ETSI EN 300 744 V1.6.1 (2009-01); European Standard (Telecommunications series); Digital Video Broadcasting (DVB); Framing structure, channel coding and modulation for digital terrestrial television. ETSI, Cedex (2009). http://www.nordig.org/pdf/NorDig-Unified_ver_2.4.pdf
5. Zhang, H., Yang, L., Hanzo, L.: IET communications: performance analysis of orthogonal frequency division multiplexing systems in dispersive indoor power line channels inflicting asynchronous impulsive noise institution of engineering and technology (2016). doi:10.1049/iet-com.2015.0702
6. Lee, C.: Advanced trends in wireless communications, pp. 327–338 (2011)
7. Gfeller, F.R.: Wireless in-house data communication via diffuse infrared radiation. Proc. IEEE 67, 1474–1486 (1979)
8. Tanaka, Y.K.: Indoor visible light data transmission system utilizing white LED lights. IEICE Trans. Commun. E86-B, 2440–2454 (2003)
9. Afgani, M.H.: Visible light communication using OFDM. In: Proceedings of the 2nd International Conference Testbeds and Research Infrastructures for the Development of Networks and Communities (TRIDENTCOM), pp. 129–134 (2006)
10. Vucic, J.K.: 513 Mbit/s visible light communications link based on DMT-modulation of a white LED. J. Lightwave Technol. 28, 3512–3518 (2010)
11. Li, H.C.: High bandwidth visible light communications based on a post-equalization circuit. IEEE Photonics Technol. Lett. 26, 119–122 (2014)
12. Haigh, P.A.: Transmitter Distribution for MIMO Visible Light Communication Systems. PGNet (2011)
13. Ghassemlooy, Z.: Indoor Optical Wireless Communication Systems – Part I: Review (2003)
14. Sibley, M.: Analysis of offset pulse position modulation - a novel reduced bandwidth coding scheme. IET Optoelectron. 5, 144–150 (2010)

On the Energy Minimization of Heterogeneous Cloud Radio Access Networks

Tshiamo Sigwele[✉], Atm Shafiul Alam, Prashant Pillai, and Yim Fun Hu

Faculty of Engineering and Informatics, University of Bradford, Bradford, UK
{t.sigwele,a.s.alam5,p.pillai,y.f.hu}@bradford.ac.uk

Abstract. Next-generation 5G networks is the future of information networks and it will experience a tremendous growth in traffic. To meet such traffic demands, there is a necessity to increase the network capacity, which requires the deployment of ultra dense heterogeneous base stations (BSs). Nevertheless, BSs are very expensive and consume a significant amount of energy. Meanwhile, cloud radio access networks (C-RAN) has been proposed as an energy-efficient architecture that leverages the cloud computing technology where baseband processing is performed in the cloud. In addition, the BS sleeping is considered as a promising solution to conserving the network energy. This paper integrates the cloud technology and the BS sleeping approach. It also proposes an energy-efficient scheme for reducing energy consumption by switching off remote radio heads (RRHs) and idle BBUs using a greedy and first fit decreasing (FFD) bin packing algorithms, respectively. The number of RRHs and BBUs are minimized by matching the right amount of baseband computing load with traffic load. Simulation results demonstrate that the proposed scheme achieves an enhanced energy performance compared to the existing distributed long term evolution advanced (LTE-A) system.

Keywords: Base station sleep · Bin packing · Cloud computing · C-RAN · Energy efficiency · HetNets · Virtualization

1 Introduction

Everyday, the number of connected devices are growing into billions and today's mobile operators are facing a serious challenge. For example, according to Huawei Technologies, in the year 2020, 100 billions of devices will be connected [1]. This will cause an increase in traffic from smart phones like iphone, android and other high-end devices like the iPad, kindle and gaming consoles spawning a raft of data intensive applications, Internet of Things (IoT) and machine-to-machine connections. As a result, fifth-generation (5G) networks have targeted to increase capacity by 1000 times, data rates by 100 times and millisecond-level delay [2]. To fulfil the capacity demands, more base stations (BSs) with a mixture of macro and small cells forming a heterogeneous network (HetNet) have to be deployed by operators, which results to a significant amount of energy consumption.

© ICST Institute for Computer Sciences, Social Informatics and Telecommunications Engineering 2017
I. Otung et al. (Eds.): WiSATS 2016, LNICST 186, pp. 223–234, 2017.
DOI: 10.1007/978-3-319-53850-1_22

This contributes to the mobile network's operating expenditure (OPEX) and emits large amounts of CO_2 which causes a greater impact to the environment.

A large amount of power within a base station (BS) is consumed by the power amplifier (PA) and baseband unit (BBU) [3]. The energy consumption of BBU implementation is getting more and more dominant in small cells due to gradual shrinking of cell size and the growing complexity of signal processing [3]. The traditional distributed long term evolution advanced (LTE-A) BSs architecture consumes a significant amount of energy and waste a lot of computing power as the BBU servers are not shared but serve each individual cell [7]. The BSs have been traditionally preconfigured to provide peak capacities to reduce outages. Nevertheless, the mobile traffic varies significantly, irrespective of the either the time of day or traffic profile and is rarely at its peak in practical scenarios [8]. Many energy-efficient schemes for wireless systems have been implemented such as BS sleeping [4–6] where offloading traffic to neighbouring BSs and then completely turning off the BS during low traffic, discontinuous transmission (DTX) where a BS is temporally switched off without offloading and cell zooming. However, current BS processing capacity is only being used for its own coverage rather than being shared within a large geographical area. As a result, during the evening, BSs in residential areas are over-subscribed while BSs in business areas stay under-subscribed. These under-subscribed BSs still consume a significant amount of energy even when they are not necessarily required to be kept active. Therefore, it is imperative to solve this problem and free up the processing capacity and save the corresponding energy.

Meanwhile, cloud radio access networks (C-RAN) have been proposed as a promising solution for minimizing energy within the cellular networks by leveraging cloud computing virtualization technology. With virtualization, baseband workload is consolidated on a minimum number of BBU servers and baseband processing is performed on virtual BBUs (vBBU) and resources are provisioned in accordance to traffic demands. C-RAN comprise of three parts: (i) remote radio head (RRH), which performs lower layer analogue radio frequency functions, (ii) BBU for digital signal processing, and (iii) fronthaul connection between the BBU and RRH. The C-RAN architecture is shown in Fig. 1. Furthermore, more energy savings can be gained from reduced air conditioning cost and reduced equipment room size. This paper integrates C-RAN in HetNets and proposes an energy efficient scheme for reducing energy consumption in C-RAN HetNets by switching off RRHs using a greedy algorithm and also switching off idle BBUs using the first fit decreasing (FFD) bin packing algorithm. The number of RRHs and BBUs are minimized by matching the right amount of baseband computing load with traffic load. The cloud based energy minimization is formulated as a bin packing problem where BS traffic items are to be packed into compute servers, called bins, such that the number of bins used are minimized. The simulations results validates the energy efficiency improvement of the proposed scheme and is compared with the distributed LTE-A system.

This paper is structured as follows: Sect. 2 discusses the related works while the system model and problem formulation is described in Sect. 3. The proposed

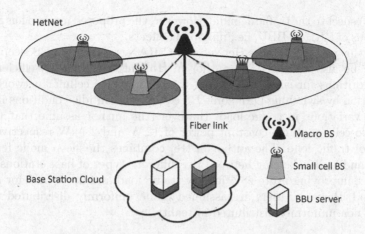

Fig. 1. An illustration of a C-RAN architecture.

scheme with computational resource models and greedy BS switching algorithm are formally are also described in Sect. 3. Section 4 provides the simulation results and discussion, while Sect. 5 provides some concluding comments.

2   Related Works

There are a plethora of solutions towards energy-efficient BSs ranging from energy-efficient hardware design, BS sleeping, to the optimal deployment of BSs [4,9]. This paper will concentrate on BS sleep which is a promising solution for minimizing energy consumption in both the radio side and cloud side of C-RAN HetNet. Authors in [10] proposed a BBU-RRH switching scheme for C-RAN that dynamically allocates BBUs to RRHs based on the imbalance of subscribers in business and/or residential areas. Even though the scheme in [10] reduces the number of BBUs required, the model performs poorly during high-traffic periods and thus still consumes a lot of energy because more BBUs are allocated to meet traffic demands. Authors in [11] developed a BBU pool test-bed using virtualization technology on general purpose processors (GPPs). The BBUs are dynamically provisioned according to traffic load. However, the paper fails to show how the number of BBUs are reduced while traffic load varies. L. Jingchu et al. [12] presented a mathematical model to quantify the statistical multiplexing gain of pooling virtual BSs. The author use a multi dimensional markov model to evaluate pooling gain considering both compute and radio resources. Nevertheless, the author have not considered energy consumption in the BS-Cloud. In [13], the authors considers the energy-delay trade-offs of a virtual BSs considering the BS sleeping approach in general IT platforms. The paper does not show how the energy savings of the virtual BSs model scales with traffic load. S. Namba et al. [14] proposed a network architecture, called colony-RAN, which has the ability to flexibly change cell layout by changing the connections of BBUs and

RRHs in respect to the traffic demand. However, the proposed method has frequent reselections of RRH to BBU, i.e., ping-pong effects.

Since this paper combines HetNet and C-RAN, research on BS sleep in Het-Nets will be also studied. The author in [15] introduce energy-efficient sleep mode algorithms for small cell BSs in a bid to reduce cellular network power consumption by switching OFF some BS equipments in idle conditions in accordance to variations in traffic load. However, the author assume that the pico and macro cells consume constant power of 12 W and 2.7 kW respectively irrespective of traffic load. The author in [16] combines the sleep mode feature of picocells and load balancing between the different types of base stations in Het-Net, hence improving up to 68% for low traffic load and up to 33% for medium traffic load. However, users are assumed to be uniformly distributed whereas users are non-uniformly distributed in reality.

3   System Model and Problem Formulation

3.1   System Model

The proposed system model is shown in Fig. 2. Consider an LTE-A C-RAN HetNet downlink system consisting of a single macro RRH (MRRH) and overlaid by several small cell RRHs (SRRHs). Assume a set of RRHs $\mathcal{R} = \{RRH_j : j = 1, 2, ..., N\}$ where N is the maximum number of RRHs and RRH_1 is the center MRRH. Define a set of users in the entire network as $\mathcal{U}$. Moreover, assume a set of computing servers in the pool $\mathcal{M} = \{GPP_i : i = 1, 2, ..., M\}$ where M is the number of physical computing servers for processing baseband signals of N cells. The global cloud controller (GCC) is located in the BS cloud and it is where the greedy BS switch off and the FFD algorithms are located. The baseband processing procedure of each RRH is divided into L tasks with a set $\mathcal{L} = \{T_k : k = 1, 2, ..., L\}$ where T_k is the kth baseband task for RRH_j. The computing processing power is measured in *Giga Operations Per Second* (GOPS). Each server has maximum capacity C GOPS. The total computing resources required by RRH_j is denoted ρ_j^{req} GOPS such that:

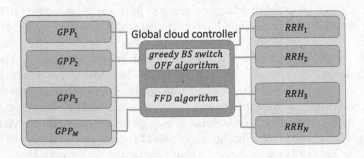

Fig. 2. System Model.

$$\rho_j^{req} = \sum_{l_0=1}^{L} \rho_{j,k}^{req}; \qquad \rho_{j,k}^{req} \epsilon (0,1] \tag{1}$$

where $\rho_{j,k}^{req}$ is the computing resource requirement for T_k from RRH_j.

Therefore, the computing resource at server S_i used by RRH_j can be calculated as:

$$\rho_{i,j}^{server} = \sum_{k=1}^{L} \xi_{i,j,k} \rho_{j,k}^{req}; \qquad \xi_{i,j,k} \epsilon \{0,1\} \tag{2}$$

where $\xi_{i,j,k} = 1$ when T_k from RRH_j is processed by server S_i and $\xi_{i,j,k} = 0$ otherwise. Tasks from RRH_j can be processed by a single server or distributed among different serves such that the constraint below hold:

$$\sum_{i=1}^{M} \sum_{k=1}^{L} \xi_{i,j,k} = L \tag{3}$$

And the BBU server processing is limited by server capacity C as:

$$\sum_{j=1}^{N} \rho_{i,j}^{server} \leq C \tag{4}$$

The energy minimization in the cloud for M BBU servers can be formulated from two components [8]: dynamic and static power consumption. The dynamic energy consumption is dependent on the amount of processing resources on the server while the static part comprises the energy consumption irrespective of traffic load, but other purposes such as coolings, etc. Now, the energy minimization problem can be formulated as:

$$\min_{\xi_{i,j,k}} \sum_{i=1}^{M} \left(\delta \sum_{j=1}^{N} \rho_{i,j}^{server} + \varepsilon_i P_{static} \right) \tag{5}$$

$$\varepsilon_i = \begin{cases} 0 & \sum_{j=1}^{N} \sum_{k=1}^{L} \xi_{i,j,k} = 0 \\ 1 & \text{Otherwise} \end{cases} \tag{6}$$

where δ is the power factor in GOPS/watts. ε_i shows the status factor of server S_i whether S_i is ON or OFF. P_{static} denotes the static power that is constant for every BBU server. Constraints are from (3) and (4).

3.2   Computational Resource Model

The baseband tasks from cells need to be quantified, i.e., they need to be mapped into computing processing in GOPS. The computing resource requirement per user per task is calculated based on the energy consumption model in [17]. The model provides energy modelling for different types of BSs such as macro, micro, pico and femto BSs. In this paper, the power equation in [17] for calculating the computing resources required for baseband tasks is adopted. Defining $\mathcal{L}$ as the set of baseband tasks and $\mathcal{X} = \{BW, Ant, Mod, Cod, R\}$ is the list of parameters affecting the scaling of baseband processing tasks, where BW, Ant, Mod, Cod and R are the system bandwidth, number of antennas used by a user, modulation bits, coding rate and number of PRBs respectively. The power equation is written as [17]:

$$P_u = \sum_{i \in \mathcal{L}} P_{i,ref} \prod_{x \in \mathcal{X}} \left(\frac{x_{act}}{x_{ref}} \right)^{s_{i,x}} \tag{7}$$

where P_u and $P_{i,ref}$ are the processing power required by user u and the processing power of reference system in [17]. The variables x_{act} and x_{ref} denotes the actual and reference values of parameters affecting baseband scaling. The variable $s_{i,x}$ denotes the scaling exponents. Users that generate traffic are randomly distributed in the cell area and the generated traffic are mapped into processing resources as per user per task. Even though there are many baseband tasks processed by a BS, this paper considers two baseband tasks for simplicity, i.e., $k = 2$: (i) Frequency-Domain (FD) processing for mapping/demapping and MIMO equalization, and (ii) Forward Error Correction (FEC) denoted by the following equations, respectively, in GOPS:

$$P_u^{FD} = \left(30Ant + 10Ant^2 \right) \frac{R}{100} \tag{8}$$

$$P_u^{FEC} = 20 \frac{Mod}{6} Cod * Ant * \frac{R}{100} \tag{9}$$

where P_u^{FD} and P_u^{FEC} are FD and FEC processing requirements, respectively, per user u per task k in GOPS. Ant is the number of antennas used per user, Mod is the modulation bits, Cod is the coding rate used and R is the number of PRBs used by u at time t. In the bin packing algorithm, the tasks per cell are packed on servers hence the processing requirements per task per cell for the two tasks is calculated as follows:

$$\begin{cases} \rho_{j,1}^{req} = \sum_{u \in U} P_{u,t}^{FD}, & \text{when } k = 1 \\ \rho_{j,2}^{req} = \sum_{u \in U} P_{u,t}^{FEC}, & \text{when } k = 2 \end{cases} \tag{10}$$

where U is the set of users within a cell.

3.3   FFD Bin Packing Scheme

A classical bin packing problem consists of packing a series of items with different sizes into a minimum number of bins with capacity C. The C-RAN resource allocation problem can be modelled as the bin packing problem where the aim is to pack items, called baseband tasks $\mathcal{L}$, from cell areas $\mathcal{R}$ into a set of servers $\mathcal{M}$ such that the number of servers used are minimized and hence the energy consumption reduction. Since the problem of finding optimal packings is NP-hard, i.e., there is no way of being guaranteed the best solution without checking every possible solutions. Amongst many other solutions, the approximation algorithm is the mostly used because of fast heuristics that generate good but not necessarily optimal packings. The approximation algorithms of FFD is considered.

The FFD algorithm illustrated in Algorithm 1 is adopted, which is a natural way of finding the approximation bin packing. In this algorithm, all bins are initially empty. Sort all item tasks in descending order. Starts with the current number of bins M and item k. Consider all bins $GPP_i : i = 1, ..., M$ and place item task $\rho_{j,k}^{req}$ baseband task in the first bin that has sufficient residual capacity. If there is no such bin, increment i and repeat until all items is assigned.

Algorithm 1. First-Fit Decreasing Algorithm

Input: a set of RRH cells R, a set of tasks L within RRH_j, their resource requirements $\rho_{j,k}^{req}$, and GPP list M, GPP capacity C_{cap}^i
Output: Number of BBUs M
Sort all RRH tasks in decreasing order of $\rho_{j,k}^{req}$.
Launch one GPP of capacity $_{cap}^i$.
for *each $\rho_{j,k}^{req}$ that arrives* **do**
> **if** *there is a server where $\rho_{j,k}^{req}$ will fit* **then**
>> Place $\rho_{j,k}^{req}$ into the left most GPP;
>
> **else**
>> Launch a new GPP;
>> Place $\rho_{j,k}^{req}$ into that GPP
>
> **end**

end
Return M

3.4 Radio Side Energy Consumption Model

The power consumption model in [17] is modified to come up with a generalized component based power consumption model of a C-RAN RRH, denoted P_j, which is formulated as:

$$P_j = \begin{cases} N_{TRX} \frac{\frac{\rho_j P_{max}}{\eta_{PA}} + P_{RF}}{(1-\sigma_{DC})(1-\sigma_{MS})}; & \text{if } 0 < \rho_j \leq 1 \\ P_{sleep}; & \text{if } \rho_j = 0 \end{cases} \qquad (11)$$

where N_{TRX}, ρ_j and P_{max} denotes the number of transmitter chains, the normalised traffic load of RRH_j^- and maximum transmission power of RRH_j. The variables P_{RF} and P_{BB} denotes the RF and BBU power consumption, respectively. The variables η_{PA}, σ_{feeder}, σ_{DC}, σ_{MS}, σ_{cool} denotes power amplifier efficiency, RF feeder losses, DC losses, MS losses and cooling losses, respectively.

3.5   Greedy BS Switch OFF Algorithm

The proposed algorithm is called the greedy RRH switch OFF algorithm and it is centralised and runs in the BS cloud inside the GCC where network information is available. In the algorithm, only the small cell RRHs are to be switch off based on a utility function $\mathcal{F}_j(PRB)$, while maintaining quality of service (QoS) i.e., maintaining the minimum datarate, r_{min}.

$$\mathcal{F}_j(PRB) = \frac{\text{number of } RRH_j \text{ PRBs occupied}}{\text{Total number of } RRH_j \text{ PRBs}} \tag{12}$$

It is assumed that there are N_{chn} available channels in every cell for transmission with each having bandwidth $BW = B/N_{chn}$ where B is the cell bandwidth. In this regard, a channel means one PRB which is allocated to each user per scheduling interval. For simplicity it is assumed that different frequency bands are used by adjacent BS so inter channel interference (ICI) has been taken care of. Thus, the minimum data rate of a user u can be formulated as:

$$r_{min} = BW.log_2\left(1 + \frac{\eta_0.P_u}{d^\alpha}\right) \tag{13}$$

where α is the path-loss exponent and $\eta_0 = G_0/N_0$ includes the effect of antenna gain G_0 and thermal noise N_0, and d is the distance from the RRH to the user. P_u is the transmission power per user. The MRRH is always kept on to maintain coverage. The algorithm runs in the BS cloud on the GCC where all information (e.g., traffic load) about other RHHs is present. At constant time intervals of 1 hour, the algorithm is invoked where the utility of all the SRRHs is calculated and the SRRH with the lowest utility first is then tested for switching OFF. The test involves checking if the SRRH traffic can be offloaded to neighbouring SRHHs or to the MRRH while maintaining the minimum datarate. If the traffic can be offloaded, then offloading is perfomed and the SRRH is then switched OFF. If the offloading can not be perfomed due to violation of QoS or due to not enough resources, the SRRH is kept active.

Algorithm 2. Greedy RRH switch off algorithm

Input: RRH traffic load information
Output: Number of switched OFF SRRHs
Define $\mathcal{R}_{off}$ as a set of switched OFF RRHs.
Define $\mathcal{R}_{on}$ as a set of active RRHs
for *each RRH* **do**
$\quad |$ Calculate the RRH utility function $\mathcal{F}(\rho_j)$
end
Sort RRHs by their increasing utility function
Test the lowest utility RRH_j for switching OFF
while $j \neq N$ **do**
$\quad$ **if** RRH_j *can be offloaded* **then**
$\quad\quad$ offload RRH_j traffic
$\quad\quad$ switch OFF RRH_j
$\quad\quad$ $\mathcal{R}_{off} = \mathcal{R}_{off} + \{RRH_j\}$
$\quad$ **end**
$\quad$ **else**
$\quad\quad$ do not offload RRH_j traffic
$\quad\quad$ keep RRH_j on
$\quad\quad$ $\mathcal{R}_{on} = \mathcal{R}_{on} + \{RRH_j\}$
$\quad$ **end**
$\quad$ $j = j + 1$
end

---

4 Simulation Results and Discussion

4.1 Parameter Settings

To analyse the performance of the proposed scheme, a simulation layout of one MRRH overlaid with 10 small cells is considered. Bandwidth of 10 MHz was considered with up to 50 users randomly generated within the MRRH and up to 5 users within the SRRH. All results using the proposed scheme are compared with the baseline distributed LTE-A system which comprises of distributed BSs with 10 individual BBU processing servers for 10 cells. The users are allocated PRB in a proportional-fair manner. Adaptive modulation and coding (AMC) scheme is used to adapt to the changing channel conditions. As the simulation runs, the values of Ant, Mod, R were captured and mapped into processing requirements and loaded into the bin packing scheme to reduce the number of servers M. For calculating the power consumption, the power factor used is $\delta = 40$ GOPS/watt and $P_{static} = 200$ GOPS as in [17]. Other simulation parameters are shown in Table 1.

4.2 Results Evaluation

Figure 3 shows the power consumption of both schemes for different traffic loads. The results show that for both schemes, as the traffic load increases, the power

Table 1. Parameters used in the simulations.

Parameter	Value
Bandwidth B	10 MHz
No. of antennas Ant	2
Modulation mod	2, 4, 6 bits
Coding rate Cod	1/3-1
Number of MRRH	1
Number of SRRH	10
Number of users per MRRH	up to 50
Number of users per SRRH	up to 5
MRRH radius	500 m
SRRH radius	40 m
MRRH transmission power	46 dBm
SRRH transmission power	30 dBm
Inter-BS distance	>1 km
BS antenna gain G_0	16 dBi
Noise Power N_0	−141 dBm/Hz
Pathloss Exponent, α	4
power factor, δ	40 GOPS/watt

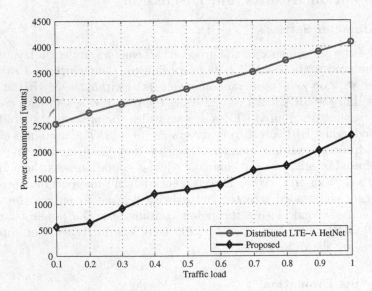

Fig. 3. Power consumption versus traffic load.

consumption increases. The proposed scheme consumes less power compared to the baseline since the proposed scheme combines RRH switch off scheme at the radio side with BBU reduction scheme at the BS cloud which both significantly reduce the overall system power consumption. The proposed scheme saves up to 44% and 78% of power at during low traffic and peak traffic respectively as compared to the baseline scheme.

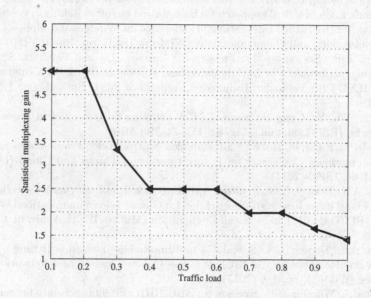

Fig. 4. Statistical multiplexing gain.

Figure 4 illustrate the statistical multiplexing gain for increasing traffic load which is calculated as the ratio of number of BBU servers used by the baseline scheme to those used by the proposed scheme. The graph shows that at low traffic period the multiplexing gain is 5 which means the baseline uses 5 times the number of BBUs compared the proposed scheme. During peak traffic, the multiplexing gain is 1.4 which means the baseline uses 1.4 times the number of BBUs as the proposed scheme due to more traffic being proposed for both schemes.

5   Conclusion

This paper presents an energy efficient scheme for reducing energy consumption in C-RAN by switching off remote radio heads (RRHs) using a greedy algorithm and also switching off idle BBUs using the first fit decreasing (FFD) bin packing algorithm. The number of RRHs and BBUs are minimized by matching the right amount of baseband computing load with traffic load. The proposed scheme saves up to 44% and 78% of power during low traffic and peak traffic periods respectively. The proposed scheme will be extended to include the separation of data and control signalling to further minimize energy consumption.

References

1. Huawei: 5G: a technology vision. In: White Paper of Huawei Tech (2013)
2. Chih-Lin, I., Rowell, C., Han, S.: Toward green and soft: a 5G perspective. IEEE Commun. Mag. **52**(2), 66–73 (2014)
3. Auer, G., Giannini, V., Desset, C., Godor, I.: How much energy is needed to run a wireless network? IEEE Wireless Commun. **18**(5), 40–49 (2011)
4. Yaacoub, E.: A practical approach for base station on/off switching in green LTE-A hetnets. In: IEEE 10th International Conference on Wireless and Mobile Computing, Networking and Communications (WiMob). IEEE, pp. 159–164 (2014)
5. Cheng, J.-F., Koorapaty, H., Frenger, P., Larsson, D., and Falahati, S.: Energy efficiency performance of LTE dynamic base station downlink DTX operation. In: 2014 IEEE 79th Vehicular Technology Conference (VTC Spring), pp. 1–5. IEEE (2014)
6. Niu, Z., Wu, Y., Gong, J., Yang, Z.: Cell zooming for cost-efficient green cellular networks. IEEE Commun. Mag. **48**(11), 74–79 (2010)
7. Sigwele, T., Pillai, P., Hu, F.: Call admission control in cloud radio access networks. In: International Conference on Future Internet of Things and Cloud (FiCloud), pp. 31–36. IEEE (2014)
8. Alam, A.S., Dooley, L. S., Poulton, A.S.: Energy efficient relay-assisted cellular network model using base station switching. In: Global Telecommunications Workshop (GLOBECOM 2012) on Multicell Cooperation (MuCo). IEEE, Anaheim, CA, USA (2012)
9. Alam, A.S., Dooley, L.S.: A scalable multimode base station switching model for green cellular networks. In: IEEE Wireless Communication and Networking Conference (WCNC), pp. 1–6 (2015)
10. Namba, S., Warabino, T., Kaneko, S.: BBU-RRH switching schemes for centralized ran. In: 7th International ICST Conference on Communications and Networking in China (CHINACOM), pp. 762–766. IEEE (2012)
11. Kong, Z., Gong, J., Xu, C.-Z., Wang, K., Rao, J.: eBase: a baseband unit cluster testbed to improve energy-efficiency for cloud radio access network. In: IEEE International Conference on Communications (ICC), pp. 4222–4227. IEEE (2013)
12. Liu, J., Zhou, S., Gong, J., Niu, Z.: On the statistical multiplexing gain of virtual base station pools. In: Global Communications Conference (GLOBECOM), pp. 2283–2288. IEEE (2014)
13. Zhao, T., Wu, J., Zhou, S., Niu, Z.: Energy-delay tradeoffs of virtual base stations with a computational-resource-aware energy consumption model. In: IEEE International Conference on Communication Systems (ICCS), pp. 26–30. IEEE (2014)
14. Namba, S., Matsunaka, T., Warabino, T., Kaneko, S., Kishi, Y.: Colony-ran architecture for future cellular network. In: Future Network & Mobile Summit (FutureNetw), pp. 1–8. IEEE (2012)
15. Ashraf, I., Boccardi, F., Ho, L.: Sleep mode techniques for small cell deployments. IEEE Commun. Mag. **49**(8), 72–79 (2011)
16. Abdulkafi, A.A., Kiong, T.S., Koh, J., Chieng, D., Ting, A.: Energy efficiency of heterogeneous cellular networks: a review. J. Appl. Sci. **12**(14), 1418 (2012)
17. Desset, C., Debaillie, B., Giannini, V., Fehske, A., Auer, G., Holtkamp, H., Wajda, W., Sabella, D., Richter, F., Gonzalez, M.J.: Flexible power modeling of LTE base stations. In: Wireless Communications and Networking Conference (WCNC), pp. 2858–2862. IEEE (2012)

Author Index

Printed in the United States
By Bookmasters